Michael Gray is twenty-seven, lives in Worcestershire and writes on rock music for many different magazines—including *Rolling Stone*, *Crawdaddy*, *Oz* and *It*—both in England and America.

Michael Gray

SONG AND DANCE MAN
The Art of Bob Dylan

ABACUS edition published in 1973
by Sphere Books Ltd
30/32 Gray's Inn Road, London WC1X 8JL

First published in Great Britain by Hart-Davis,
MacGibbon 1972
Copyright © Michael Gray 1972

ISBN 0 349 11540 0

Set in Intertype Times

*Printed in Great Britain by Cox & Wyman Ltd,
London, Reading and Fakenham*

Thanks

To Bob Jones, for much encouragement and patience in formative days; to Christine Seville, for all her time-consuming and noble work; to Paul and Anna Harvey, for more kinds of help than I could possibly catalogue; and, most of all, to Sue.

Acknowledgements

I must also record my indebtedness to Steve MacDonogh, for allowing me to plunder his own work on links between Dylan and Browning; and to the published work of Alan Lomax and Paul Oliver, on which I have leant with obvious heaviness in what follows.

The author and the publishers also desire to express their thanks to the undermentioned copyright owners for the use of material written and composed by Bob Dylan.

Quotations are taken from Bob Dylan recordings and may, in some cases, differ from the printed versions.

DESOLATION ROW (© 1965 by M. Witmark & Sons, U.S.A.)
BABY I'M IN THE MOOD FOR YOU (© 1963 by M. Witmark & Sons, U.S.A.)
A HARD RAIN'S A-GONNA FALL (© 1963 by M. Witmark & Sons, U.S.A.)
TALKING NEW YORK (© 1962 by Duchess Music, U.S.A.)

SONG TO WOODY (© 1962 by Duchess Music, U.S.A.)

I SHALL BE FREE (© 1963 by M. Witmark & Sons, U.S.A.)

TALKING BEAR MOUNTAIN PICNIC MASSACRE BLUES (© 1962 by Duchess Music, U.S.A.)

*ALL ALONG THE WATCHTOWER (© 1968 by Dwarf Music, U.S.A.)

FREIGHT TRAIN BLUES (not by Bob Dylan)

JUST LIKE TOM THUMB'S BLUES (© 1965 by M. Witmark & Sons, U.S.A.)

BALLAD OF A THIN MAN (© 1965 by M. Witmark & Sons, U.S.A.)

WITH GOD ON OUR SIDE (© 1963 by M. Witmark & Sons, U.S.A.)

*LAY, LADY, LAY (© 1969 by Big Sky Music, U.S.A.)

BALLAD OF HOLLIS BROWN (© 1963 by M. Witmark & Sons, U.S.A.)

WHEN THE SHIP COMES IN (© 1963 by M. Witmark & Sons, U.S.A.)

COUNTRY PIE (© 1969 by Big Sky Music, U.S.A.)

THE BALLAD OF FRANKIE LEE AND JUDAS PRIEST (© 1968 by Dwarf Music, U.S.A.)

DON'T THINK TWICE, IT'S ALL RIGHT (© 1963 by M. Witmark & Sons, U.S.A.)

IT AIN'T ME, BABE (© 1964 by M. Witmark & Sons, U.S.A.)

RESTLESS FAREWELL (© 1964 by M. Witmark & Sons, U.S.A.)

*TONIGHT I'LL BE STAYING HERE WITH YOU (© 1969 by Big Sky Music, U.S.A.)

I THREW IT ALL AWAY (© 1969 by Big Sky Music, U.S.A.)

ONE MORE NIGHT (© 1969 by Big Sky Music, U.S.A.)

ALL I REALLY WANT TO DO (© 1964 by M. Witmark & Sons, U.S.A.)

VISIONS OF JOHANNA (© 1966 by Dwarf Music, U.S.A.)

JOHN WESLEY HARDING (© 1968 by Dwarf Music, U.S.A.)

ONLY A PAWN IN THEIR GAME (© 1963 by M. Witmark & Sons, U.S.A.)

PLEDGING MY TIME (© 1966 by Dwarf Music, U.S.A.)

IT TAKES A LOT TO LAUGH, IT TAKES A TRAIN TO CRY (© 1965 by M. Witmark & Sons, U.S.A.)

MAN OF CONSTANT SORROW (© 1962 by Duchess Music, U.S.A.)

BOB DYLAN'S DREAM (© 1963 by M. Witmark & Sons, U.S.A.)

ABSOLUTELY SWEET MARIE (© 1966 by Dwarf Music, U.S.A.)

ROCKS AND GRAVEL (© 1963 by M. Witmark & Sons, U.S.A.)

SITTING ON A BARBED WIRE FENCE (© 1970 by Warner Bros. Music, U.S.A.)

HIGHWAY 51 BLUES (not by Bob Dylan—written by C. Jones)

TEARS OF RAGE (Words by Bob Dylan, Music by Richard Manuel) (© 1968 by Dwarf Music, U.S.A.)

LOVE MINUS ZERO/NO LIMIT (© 1965 by M. Witmark & Sons, U.S.A.)

TO RAMONA (© 1964 by M. Witmark & Sons, U.S.A.)

LET ME DIE IN MY FOOTSTEPS (© 1963 by M. Witmark & Sons, U.S.A.)

TOO MUCH OF NOTHING (© 1967 by Dwarf Music, U.S.A.)

POSITIVELY 4TH STREET (© 1965 by M. Witmark & Sons, U.S.A.)

*PEGGY DAY (© 1969 by Big Sky Music, U.S.A.)

OPEN THE DOOR, HOMER (© 1968 by Dwarf Music, U.S.A.)

THE GATES OF EDEN (© 1965 by M. Witmark & Sons, U.S.A.)

SUBTERRANEAN HOMESICK BLUES (© 1965 by M. Witmark & Sons, U.S.A.)

TOMBSTONE BLUES (© 1965 by M. Witmark & Sons, U.S.A.)

TEMPORARY LIKE ACHILLES (© 1966 by Dwarf Music, U.S.A.)

MOST LIKELY YOU GO YOUR WAY (AND I'LL GO MINE) (© 1966 by Dwarf Music, U.S.A.)

BOB DYLAN'S 115TH DREAM (© 1965 by M. Witmark & Sons, U.S.A.)

LEOPARD-SKIN PILL-BOX HAT (© 1966 by Dwarf Music, U.S.A.)

MILLION DOLLAR BASH (© 1967 by Dwarf Music, U.S.A.)

DRIFTER'S ESCAPE (© 1968 by Dwarf Music, U.S.A.)

TALKING WORLD WAR III BLUES (© 1963 by M. Witmark & Sons, U.S.A.)

CAN YOU PLEASE CRAWL OUT YOUR WINDOW? (© 1965 by M. Witmark & Sons, U.S.A.)

IT'S ALL OVER NOW, BABY BLUE (© 1965 by M. Witmark & Sons, U.S.A.)

MOTORPSYCHO NITEMARE (© 1964 by M. Witmark & Sons, U.S.A.)

LO AND BEHOLD! (© 1967 by Dwarf Music, U.S.A.)

NOTHING WAS DELIVERED (© 1968 by Dwarf Music, U.S.A.)

MINSTREL BOY (© 1970 by Big Sky Music, U.S.A.)

THE CHIMES OF FREEDOM (© 1964 by M. Witmark & Sons, U.S.A.)

I PITY THE POOR IMMIGRANT (© 1968 by Dwarf Music, U.S.A.)

THE WICKED MESSENGER (© 1968 by Dwarf Music, U.S.A.)

*JUST LIKE A WOMAN (© 1966 by Dwarf Music, U.S.A.)

HIGHWAY 61 REVISITED (© 1965 by M. Witmark & Sons, U.S.A.)

PLEASE, MRS. HENRY (© 1967 by Dwarf Music, U.S.A.)

MR. TAMBOURINE MAN (© 1964 by M. Witmark & Sons, U.S.A.)

Contents

To Linda Thomas; to Paul and Anna; and to Sue

List of Illustrations

1 Bob Dylan in 1963

2 In Paris, 1966 (Azoulay: Paris Match; Camera Press London)

3 In Sydney, Australia, 1966 (John Fairfax & Sons Ltd)

4 At the Isle of Wight Festival, 1969 (Camera Press London)

5 At the Bangla Desh Benefit Concert, Madison Square Gardens, 1971 (Joseph Sia)

6 At the Mariposa Festival, 1972 (Martin Colyer)

7, 8, 9, 10 At the Band's New Year's Eve concert, Academy of Music, New York City, 1971–2 (Joseph Sia)

The author and publishers gratefully acknowledge permission to reproduce the photographs listed above.

'I think of myself as just a song & dance man.'
Bob Dylan, 1969

'Never trust the artist—trust the tale.'
D. H. Lawrence, 1924

Preface

A book on Bob Dylan is still a surprisingly rare thing to come by. There must have been a few teeny-books rushed out in American paperback editions since Dylan succeeded to the difficult position of mass-media availability seven or eight years ago; there have also been a couple of biographies. In none of these books has there been anything significant about the man-as-artist or his work.

In that I have tried, in this book, to cover exactly these subjects, and to cover them as fully as possible, then certainly what follows is uncommon. If it is also considered to be of any importance, I hope this will be for reasons other than its novelty—reasons associated with real merits, not with my good intentions.

To dispose of these intentions, I want to say this: that I am not a folk-music fanatic, nor a hippy; and that I am not American, nor a professional academic. That ought to eliminate a certain amount of sectarian machination.

1

Bob Dylan's Art: Introduction

I should make it clear at once that my concern relates more to a preoccupation with, and knowledge of, literature than music, though I have tried to take a proper account of both in what follows.

After all, Dylan uses much more than language in his art: his words are presented not as poems but as parts of songs. This is not to suggest that Dylan is no poet—but simply to remember that he is certainly a composer, and a singer too, at the same time. Where some attempt is made to isolate the words—to study verses like stanzas of poetry proper—it ought to be kept in mind that the selection and organization of Dylan's language is governed by the artistic disciplines of a medium not solely linguistic or literary. It cannot be emphasized too strongly that Dylan's finished works of art are his recordings—that like his vocal performances and his music, his words are just ingredients.

To lift off the lyrics (using that word in the song-writing sense) is to disrupt the intimacy of connection between words and music. Structurally, the words of a song differ necessarily from those of a poem. They are not the sole arbiters of their own intended effects, rhythmically or in less technical ways.

In print, the rhythmic pattern of the following lines, for instance, might be as indicated here:

> Einstein disguised as Robin Hood
> With his memories in a trunk ...

whereas in context—the context of the song as recorded (it is *Desolation Row*, from the 1965 album 'Highway 61 Revisited')— the rhythmic pattern is this:

Einstein disguised as Robin Hood
With his memories in a trunk...

I am suggesting the kind of thing that must be borne in mind if we approach analysis, and not that no analysis should be tried. Too many of those who stand by Dylan's art as they see it contend, apparently as proof of its rare quality, that it cannot or should not be analysed. Add to this the mass uneasiness which talk of "literary criticism" produces at the present time and one has enough to explain, in the rush of "enthusiasm", the lamentable absence of critical concern which has greeted Dylan's work.

To analyse is first to find a context, which involves asking definite questions. Who are today's artists? What, of real consequence, has appeared since the work of D. H. Lawrence? This book tries to explain why my answer has to be that Bob Dylan is the artist who has vitally enhanced our perceptive abilities in the last ten years. A great artist.

It seems so obvious to me, in consequence, that by the beginning of the twenty-first century, and for a long time after that, those who want to understand the generation which has been growing up in the West in the 1960s and 1970s to alter the rest of our times, will find it vital to study Bob Dylan's art very closely.

It is, of course, hard to make firm contemporary judgements— yet for precisely the reasons which have enforced my sense of the difficulties involved, it is necessary to state a case for Dylan *now*. I have cited Lawrence deliberately—conscious that he provides, unhappily, an example of an artist who went uncredited for far too long by the generations he was addressing so urgently. Dylan gives no such impression of being a sage in haste, and in many ways has hardly gone uncredited: but it would be a comparable disaster were a knowledge of Dylan's work to remain confined to those who explore it at the moment. I have tried, therefore, in what follows, to assess the great value of Bob Dylan's art—and so to get it more widely listened to and discussed.

Eight years ago, rock music was largely despised by the mass of those American and British students who follow it so devotedly today. Though they have since been put right on this— largely at Dylan's instigation—the older intelligentsia has not caught on. It has in the end recognized that films can be works of art, but rock music—no, surely not, not that!

So ignorance widens the generation breach. A student of today who can move calmly from, say, a consideration of Edmund Spenser to one of the Rolling Stones gets told that such facility is, deplorably, symptomatic of what T. S. Eliot called "the dissociation of sensibility". This simply exposes a similar limitation to that under which the Victorian critic struggled. Think of poor, brilliant Matthew Arnold, breathing in the sexual panic of his times and so deciding that Chaucer's work, because it showed no such panic, was "lacking in high seriousness".

It is time it was more generally recognized that to use rock music, as Dylan has done, is not to be, *ipso facto*, lacking in such high seriousness; and the corollary of this is to analyse, not shudder at, what Dylan has achieved.

*   *   *

There is a sense in which, more fully than F. Scott Fitzgerald did, Dylan has created a generation. For those of us within that generation, the possibilities of our inner lives have been intrinsically enhanced by the impingement of Dylan's art—by the impact of his consciousness on ours. The point that needs equal emphasis is that this impact, this impingement, need not be, as direct experience, exclusive to one generation, any more than the effects of Dylan's achievement, as indirect experience, can be discounted as a vital part of contemporary, changing, everyday life.

Whenever an artist of such real power emerges, there is a fatalistic desire, on the part of those who appreciate it, not to analyse but to submit. People can hardly be expected to question critically the quality of the artist's achievement when they are so much more concerned with the style of their own surrender to it. The critical questioning is necessary, though, if, unlike politicians, we are concerned about the direction in which our civilization moves as well as with its methods of getting along. There is a collaborative process involved in art's impingement: the artist's work must be receptively approached before it can function fully.

I am not arguing that Dylan's work has been ignored on every level, but it is the case that though the Underground, obviously, has picked up on it, the real impact of Dylan's art has passed unnoticed by both the literati and the mass-media, while that other impact—the impact of the showbiz phenomenon—has been far from ignored. Dylan has been interviewed, his concerts written up, his records reviewed, with relish and persistence; but reviews and interviews are rarely designed for analysis so much as for a kind of flippant prying. The review is as far removed from real criticism as is the interview from real dialogue.

In Dylan's case there has been plenty of this superficial Message-Hunting. It provokes, in the artist, an appropriate defensiveness:

DYLAN: ... I do know what my songs are about.
PLAYBOY: And what's that?
DYLAN: Oh, some are about four minutes, some are about five minutes, and some, believe it or not, are about eleven or twelve.

The kind of insensitivity which lends itself readily to the interview is, of course, an occupational malaise. The journalist cannot afford the time or the perceptions needed for telling the truth—or even recognizing it. He is trained to extract stories from life, to produce inaccurate outdated timetables of miserably external events, and to deny, in the process of extraction, the centrality of individual experience. And then again, editors must "give the public what it wants". The artist is the inevitable enemy of the journalist because he stands absolutely on the other side from any such obligation.

Dylan, of course, is hardly the only man to speak out honestly against what adds up to the contemporary dehumanizing process —a process of discrediting imagination, of removing, in schools and via the media, any assertion of real individuality, and of obliterating our resources for a valid human dignity.

One must, though, distinguish between intention and effect in such a "speaking out". The phrase has qualitative implications. I don't know what Nietzsche had in mind when he wrote that people should not know more than they can creatively digest, but I take it as recognizing that, for example, while the polemicist offers "Freedom"! as a slogan and can communicate no more than the hysteria of the *word* to his audience, the creative artist can offer in his vision the living experience of freedom as a real force. Like the man said, all art is propaganda, but not all propaganda is art.

It is this power of the artist's which lends his ability to "speak out" its quality. Great art is highly effective art; and Dylan's comes into this category. He seems to me better equipped creatively to "speak out" for life and growth than any of his contemporaries.

What Dylan does not do—and consequently, whatever the mode of approach, the journalist's Message Hunt must fail—is consciously to offer a sustained, cohesive philosophy of life, intellectually considered and checked for contradictions. What I think he does offer is the artistic re-creation of the individual's struggle in our times—a vision of life within chaos—a very contemporary, and yet universal, vision for the English-speaking world. His work is truly educative, and thereby truly entertaining. Its virtue lies not in the immediacy, or pace, but in the perceptiveness of what it offers. It is too much like faint praise to say that Dylan adds a fresh voice to the cluster of modern writers' attempts to deal with the problem of loss of identity and individuality. At its best, Dylan's work possesses much more than freshness: it has that clear individually-disciplined integrity which is capable of "representing the age" and competent, therefore, to go beyond and outside it— to clarify by focusing, with a vital intelligence, on its confusions.

From the most elementary consideration of Dylan's art it is plain how different is its capacity from a facility for collating a few common denominators of sentiment to which everyone feels susceptible, as (say) the Beatles did. The process whereby *their* work functioned engaged no individual consciousness: it was "dealing in the known and the cheap" and sustained its pretence at a connection with the individual focus only by the careful preservation and inclusion (to a formula) of an ostensibly *playful* eccentricity. Lennon and McCartney were self-stylized "amateur" parallels of Walt Disney. They used their own persona as Hollywood used Bambi, with Ringo—forgive the pun—as a cute Liverpudlian Thumper.

It follows that the *rapport* which *this* level of evocation produced applauds, in effect, a fundamental and wilful ignorance. The Beatles offered glossy sketches of a world that we must fool ourselves into seeing: a world that could be "if only"—or "once upon a time". What they ignored, and what Dylan always deals with, is the human world as it really is.

At one time Dylan wrote songs explicitly "about" war, exploitation and suffering. That he no longer does so is not a mark of any lack of concern—of any retreat from responsibility. As Jon Landau has pointed out, Dylan could not have written (Lennon-

McCartney's) *Fool On The Hill* contemporaneously with the Vietnam war. The imagination, however wistfully or humorously engaged, must connect with the real spirit of the age; *Fool On The Hill*, *Lucy In The Sky With Diamonds* and the rest connect only with a self-indulgent falsity.

In contrast, an early Dylan song like *A Hard Rain's A-Gonna Fall*, with its clear didactic glimpses:

> I met one man who was wounded in love
> I met another man who was wounded in hatred

—evinces the same kind of exploratory awareness which has matured, not disappeared, in Dylan's later work.

On a political level, in any case, Dylan's work has become more important as it has moved beyond the early explicit rhetoric. Compare *The Times They Are A-Changin'* with *Desolation Row*. As Nigel Fountain has expressed it, whatever happened to all the senators and congressmen who were supposed to heed the call? Dr. Filth is still around. With his later work, in fact, Dylan is politically *ahead*, almost a kind of pied piper of dissent. It can be said of the ("non-political, non-progressive") album "Self Portrait", 1970, that once again, Dylan had anticipated the direction in which the New Left in America must move. While the Weathermen were increasingly an isolated, alienated, psychotic group bereft of any public support, Dylan was directing the hip/aware/active crowd towards the American white working-class masses, via their music—and doing so at a time when the New Left needed to move precisely in the direction of those workers.

There is, then, a fundamental sense in which Dylan cannot be placed alongside most heroes of the mass-media: he is incapable of that falsity of consciousness, that bland superficiality on which they depend, and which they purvey to the ulcerated tribesmen of McLuhan's global village.

In this achievement, Dylan proves how right a part of McLuhan's thesis is. It *is* true that Dylan's vast young audience has been attracted by the medium as well as the message, indeed that the two are bound up. It is true that the kind of thinking, the kind of perceiving, spawned by the old print technology seems increasingly foreign to those whose real attention is caught by the audio-visual media; that because the TV set and the record-player are more vocal and articulate parts of people's homes than their parents are or were, so now the home is open-ended and "all the world's a stage". It is true too that the traditional education system is at last being seen as a pathetically outdated imaginatively bankrupt, mind-shrinking affair. And while schools, along with much else that is crumbling, stand for categorization, detachment and what Mailer calls "the logic of the next step", so electric technology "fosters and encourages unification and involvement". And the medium Dylan works in is the most powerfully attractive form of electric technology yet available—since, that is, films still involve having to sit in cinemas, and TV is in the hands of those Dylan once called "men and women who look like cigars—the anti-happiness committee".

At least one wheel has come full circle. Folk-music married to poetry has been reasserted; in Dylan, as indeed in Bunyan before him (see Chapter 3), the sub-cultures have surfaced.

This is not hard to explain. Dylan's generation has packed together its discoveries of innumerable "sub-cultures" and re-formed them into chaotic, kaleidoscopic but living experience. The contemporary student of, say, literature, gets far more from a life only peripherally concerned with the cultural mainstream than does his professor, who never stops swimming in it. The student has, with a free intelligence, derived a dynamic vision from rock music, cinematic experiment, comic books, communal living, philosophy, existential politics, trips (upon the tambourine man's magic, swirling ship), and an early tacit recognition that the cultural mainstream has done little, in our times, to combat the moral and imaginative imbecility of the Great Society and its Establishment intelligentsia. As Mailer has said of this generation:

Their radicalism was in their hatred for the authority—the authority was the manifest of evil to this generation. It was the authority who had covered the land with those suburbs where they stifled as children while watching the adventures of the West in the movies, while looking at the guardians of dull genial celebrity on television; they had had their minds jabbed and poked and twitched and probed and finally galvanized into surrealistic modes of response by commercials cutting into dramatic narrative, and parents flipping from network to network—they were forced willy-nilly to build their idea of the space-time continuum (and therefore their nervous systems) on

23

the jumps and cracks and leaps and breaks which every pheno-menon from the media seemed to contain within it.

Under these conditions, the very term "sub-cultures" becomes meaningless. Everything connects and makes redundant the sorts of distinction implied by the term. It is to this re-processing that Dylan's work so eloquently testifies, and I think it true to say that it is in this context that an understanding of his art can best be attained.

What follows is an examination of different aspects of that art.

2

Dylan and the Folk Tradition

*"Strap yourself to a tree with roots
You aint goin nowhere."*

When Dylan first went East and arrived in New York, at the start of the 1960s, the repertoire and the styles of delivery he brought with him provided a culture-shock not only to Sinatra-tuned audiences but also to the patrons of the many small "folk clubs" then in bloom around Greenwich Village. As he recalls the latter's reaction, it ran as follows:

> You sound like a hillbilly:
> We want folk-singers here ...

The point, and it is made here with a characteristic lightness of irony, is of course that Dylan was a folk-singer; and to learn how his early work was received is to understand the various misconceptions that obtained in New York at that time and which, from New York, spread (though not back into the Appalachians) via college circuits and out across the Atlantic.

To sound like a "folk singer" you were supposed to be smoothly ingenuous, Angry and, above all, Sensitive. It is hard to pin down precise criteria but I think it's enough to say that Peter, Paul & Mary passed the test. With a name like that, how could they fail? They were the Greenwich Village ideal—white, clean and middle-class to the point of cultivated preciousness. They had all the essentials of what was required: a coyness and a bourgeois gentility that functioned as a kind of marketable post-adolescent reproach.

The young, white, middle-class Americans to whom such personae appealed were thus provided with a handy collective psyche —a palliative to all kinds of inadequacy. This was encouraged and strengthened, moreover, by the arid folk preservation movement,

25

which judged its music on "purity of style", regardless of quality of content. A formidable alliance. If one could only keep away the hillbillies, one could fill out one's life amiably enough with an indulgent, deadening orthodoxy.

This did not suit Dylan. His first album consisted mainly of his own impressionistic arrangements of modern-traditional songs (songs like Blind Lemon Jefferson's *See That My Grave Is Kept Clean*[1]) performed without any "gentility" and with a voice that, far from suggesting a soul-mate for Peter, Paul or Mary, suggested some octogenarian Negro singing personal blues at the back of his shack. The blurb that went out on the album could quite plausibly call Dylan the newest voice in the country blues tradition.

In fact Dylan's recordings of folk material are very much more extensive than those officially released suggest, but here I want to concentrate on this first official album as a unit, a collection, which stands up by itself.

It is a brilliant debut—a performer's *tour de force*—but not, of course, without its flaws. What it reveals and what were the intended statements do not always coincide; and, in the way in which they differ, they show up a confusion of purpose which proves a personal sincerity yet perhaps denies an artistic one. Nevertheless, the album served as a fine corrective for Greenwich Village: it was the opposite of effete.

There are tracks that ring a little false. On Dylan's rendition of the spiritual *Gospel Plow*, for instance, the death-wish of the young man (Dylan was 20) may be genuine but the evocation is not: wrongly, it relies on a pretence at the experience of age to "justify" that death-wish. So that what comes through is a clumsiness of understanding as to what the artist requires of himself.

Yet what comes through from the album as a whole is a remarkable skill and more than a hint of a highly distinctive vision. Indeed, taken in the context of what was happening at the time—American folk culture all but obliterated and a stagnating "folk" cult established as if in its place—Dylan's first album can hardly be faulted without the critic being much in debt to pedantry.

I've already referred to Dylan's use of irony in *Talkin' New York*. The same asset appears again, and to greater effect, in the other self-composed song on the album, the reflective *Song To Woody*. Here, the irony closes the lyric:

Here's to Cisco and Sonny and Leadbelly too[2]
And to all the good people that travelled with you
Here's to the hearts and the hands of the men
That come with the dust and are gone with the wind.

I'm a-leavin' tomorrow but I could leave today
Somewhere down the road someday ...
The very last thing that I'd want to do
Is to say I bin hittin' some hard travellin' too.

Clearly, to say he'd been hitting some hard travelling too is not the last thing Dylan would *like* to be *able* to do.

It is with those final lines—which get their special strength not just from the understatement but from the carefully clipped reluctance of the cadence—that we get a fresh focus on the whole theme of the song. And at the same time, we still hear the echoes of all those delicate rushes of confidentiality which, throughout the lyric, establish its tone.

There are other aspects of the song which contribute to its appeal. There is the frank if implicit statement of what is, on Dylan's part, a plea for an innocent drop-out and the concern to find a new allegiance in the "hard travellin' " ethos. Again, there is a delicacy in handling this—a balance struck in perceiving both the harsh reality and the romantic flavour of this ethos. The song not only reflects Guthrie faithfully but assesses his real but disappearing America from Dylan's, the young man's, perspective. We are offered a highly intelligent understanding of the subject.

This comes over, equally, in the rhythmic balance of the lyric—look at the third and fourth lines, the seventh and eighth, and so on; and likewise, the wind and the dust are there in the song's construction. Lines and syllables take the form of a list: the suggestion is one of restless movement within a preordained pattern of repetition. The sharecropper's life-rhythm.

In Guthrie's triumphant autobiography, *Bound For Glory*, we see him travelling around with the homeless families who are also the heroes of Steinbeck's *Grapes of Wrath;* and while recalling one particular encounter, Guthrie quotes one of his own songs, *Pastures of Plenty*. Appropriately enough, Dylan's tribute reworks this. One of Guthrie's verses runs:

I work in your orchards of peaches and prunes
Sleep on the ground 'neath the light of the moon
On the edge of your city you see us and then
We come with the dust and we go with the wind.

Dylan's alteration of that last verb, from "go" to "are gone", is sufficient to indicate his very inward awareness that the era which produces such men is all but over.[3]

Elsewhere, Dylan can use the *tone* of Guthrie's autobiographical writing unaltered, can capture it exactly, in song. The chaotic scurrying around of cram-packed humanity which Guthrie describes so well (particularly in the sequence on the box-car ride that opens and closes his book) is done *precisely* in this way (from Dylan's unreleased 1962 song *Talking Bear Mountain Picnic Massacre Blues*):

> Dogs a barkin', cats a-meowin'
> Women screamin', fists a-flyin', babies cryin'
> Cops a-comin', me a-runnin'
> Maybe we just better call off the picnic.

That is Woody Guthrie's voice.

Alan Lomax wrote of Guthrie that ". . . he inherited the folk tradition of the last American frontier (western Oklahoma) and during his incessant wandering across the U.S. he has recomposed this tradition into contemporary folky ballads about the lives of the American working class. Some of these songs have already passed into oral circulation. Many more will do so. No modern American poet or folk singer has made a more significant contribution to our culture."

If Dylan's debt to Guthrie is, as he admits, substantial it is not in essence merely derivative. A few people could have gained—can have gained—so much from Guthrie's work (or life-style), even though that work is so impressively among the best of the American folk-art accessible to us from the pre-1960s. When Dylan sings that

> I'm seein' y'r world of people and things

he is too modest: he has not so much seen as re-created.

Nevertheless, Guthrie's influence can be traced much further

28

through Dylan's work than simply to the tribute-song we've been discussing. Elsewhere on the latter's first album we recognize Guthrie's subject-matter—the hobo's America—and Guthrie's humour. In the famous Dylan "protest songs" of his second and third LPs (*Blowin' In The Wind; Masters of War; The Times They Are A-Changin'; Oxford Town;* and others) it is largely Guthrie's idealism. And it must have been Guthrie, rather than Dylan's somewhat amorphous "first idol", Hank Williams, who impressed upon Dylan, by his example, the seminal need of the artist to stand alone, true to his individual vision.

Like his early "hillbilly sound", this sense of responsibility to oneself and to one's art was not understood (it is not surprising) by Greenwich Village/Newport Folk Festival devotees. Even when the Protest Phase was rampant, most of its fans preferred it with jam: preferred the sweeter versions of the *Blowin' In The Wind* kind of song, by—the example is inevitable—Peter, Paul & Mary. There were, in fact, over sixty different recorded versions of that particular song, all performing the same function: anaesthetizing the Dylan message. Columbia Records (CBS), being in it for the money, were caught both ways: on the one hand they forced the suppression of his *Talking John Birch Society Blues* and at the same time they found it necessary to mount a campaign with the somewhat mournful slogan *Nobody Sings Dylan Like Dylan.*

In fact, of course, the "protest" group of songs is not of outstanding quality: Dylan's performances of them can do little more than partly compensate, as it were, for the lack of anything in them but "messages". Much of this early Dylan social commentary appeared at the time, and appears more so in retrospect, obvious and consequently naïve. It is not just the clichés that mar these songs but—along with their obviousness—the assumption that cliché is necessary for emphasis: the assumption that the listener must be spoon-fed, if not force-fed. Dylan is giving us rhetoric, not art. In contrast, where societal comment is present in his later work—as for instance in the 12-minute *Desolation Row* on the "Highway 61 Revisited" album—Dylan's critique is always offered in a form dictated by a most formidable art and not by an anxiety based on lack of trust in the listener.

We have already seen from *Song To Woody* that the early Dylan was aware of such criteria; his early folk-protest-conservationist audiences were not. Here was a folk singer, by any sane definition of the term, who was first upbraided with the hillbilly tag and then, because he had written *Blowin' In The Wind*, made the victim of a public idolatry, misplaced and misconceived: an idolatry which demanded that he keep on writing that song, again and again, for the rest of his artistic life. When he broke away from this, the response was again an upbraiding. Ironically enough, because of the direction in which Dylan set out, the new approach went like this: you sound like a pop-star: we still want folksingers here.

The utter blankness of such a response was made graphically clear at the 1965 Newport Folk Festival. By this time exploring an electric sound, Dylan appeared with his electric guitar. The audience took this as a parading of the intention to "sell out". The songs he sang, which did not include the "protest" group, were at first greeted by hostile silence. Eventually, the audience shouted its inarticulate objections and Dylan walked off the stage. He was, in the end, persuaded to return and reappeared, this time with his old, acoustic guitar. The audience members assumed that they had disciplined their recalcitrant idol into submission—and it sufficiently condemns their intentions that this pleased them. It was, in any event, a short-lived assumption, for Dylan sang only one more song—the aptly-titled and derisive (in context) *It's All Over Now, Baby Blue*.

Such an explicit lesson should not have been necessary. The whole controversy about Dylan's songs and styles reveals a fundamental misunderstanding of his claim to be an artist, and an almost total failure to appreciate the traditions of folk culture which Dylan's work has, with varying degrees of prominence, always displayed.

I don't think it necessary to spend long on the first point—on defining what American folk music is and is not. Traditionally, it has been that day-to-day music created by the people and for the people, rather than that created by and for small, educated elites. It gives form to the democratic ideal. It moves below the mainstream of culture, the flow of which is sustained and altered by the small elites. It is a cohesive and natural sub-culture (if, for convenience's sake, we concede here to the traditional elitist perspective on it).

In the present century, of course, this music of the ordinary American people has become radically less regionalized. The slump and dust-bowl times provided a focus on the "inevitable" transition from the American family's adherence to regional ties to the dislocating removal of most of this insularity and its replacement by a more rational and uniform consciousness. As the people moved from the farms and small communities, folk music moved to the media.

On the other hand, though the way of life from which folk music flowed naturally has essentially disappeared, the radical changes of environment which have been forced upon millions of Americans by an ailing capitalist system have to some degree acted as stimuli to self-expression—however defensive that impulse must now be—and thereby as a regenerative influence on the creativity of ordinary people. Urbanized life has altered but none the less maintained the means of invention of music and song undreamt of in the Cole Porter philosophy. This we can still plausibly call folk art—and we can find it characterized at its best by pertinent themes, and vital sensibilities.

Alan Lomax, America's pre-eminent expert on folk music, wrote (in noting the effects of such environmental changes) that

> ... there are aesthetic needs that Hollywood and Tin Pan Alley do not yet know how to satisfy. Tomorrow the Holy Rollers, the hillbillies, the blues shouters, the gospel singers—the Leadbellies, the Guthries ... who have formed our twentieth-century folk music, will be replaced by other folk artists ... [who] will give voice to the deep feelings and unspoken needs of their own time, as have all the folk-singers of the past.

Future or past, folk music must flow naturally from the lives of those who participate in it. When such lives were eked out traditionally, in country communities, the primary material—to shelter in and to work with—was wood. This was the simple reason for the centrality of the acoustic guitar in folk music. Now that people buy their environments in units of electric technology, folk culture has new material to work with. The serious contemporary artist cannot ignore the technology that surrounds him and shapes his life-style; and he has every reason to utilize it not only for his art but also in the interests of the clear duty to reach an audience.

A consideration of the issues involved in all this—which the black folk artists of twentieth-century America have always understood—ought to have been fired into being by the changing

31

direction of Dylan's art, even among those who have decided—either in the context of folk music or in the wider context of "Art"—that because a man goes out to his audience competent not only with a pen but also with microphones and studios and sound-effects and electric instruments, he must *ipso facto* be a fraud.

To dispute the validity of "going electric" in folk music seems to me to disregard the responsible resources of artistic work; and the attempts of the "purists" to "preserve" folk music from such moves can only, where successful, act to the detriment of folk music's potential for growth.

Two final observations here: firstly that to insist on all this is not to argue that the electric guitar, for instance, is essential all the time nor to suggest that the issue at stake is one of trendiness versus the old-fashioned; and secondly that other issues raised here —for instance, that of the borderline area between folk art and "art proper" (between the sub-culture and the mainstream)—are returned to at a later point. It seems more appropriate here and now to concentrate on the specific folk music roots, traditional and modern, in Dylan's work.

When American life was wholly localized and regional, there were four main types of American folk music (apart from the traditions preserved by foreign-language immigrants, on which I can't see —though the fault may well be mine—that Dylan has drawn). These four were: Yankee, Southern Poor White, Cowboy and Black. All four figure strongly in Dylan's art, if in very different guises as that art has matured.

The Yankee, who first sang on packet ships and there revived the sea-shanties that had dropped out of circulation in the British Navy, adapted his songs to the newer environment when working in the forests that stretch from Maine to Dylan's home-state of Minnesota. The nature of this life and work produced a tradition of song in which the workman was a hard and grimly realistic hero. A less "reflective" Hemingway ideal.

The Yankee backwoodsman sang in a hard, monotonous, high-pitched, nasal voice; his songs used decorated melodies in gapped scale structures; and words mattered more than tunes.[4] Those familiar with Dylan's early work will recognize aspects of it, both of style and content, in that description. Indeed, the close relation much of the early Dylan output keeps with this Yankee tradition is what makes that output difficult to attune to, not only for adults trained by Gilbert and Sullivan (in which the words are decadent nonsense and a-tune-you-can-hum is the main ingredient) but also for the pop-orientated teenager.

There is perhaps little more in the Yankee tradition that claims Dylan as its modern voice. Although a song such as his *Lonesome Death of Hattie Carroll* makes "an ordinary worker" into a kind of heroine, Dylan makes this happen as a device, not an end in itself: a device for strengthening an essentially political and social polemic. He does the same with Medgar Evers and his killers in *Only A Pawn In Their Game*: the two men are just pawns in Dylan's "game". On the other hand, *North Country Blues* much more nearly exhibits a traditional Yankee perspective, in that it deals very consciously with a working community's suffering, albeit treated through the story of one family's misfortunes, and with that community's annihilation. The song provides a timely epitaph to the destruction of the folk culture such a community produced, while getting the dynamics of its construction from that kind of culture. When, on the much later album, "Self Portrait", Dylan returns to a Yankee song, *Days of '49*, he offers it quite rightly as a museum-piece even as he breathes new life into it.

Beyond this, however, there are, elsewhere in Dylan's work, strong points of adherence to the Yankee tradition as regards technique. For instance, this kind of language-juggling—from *Katy Cruel*—has provided a stimulus to Dylan's own linguistic inventiveness:

> O that I was where I would be
> Then would I be where I am not
> Here I am where I must be
> Go where I would I can not.

It is a convention of mock confusion, and Dylan acquires it, and uses it. One can trace its development in his songs, from the early use of it—device used as device—where it remains straight mock confusion, to his frequent later plays on drug confusion. There is the buoyancy of the juggling in his adaptation of *Freight Train Blues*, on his first album:

> My father was the fireman and my mother dear
> She was the only daughter of the engineer

33

> My sweetheart loved the brakeman an' it aint no joke
> Seein' the way she keeps a good man broke

and in contrast the equally word-stumbling *Just Like Tom Thumb's Blues*, from Dylan's sixth album, "Highway 61 Revisited":

> If you see Saint Annie, please tell her thanks a lot,
> I cannot move, my fingers, they are all in a knot,
> I don't have the strength to get up and take another shot,
> And my best friend my doctor wont even tell me what
>   it is I got.

Granted, the change is a drastic one in many ways. *Freight Train Blues* states a clear situation in a deliberately complicated way—as does the stanza from *Katy Cruel*; *Tom Thumb's Blues* states relatively clearly the complications of the predicament described. In the first song, the confusion is a smoke-ring created and then blown away by the lyric alone; in the second, it is the message itself, established by the music and the delivery as well as by the words. (This overall reliance is emphasized in the version of the song recorded in concert in Liverpool, May 1966, and issued as the B-side of the *I Want You* single.[5])

Despite the differences, however, both *Tom Thumb's Blues* and the early *Freight Train Blues* are inspired by the same mode of theatrical stylization. They both show a common intent and a common convention. The link between them is made clear enough by looking at another song from "Highway 61 Revisited", the much-esteemed *Ballad Of A Thin Man*.

This song has often been seen as a cruel, hard-line attack upon un-hip people, on the people who will not recognize that the times have been a-changing. If this was indeed its frame of reference, the song wouldn't merit much attention, except by the most paranoid kind of hippy. But it is not a song that merely condemns others—either for being fascists, or fuddy-duddies, or indeed for being lost. In fact, "condemns" is not the right word at all. *Ballad Of A Thin Man*'s importance is that it deals with a universal experience—the feeling of a loss of identity and the mind's attempt to overcome the consequent sense of debility. There is no condemnation of the many, or the old, nor any corresponding implication of praise for the trendier, younger few. The song implicates its narrator quite consciously and so makes clear that we are each of us the Mr. Jones whose confusion we witness:

> You raise up your head
> And you ask is this where it is?
> And somebody points to you and says
> It's his
> And you say what's mine?
> And somebody else says
> Well what is?
> And you say Oh my God, am I here, all alone?
>
> Because something is happening here
> But you don't know what it is,
> Do you, Mr. Jones?

The confusion there is all-embracing, and so it gives us the sense of the link mentioned above in that its confusion straddles both the language and the subject-matter. One notes, in particular, that superlatively ambiguous question "Well what is?", which the listener first takes as the simple retort to Mr. Jones' plaintive "What's mine?" but which then comes across with its second and deadlier meaning—"Well, what *is*?"—and so demolishes even those few certainties that seemed unquestioned earlier.

*   *   *

Southern Poor White folk music, hillbilly mountain music, the music of the settlers—which was the second of the four main American folk traditions—consisted of hybrids. Its songs fused Scots, Irish and English influences and yet expressed a new-world pioneer milieu. Songs like *Come All You Virginia Girls*; *Old Blue*; *I Love My Love*; *Went Up On The Mountain*; and *Pretty Saro* reflected normal life all across the southern backwoods, and testified to the cultural bonds between Poor Whites as far west as Texas and Oklahoma.

It was a tradition linked fundamentally to Calvinist precepts —to the passionate belief in sin, the concern for individual salvation and the surety of a God On Our Side. Uncle John, from Oklahoma, in *Grapes of Wrath*, is in this sense the compleat descendant of the pioneers who constructed the tradition.

Whether this tradition impinged on Dylan in childhood—his was a suitably small-town community—or in adolescent travelling or even simply in listening to the radio, one doesn't know; but at any rate, its eccentric and fascinating hybrid songs certainly did reach him somehow.

With its vital mixing of ancient and fresh vocabulary and its truly pioneering grammatical freedom, this tradition offered what is the real core of folk song, a conserving process which is at the same time creative; and in his use today of that fundamental life-force, Dylan is the great white folk singer. He has drawn on this tradition in two ways: he has used its established characteristics for some of his own song-structures, and he has used its very lively inventiveness as a source of strength for his own.

His adaptation of the traditional Scottish song *Pretty Peggy-O*, on his first album, gives a Texas accent a central rhythmic purpose. The guitar-work and melodic structuring on *The Ballad Of Hollis Brown* are straight from the Appalachians, where such forms and modes had evolved, in comparative isolation,[6] over a period of almost two hundred years. And a traditional song such as *East Virginia* reflects the brooding about death which Dylan echoes throughout his first album (and sometimes in later work) and which is rooted as much in the orthodoxy of Calvinism as in black folk culture.

The Calvinist precepts are not, of course, taken up wholesale by Dylan: rather, he takes up the challenge, the encapsulating threat, of these ideas. In *With God On Our Side*, which appeared on his *Times They Are A-Changin'* album towards the end of his flirtation with the protest movement, it is the early part of the song, and not the later homilies on world wars and atom bombs, that is of real and lasting interest. It gives us Dylan assessing the inroads of pioneer religiosity on his own sensibility:

> O my name it means nothing
> My age it means less:
> The country I come from
> Is called the Mid-West.
> I was taught an' brought up there
> The laws to abide
> And that the land that I live in
> Has God On Its Side ...

36

There is an extraordinary sweep of implicit experience in those first four lines. The sense of the narrator's context—his sense of history and therefore of identity—makes itself felt quietly and yet with impact. The careful omission of any "but" or "yet" or "and" between the second and third lines has a striking and forceful effect. This creation of effect by what is lacking, not by what is there, is characteristic of much Dylan material, and gets a fuller discussion later in this book.

The verse just quoted also provides an obvious dismantling of the Calvinist doctrine contained in the song title: and it is a pity that as the later verses draw nearer and nearer to the "protest" formula, this dismantling becomes correspondingly heavy-handed. In contrast, this first verse has a truly compelling delicacy. And it is able to give us very finely the narrator's sense of the intellectual and moral pressure of his upbringing in terms of "folk education". The third and fourth lines refer to the listener, again with a considerable poise of implication, to the seeds of folk lore blown over by travel and by time from New England and its neighbours. Clearly, those two lines do not provide a mechanically-inserted or merely peripheral piece of information. Dylan is stating his awareness that the country he comes from has its claims upon him, and upon his art, for both good and bad. (He nowhere draws more on his background familiarity with Calvinistic folk life than in his beautifully poised, pinched delivery on the unreleased *Quit Your Low Down Ways*—a definitive cameo, as he does it.)

Lastly, Dylan returns to Appalachian music on his 1970 double-album, "Self Portrait", to give us an odd but effectively atmospheric version of the traditional song *Copper Kettle*. As with all the music he touches on this collection, he brings back to life the spirit of the age that the song is all about, and does it immeasurably better than those purists to whom his version (it has violins and women on it! !) is anathema. And as if to emphasize further his ability to do this sort of thing, the same album offers a Dylan composition, *Belle Isle*, which reaches back even further into the traditional folk past, invoking those purely Gallic origins which are part of the founding ingredients of America's Southern Poor White music.

* * *

The Cowboy music tradition was, like the Southern Poor White, a hybrid, though of a different and more simple kind: it was basically an amalgam of Southern and Yankee brands of folk. In Lomax's phrase, "the cowboy singer was a Yankee balladeer with a southern accent". And though the wildest of his predecessors have been discarded by popular history,[7] the cowboy himself remains substantially the hero of the American dream.

As with the hillbilly genre, Dylan uses the cowboy tradition in two ways. He uses the structures and conventions, and he uses the atmospheric essence. This essence is the lyric magic that first takes its being from the "noble" struggle of hard-living men in a hostile work environment (and later, much more famously, from the communion of the individual with his own loneliness in the environment of the great western plains). A traditional sample of the hard-struggle song is this:

> Our hearts were made of iron, our souls were cased with
> steel,
> The hardships of that winter could never make us yield,
> Our food, the dogs would snarl at it, our beds were in the
> snow,
> We suffered worse than murderers up in Michigan-i-o.

That recalls, in Dylan's output, more than his delighted use of that last rhyming device in his version of *Pretty Peggy-O* ("He died somewheres in Loos-i-ana-o"). We can easily envisage Dylan singing—say, on "Self Portrait"—the lines just quoted. Phrases like "our food, the dogs would snarl at it" are well within what we've come to know as Dylan's scope. And to think back to *Song To Woody* is to recognize a rhythmic effect similar to that achieved in the above, on phrases like "Here's to the hearts and the hands of the men".

This same flavour is prominent again in Dylan's *Ballad Of Hollis Brown*—even though there the sense of community is taken outside the song's characters and exists solely between the narrator and his subjects (and is only a one-way awareness, for the narrator's sympathy cannot reach their loneliness):

> There are seven breezes blowin' all around the cabin door
> Seven breezes blowin' all around the cabin door
> And somewhere in the distance a cold coyote calls.

A very different song, though from the same Dylan album, draws just as firmly on the idea of the hard struggle of good-hearted men to overcome adversity. The song is *When The Ship Comes In,* and it is a tribute to Dylan's intelligence and artistry that he can use the strengths of this theme from this tradition in the utterly different context, in this song, of a moral struggle, without any loss of poise. It is a much under-rated song.

Part of its tremendous appeal comes, of course, from its tune and from Dylan's performance. Throughout the song, these two elements combine, and combine with the words, to sustain a maximum effect and energy (as, for instance, when we come to that simple word "shout" in the last verse: the voice does indeed break into a shout, a celebratory exclamation, and hits the word as the tune hits, for it, the highest note in the verse).

Even as mere words-on-the-page, though, the song has a distinctive and distinguished charm, very much its own—like a glimpse into a world both real and unreal: morally mature (if severe) yet childlike in conception.

The internal rhyming is so effective, driving the vision along in the rhythm of the oncoming ship as it meets, again and again, relentlessly, the swell of the sea:

> And the song, will, lift, as the main, sail, shifts
> And the boat, drifts, ...

Moreover, this internal rhyming collaborates perfectly with the alliterative effects (as well, of course, as with the tune):

> Then the sands will roll out a carpet of gold
> For your weary toes to be a-touchin'. . .

Never once does this immense charm come across as simplistic or faulty, and this is a more than merely technical achievement. The childlike allegory that Dylan is offering comes over, in fact, as a quite unexceptionable moral cleanliness—a convincing wisdom.

This not only redresses anger; it yields a positive and spirited apprehension of the new age's possibilities (which, other differences aside, sets it very much apart from, and qualitatively beyond, say, *The Times They Are A-Changin'*):

> Oh the fishes will laugh as they swim out of the path
> And the seagulls, they'll be smiling ...

And the sun will respect every face on the deck
The hour when the ship comes in.

Political yearnings do not sweep aside more ordinary joys envisaged: to talk of the joy of having sand between your toes, to
feel glad of the imagined sympathy of fishes as well as of the
overseeing of "the ship's wise men", and to conceive, in the midst
of creating a mood of general anticipation, a fancy demanding
such a particular image as that of a smiling seagull face—this is
to encompass a wise and salutary statement of hope. (Indeed, an
alternative interpretation of the song consists in seeing it not as a
political dream at all but as an allegorical statement of personal
hope: as, in fact, the fantastic dream-corollary of *Boots of Spanish
Leather*.)

It accords with this achievement—this sustained control—that
Dylan avoids painting "the foes" as demons or fools. They are
big enough to hold on to a certain dignity where the allegory goes
biblical; and yet, beyond this, the apparently childlike vision
applies to them too, humanizing them even as it condemns:

> Oh the foes will rise with the sleep still in their eyes
> And they'll jerk from their beds and think they're dreamin'
> But they'll pinch themselves and squeal and know that its
>   for real
> The hour when the ship comes in.

As even this perfunctory glance shows, Dylan has taken us a long
way, in *When The Ship Comes In*, beyond the cowboy tradition
on which the song is based; and in any case, its basis is in the less
recognizable of the two cowboy types. What needs to be considered
now is Dylan's relation to the other type: that which corresponds
to our image of the cowboy hero, that which is bathed in the
romantic lyricism of saddle-sore silent men set against lonesome
prairies and plains.

The traditional song *I'm A-Ridin' Old Paint* well represents
the genre:

> Now when I die don't bury me at all
> Just saddle my pony, lead him out of the stall
> Tie my bones in the saddle, turn our faces to the west
> And we'll ride the prairie that we love best.

If Dylan had used that as it stands we should, before "Self Portrait" at least, have considered it surprising and even dishonest. Dylan adapts before he uses, and the only exceptions apart from the "Self Portrait" traditional songs—which in any case, as we've noted, aren't left entirely to themselves—are early on in his career.

It isn't surprising, therefore, that Dylan never actually rides a horse (or a pony) through his songs. Indeed, the only Dylan recording which uses clippety-clop noises is the one called, ironically enough, *You Aint Goin' Nowhere* (the unreleased version).

The horse, in fact, is really less important to the cowboy genre than the ethic of noble misanthropy which womanlessness imposed. When a pattern of abstinence, bar-room tarts, abstinence is the enforced norm in a working man's life, a certain defensiveness is bound to develop in his ethical stance. So the cowboy nurtured an internal restlessness into something bigger than himself. His home became the Big Wide West—and he always felt compelled to be "movin' on". And how easy it was for this spirit to pass from the nineteenth-century cowboy to the twentieth-century professional hobo.

Dylan takes this up, sometimes comically, more often with a plausible earnestness. The comical example that springs to mind is from *Country Pie*, on the "Nashville Skyline" album:

> Saddle me up a big white goose!
> Tie me on her and turn her loose!
> Oh! me, oh! my—
> Love that Country Pie!

which we can take as a sympathetic send-up of the traditional song just quoted.

Dylan's more serious expressions of this compulsion to move on, to not get entangled, are numerous. On "Self Portrait" he relaxes—as he does more conspicuously and perhaps less wholeheartedly on *Country Pie*—and handles Clayton's famous *Gotta Travel On* as the archetypal statement it is. In other words, he lets the words remain as simple as they are and puts the song across as music: and that music rides on beautifully. In contrast, he gives voice to the same roving compulsion in the disarming aphorism that brings his *Ballad Of Frankie Lee And Judas Priest* to a close on the "John Wesley Harding" album:

41

... don't go mistaking Paradise for that home across the road.

When we come to Dylan's more concentrated and sustained expressions of this same theme, of this negative-positive moral, we find, I think, that their plausibility derives from their being always addressed to a particular woman or specific entanglements of which the narrator understands the full worth. It is never, in Dylan's hands, a merely boastful theme—never a Papa Hemingway conceit, an I'm-too-hot-to-hold bravado. The opposite impulse, the desire to stay and be entangled, is always felt to be present, though it cannot (until "Nashville Skyline") win.

We have this formula in *Don't Think Twice, It's All Right*, from the second Dylan album, a song based, for its tune, on Johnny Cash's composition *Understand Your Man*:

> I'm a-thinkin' and a-wond'rin', all the way down the road,
> I once loved a woman—a child, I am told:
> I gave her my heart but she wanted my soul
> But don't think twice, it's all right.

The same integrity of spirit underlies the 1964 song *It Aint Me, Babe*:

> You say you're looking for someone
> Who'll pick you up each time you fall,
> To gather flowers constantly
> An' to come each time you call:
> A lover for your life an' nothing more—
> But it aint me, babe,
> No, no, no, it aint me, babe,
> It aint me you're looking for, babe.

In the first of those two examples, there is a hint of direct reproach, yet the narrator's own doubts give this a redressing balance. The title line is, in that verse of the song, deliberately addressed to the narrator himself. In the second example above, doubt is unnecessary because behind the narrator's careful assessment of the woman involved there is an element of compassion for her needs, and a consequent determination on his part to acquit himself fairly.

There are many more instances of Dylan's using this "gotta travel on" spirit. Perhaps his most directly autobiographical state-

42

ment of it comes in the hastily-composed yet excellent *Restless Farewell*, with which he closes his "Times They Are A-Changin'" album. Within the same collection, that word "restless" is taken up again in a song Dylan has revisited often since, the lovely *One Too Many Mornings*:

> It's a restless, hungry feeling that don't mean no one no
>   good[8]
> When ev'rything I'm sayin' you can say it just as good
> You're right from your side. I'm right from mine:
> We're both just one too many mornings
> An' a thousand miles
> Behind.

Often, then, this restlessness runs into what is for Dylan a search for the ideal, for nothing less than the perfect. It is only when we reach as far through his career as the "Nashville Skyline" album that we find this search largely discarded. On the whole, the mood of this album is against this restlessness. Consciously, at last, an imperfect love can be accepted as salvation.

The last song on the album brings this out most explicitly: *Tonight I'll Be Staying Here With You*. As its title suggests, it's a deliberate announcement of the fall from restlessness. The habit of always moving on has been kicked and the impulse to stay has at last succeeded:

> Throw my ticket out the window
> Throw my suitcase out there too
> Throw my troubles out the door
> I don't need them any more
> 'Cause tonight I'll be staying here with you
>
> I should have left this town this morning
> But it was more than I could do
> Oh your love comes on so strong
> And I've waited all day long
> For tonight, when I'll be staying here with you.

In the first of those verses, we get the direct announcement; and the first three lines give us the gestures that go with it (and those of us steeped in the legends of rock music might well be reminded, by those lines, of Little Richard throwing his gold and jewelled

43

rings over Sydney Harbour Bridge as he announced his intention, years ago, to follow the Lord instead of Mammon).

Similarly, that "should have left this town this morning", in the second verse, is a reference to the old travelling compunction now renounced, not merely to some particular journey's schedule. And correspondingly, of course, the point of the title line is that it isn't just tonight; the narrator has come to rest. Not even the train whistle heard in the distance can lure him back to homeless sojourns now.

Two further points are raised by this song, both of which take us away from the strict context of the cowboy ethic in which it has so far been seen. However, the digression it takes to discuss these two points seems fairly necessary.

First, there is the question of whether each individual work of art must stand alone—because we have only discussed *Tonight I'll Be Staying Here With You* in the context of other, earlier Dylan songs. The consideration given it above has implied, and quite rightly, that its importance lies in its reversal of the *Gotta Travel On* philosophy. If we didn't see the song as part of a pattern in Dylan's output, if we hadn't come across Dylan before and we found it simply as a song on its own, a song by itself, would it merit any real attention?

Probably not. But Dylan has clearly rejected the things-must-stand-up-by-themselves proposition; in consequence it would be, I think, missing the point for the critic and the listener to try to adhere to it. In any case, even if Dylan himself attempted such an adherence, he could never succeed. No work of art stands alone: it is created in a context—involving the things that inspired it, and so on—and on completion is at once assimilated into other contexts: not least into the context of the whole pattern of works of art which the very fact of its emergence, as Eliot pointed out, disturbs and changes. Moreover, no art theorist can, as it were, disallow specific references by one work of art to others. Eliot's own *Wasteland* is full of such references; and, to take a much smaller example, that chorused "No, no, no" in Dylan's *It Aint Me Babe* includes a passing reference to that once-famous 'Yeah, yeah, yeah" in the Beatles' song *She Loves You*. If *It Aint Me Babe* reverses *She Loves You*, there's no reason why *Tonight I'll Be Staying Here With You* should not depend on a reversal of the theme of *It Aint Me Babe*.

44

In fact, Dylan takes this particular theme-reversal further, and in doing so relies even more heavily on the context of his own bygone opposites. In "Self Portrait" he gives us his own version of *Let It Be Me* (French tune, American lyrics) which was a smash for the Everly Brothers years before—and in recording this song the year after giving us *Tonight I'll Be Staying Here With You*, Dylan is emphasizing his new-found lack of restlessness; for it begins:

> I bless the day I found you ...

and in a sense Dylan has rewritten that song, by giving it an importance which derives precisely from his placing it so firmly inside the context of his own writing, his own output, his own creative spectrum.

When I first heard *It Aint Me Babe* I specially liked that line "A lover for your life and nothing more" because in pop songs there never was anything more: to be a "a lover for your life" was the ultimate ideal. For me, then, *It Aint Me Babe* was good in the context of this contrast; and five years of Dylan output later, *Tonight I'll Be Staying Here With You* is good in that it can make use of its contrast to *It Aint Me Babe*. It's not a step back, it's another step beyond—and it is in this same spirit of achievement that Dylan can reintroduce that "I bless the day I found you" in *Let It Be Me*, so that despite its being an old pop song it, too, under Dylan's auspices, shows the same progressive second step. It parallels "Throw my ticket out the window".

This brings us round to the second digressionary point that needs mentioning—namely, the question of the acceptability and effectiveness of the ultra-simplicity of language in which Dylan deals in these new/newly-used homecoming songs. It was, after all, quite a shock, on a first play of "Nashville Skyline", to hear Dylan singing lines like that (already quoted above) from *Tonight I'll Be Staying Here With You*: "For your love comes on so strong". And when we come to the middle-eight of that song, we find Dylan coming on even stronger with this "new" language:

> Is it really any wonder
> The love that a stranger might receive?
> You cast your spell and I went under
> I find it so difficult to leave.[9]

45

Once more, we have to look at this in the context of Dylan's other work. Only against such a background can we ask or begin to answer our instinctive question: What is he playing at?

One "answer"—one comment at least—was given in an interview with Doug Kershaw (revered Nashville violinist who appears on Dylan's "Self Portrait" album) which Patrick Thomas conducted for *Rolling Stone* magazine and which is partly reproduced in the postscript to Chapter 8 (pp. 283–4). Another useful comment on the same issue is offered by Geoffrey Cannon's review, in the *Guardian* of June 26th, 1970, of "Self Portrait". Cannon sees the "You cast your spell and I went under" kind of language in another context also:

> ... the coup of "Nashville Skyline" [was] to demonstrate that proverbs are aphorisms when used (as they always are, except in books) by a particular person to a particular person, in a place and a time. It's human context, not verbal dexterity, that lets words, especially words of love, work.

That account is a little dangerous, of course: we shouldn't be talked into gracing any old pop writer's clichés with the descriptive term "proverbs"; nor is it anything but silly to pretend that the widespread dissemination of such clichés is anything but irresponsible—it trains people to think, not just speak, in platitudes, and thereby it trains people not to think at all. Yet there is a sense in which Cannon's argument does apply to a Dylan song such as the "Nashville Skyline" one we've been looking at. When Dylan sings "For your love comes on so strong" he is effectively saying that that phrase will do as well as any to cover that small part of his feelings which he can hope to put into words. And when he says that, he is rejecting a self-image of Dylan the brilliant poet in favour of a concept of himself as an ordinary man coping with love. That is how such phrases work, that is what justifies things like "You cast your spell". It shouldn't be necessary to emphasize that this is not Dylan patronizing, or condescending to, the ordinary mind; it is a confession, candid and accepting, that he is, in ways that it matters to be honest about, an ordinary man himself. It is, from a different perspective, part of the process whereby, by the time of the "Self Portrait" album, Dylan has detached his own legend substantially from his material.

To return, now, to where we left off. Love doesn't always come

Dylan's way on "Nashville Skyline", but it does provide the focus of his desire. The second verse of the quiet *I Threw It All Away* —the "it" being love—echoes the cowboy ethos succinctly by using, as his image for the discarded love's value, the scenery the lonesome traveller has around him in place of love:

> Once I had mountains in the palm of my hand
> And rivers that ran through every day—
> I must have been mad, I never knew what I had
> Until I threw it all away.

The emphasis there is on the problem of choice, but the choice propounded is again that between loving and moving on.

It may be said that there are much stronger influences in all this from modern country music (country-'n'-western, as it is still called in England) than from the older traditional material. Let's not quibble too much about that: it is from the traditions that the modern amalgam derives, and in any case it is hardly possible to draw a line through some year in American history and say that behind the line stands virginal tradition, and in front the whore of Nashville. Certainly, it is necessary to look at both—although not in the spirit suggested by my analogy—because there is more in Dylan's country pie than cowboy classics revisited (as we have seen) and more, equally, than the bland successors of Hank Williams can match. More too than modern voices with styles or techniques of their own—the Roger Millers, Glen Campbells, Buck Owenses and Jerry Lee Lewises.

It isn't denigrating Jerry Lee—who is a fine singer and a very fine pianist—to say that even the Dylan songs most reminiscent of his work are less performances and cameos in his idiom than attempts to bring a new disciplinary precision to that idiom. The two songs I have in mind are *Down Along The Cove*, from the superlative "John Wesley Harding" album, and *Living The Blues*, from "Self Portrait". It isn't possible to illustrate the "new disciplinary precision" that sets them beyond Jerry Lee Lewis's work by pointing at the lyrics, because in each case Dylan achieves this through the music. In *Down Along The Cove*, for instance, it is done almost entirely through the drumming and guitar-work.

At the same time, one of the many things that "Self Portrait" and the like can send us back to with a heightened appreciation is certainly Jerry Lee Lewis's old country B-side material—material

like Hank Williams' *Cold, Cold Heart* cut for the legendary Sun
label in Memphis and issued as the flip of *It Won't Happen With
Me* in 1961.

As for the Dylan song that most clearly registers Hank Williams
himself—*One More Night*, from "Nashville Skyline"—it too includes far more than its ostensible inspirator can offer.

The tune of the verses, though not of the middle-eight, is that
of an old English popular song. Correspondingly, the lyric is not
only consciously "unoriginal" but actually recalls other lyrics:

> Oh it's shameful and it's sad
> I lost the only pal I had
> I just could not be what she wanted me to be
> I will turn my head up high
> To that dark an' rollin' sky
> For tonight no light will shine on me
>
> I was so mistaken when I thought that she'd be true
> I had no idea what a woman in love would do:

That couplet beginning "I will turn my head up high" comes
straight from the traditional cowboy song *Lonesome Prairie*,
except that in the original as we know it "the dark" stands in
place of Dylan's "that dark". There is a less exact but none the
less striking resemblance also between Dylan's last verse and a
part of the famous oldie *Blue Moon Of Kentucky*—and this is a
resemblance that goes further than the lyric. Dylan's use of the
tune at this point, and the whole tone of his delivery, suggest
that Dylan has a copy of the very early Elvis recording of the
Blue Moon Of Kentucky song. In any case, the words are con-
vergent. Dylan's last verse runs:

> One more night, the moon is shinin' bright
> And the wind blows high above the tree
> Oh I miss that woman so,
> I didn't mean to see her go
> But tonight no light will shine on me.

and *Blue Moon Of Kentucky* says the same.

Perhaps this helps to identify the light for which Dylan's narrator
waits, and waits in vain. At the root of it, of course, there is the
simple idea that moonlight cannot penetrate the heart love has

abandoned; the trouble is that Dylan's lyric is not just a continual re-phrasing of this idea but a continually confused one. Only in the middle-eight do we get any real precision of phrasing:

> I was so mistaken when I thought that she'd be true
> I had no idea what a woman in love would do:

and that indeed has a remarkable economy of statement, which belies its apparent ordinariness. In the rest of the song, though, there is a noticeable slackness of structure—heightened, moreover, by the absence of slack in the music.

Yet Dylan's lyric does offer the flash of wit in that word "pal" in the second verse. This does more than give us a sudden smile at the whole genre the song represents: it also lends a subtle support to the line that follows it, in referring us back to much earlier Dylan songs. "I just could not be what she wanted me to be" plus "only pal I had" equals

> All I really want to do
> Is baby be friends with you

—which was the sentiment that opened Dylan's 1964 album, "Another Side Of Bob Dylan".

But that sentiment is only momentarily recalled by that second verse. The focus of the song is not the same as in *All I Really Want To Do,* as its middle-eight insistently confirms. A true friend? A true love? And doesn't this affect "the light", by colouring the listener's idea of how the pathetic fallacy might be at work?

In the end, regardless of its imprecisions, the song gives us the cowboy genre lightly and attractively enough under that dark and rollin' sky.

Another aspect of the cowboy tradition is its special fondness for heroes, and Dylan comes to this on the "John Wesley Harding" album, as he reaches back into America's past for the secret strengths of her myths. The album is a "retreat"—a turning away —from the chaos of the modern urban intellectual's burden; yet clearly it is a regenerative spirit that drives Dylan to search back as he does. He engages, in this album, in a desperately serious struggle to free himself—and subsequently to free us—from the debilitating predicament our fragmented sensibility has placed us

49

in; the predicament Dylan defined on his previous album, the druggy, urban, chaotic, compelling "Blonde On Blonde". *Visions Of Johanna* summed up this mess:

> We sit here stranded
> We all doin' our best
> To deny it . . .

As Dylan comes, then, in "John Wesley Harding", to the myths and extinct strengths of America, he explores the world of the cowboy as well as the pioneer. The man in the title song is a cowboy, and, indeed, a hero.

It is a modest exploration, in that the cowboy-outlaw is not an unusual subject for hero-treatment; but what a delicate, subtle portrait the song offers. It is all so simple, so straightforward (like the system of values we have come to associate with the cowboy world): a ballad that tells the story of its hero's exploits. Yet at the end one still has no idea what actually happened, nor any clear indication of the narrator's attitude. One is given clues but no bearings. It was never like this when Tennessee Ernie Ford sang *The Ballad of Davy Crockett*.

The song's economy of organization and language is noticeable at once. There is no use of simile and no reliance on images or symbolism. Following that, we notice a corresponding lack of what may be called "moral centre". Each statement in this ostensibly bare narrative is placed in egalitarian conditions and demands an equal scrutiny. Nine of the twelve lines provide what could be taken, at first glance, as testaments to the hero's worth and virtue: yet actually none is free from significant ambiguity—and these equivocations, collectively, have a piercing eloquence to offer.

> John Wesley Harding was a friend to the poor

In what way? To what extent? The claim has, deliberately, no core behind its apparent bluntness. It refrains from contradicting the suspicion that Harding's name could be added to a long list of men whose lives and interests are spent in opposition, effectively, to the lives and interests of the poor but to whom it is advantageous to seem to appeal. Plenty of hero-reputations depend upon this pretence.

As for those two very reasonable questions raised by that first line of *John Wesley Harding*—a friend in what way? and to what extent?—they are in no way answered by the rest of the song.

> All along this countryside he opened many a door

We could put similar questions in response to that—and be met by a similar blank. The line opens no doors for us.

It works, as intended, by yielding an echo which lingers throughout the song: the echo of a second empty claim. To it must be added the corresponding echoes of the other claims that confront us. As we meet them, the next is this:

> But he was never known to hurt an honest man.

Dylan chooses the negative form of expression; and the consciously reductive intention this reveals gets reinforcement from further negatives in the song; and it ends by giving us a pile-up of three of them:

> But no charge held against him could they prove
> And there was no man around who could track or chain
>   'im down
> He was never known to make a foolish move.

Not only is all this presented carefully in the negative, but it all serves to emphasize the deliberate vicariousness of the testimony we're given: "He was never known to ...; He was never known to ...'

Back in the first verse again, the fourth line is linked to the third in such a way as to discredit any inference of virtue from either when they are considered together. He opened many a door but he was never known to hurt an honest man. That word "but" gives the statements either side of it a cynical focus which the substitution of "and" could have avoided had Dylan's intention been different (had Dylan's approach, for instance, been Hollywood's).

The following lines add precisely nothing to our picture of the hero's character:

> 'Twas down in Caynee Coun'y, the time they talk about ...
> And soon the situation there was all but straightened out ...
> All across the telegraph his name it did resound;

and the inferences to be made do not concern his heroism, his

51

virtue or his good deeds. They concern the far less earth-bound strengths of his fame and reputation. There is, again, a consciously reductive intention on Dylan's part: the intention of repeating, and giving a collective weight to, the idea that Harding had a reputation for ... and then the vague list: lending help, opening doors, refraining from injuring the honest, almost straightening out some utterly unspecified "situation", not getting tracked down, and, lastly, looking after himself cleverly. Moreover, this repeated insistence on Harding's reputation casts a doubt on the veracity of what is being insisted upon. Thus Dylan trades on our methinks-he-doth-protest-too-much reaction, in order to increase further our sense of the empty centre of the story.

Two of the lines—but only two—work in a different way. One—

> With his lady by his side he took a stand

—adds to those echoes of the unspecific in the way that other lines do, by that flamboyantly vague phrase "he took a stand"; but it creates, with the other half of the line, an almost explicit condemnation. Within the cowboy ethic, the hero should neither have needed his lady by his side to give him his courage nor have placed her inside the danger-zone.

The other line—"He travelled with a gun in every hand"— goes further. The wit of that phrase "in every hand" serves quietly to highlight Harding's inadequacy. Such a reliance on his weapons (reminiscent, now, of the gun-stroking scene at the beginning of the *Bonnie and Clyde* film) seems to suggest a hint of something rather discreditable. And in support of this, the phrase acts as a reference back to Dylan's earlier song *With God On Our Side*:

> And the names of the heroes
> I's made to memorise
> With guns in their hands.
> And God on their side.

These two differently-functioning lines, concerning the hero's guns and lady, are the least successful in the song. They are relative failures because for the criticisms of the song's hero to take their full effect, the listener must swap contexts. The first of the two demands consideration strictly within the context of the cowboy milieu, so as to get a response roughly along the lines of "Davy

Crockett would never have made a stand with his lady there beside him" (and for this one can forget the rest of Dylan's work without any loss of understanding); the second of the two lines demands consideration both in a wider than cowboy context— for "gun" is the nearest thing to a symbol in the song—and also perhaps necessarily inside the context of Dylan's other work.

It is not, however, from these two lines of near-explicit criticism that *John Wesley Harding* gets its power. This comes emphatically from Dylan's carefully constructed "echoes of the unspecific", as I have called them—and these are indeed eloquent. In its three short verses, the song offers a keen critique of values pertinent not only to the nineteenth-century cowboy's world but to the heirs of that bygone civilization in contemporary America. The clichés of thought exploded so precisely in the song are still in the way today; but Dylan has done battle with them. *John Wesley Harding* joins with the rest of the album of that name to give us, through this "battling", Dylan successfully engaged in the mature artistic attainment of reconstruction and revaluation: Dylan at his most seriously and intelligently creative.

*　　　*　　　*

We come, now, to the question of his relation to the black folk music tradition.

Black folk music began by reflecting the basic dream of release —and yet it first impinged upon white America as a novel, engaging entertainment (which is as telling an introduction to the history of race relations on that continent as the attempt to wipe out the Red Indian). The distinctive, animated dancing of the slave won the attention and applause of his owner. Then enforced initiation into the prosaic mysteries of the Protestant tradition gave rise to spirituals which reflected a double burden: chains plus Original Sin.

These spirituals were first studied and collected by campaigners for the abolition of slavery, whose aim was to prove that the black man had a soul and should therefore be set free. Since then, the influence of white and black folk music on each other has been substantial. The black, although preserving African modes of tune and rhythm, has adopted many Celtic musical conventions even while retaining the habits of improvisation and adaptation and the endless repetition of short, sharp phrases. Owing to

African influence, correspondingly, white folk music has become increasingly more polyphonic and polyrhythmic.

The blues, which emerged in the present century, is therefore not entirely black: it relied on newly-found Afro-American dialects, "spoken" through the guitar as well as the voice, latterly (but not always) in a 3-line, 12-bar verse pattern. Those black movements in America which are today pursuing back-to-Africa philosophies would have to ditch the blues were they to "purify" their cultural heritage—and that would be a tragedy not only for the middle-class whites who have "discovered" the blues in the last fifteen years but also for large numbers of black Americans.

The blues mingles black and white (what a phrase to have to use!) in other ways too. A song such as the old *Blowin' Down The Road* illustrates the common ground which had, by the time of the New Deal, developed both musically and socially between the Negro and Poor White. This was the seminal folk song of the depression and New Deal period. In form and origin a blues number, it became of expressive importance to millions of displaced Whites. The *Grapes Of Wrath* people understood the blues: and they probably understood the black man better than he is understood today.

Woody Guthrie, anyhow, in his autobiography describes the experience of those times in a noticeably duo-racial way. The box-car ride of the opening and closing chapters is one in which Blacks and Whites are so jumbled together as to disarm any racial distinctions: they are all men who share the same nomadic discomforts: they are all looking unsuccessfully for a living; they are all outside the cop-protected communities:

"And remember—take an old 'bo's word for it, and
stay th' hell out of the city limits of Tucson."
"What kind of a dam town is this, anyhow?"
"Tucson—she's a rich man's bitch, that's what she is, and
nothin' else but."

This same situation is handled again in the Guthrie song quoted earlier in this chapter. "On the edge of your city, you see us and then/We come with the dust and we go with the wind."

Both white and black are hungry, poor, "a problem", the pawns of an economic game that demands unemployment for flexibility of labour—and therefore high profits—yet attacks, economically

54

and socially, the people who have to provide its unemployment pool.

This kind of common ground of situation reduces the difference between black and white perception. Guthrie's pen-and-ink sketches, which are included in his autobiography, feature people not easily classifiable by race—and indeed his sketches of himself make him look, if anything, more Negroid than Caucasian. And in the text he cites only one instance of racial prejudice amongst the hobo community, and this he dismisses more as a matter of course than of conscious principle.

Dylan, then, inherited black folk traditions not entirely from the outside—not as a separate form but as ever-present influences on other hybrid forms. This inheritance shows clearly right from the start. As Wilfred Mellers has expressed it (*New Statesman*, July 11th, 1969),

> In the first phase of his career ... [his] musical materials were primitive: model white blues, hill-billy, shaker songs and hymns, with an interfusion of (pentatonic) black holler, relating the young white outcast to the Negro's alienation.

And, as we've implied, Guthrie had in any case taught him that relation. Thus, artistically, Dylan the middle-class white Minnesotan anticipated the present (uneasy) attempts of the militant hippies to hold hands with Black Power.

The strands for Dylan are pulled together by his *Only A Pawn In Their Game*, a song written after the murder of Medgar Evers. The Poor White is the pawn:

> From the poverty shacks he looks
> from the cracks to the tracks
> and the hoofbeats pound in his brain
> and he's taught how to walk in a pack, shoot in the back,
> with his fist in a clinch,
> to hang and to lynch,
> to hide 'neath a hood,
> to kill with no pain;
> like a dog on a chain,
> he aint got no name,
> but it aint him to blame:
> he's only a pawn in their game.

Dylan, however, comes closer to black culture than is suggested by this "holding hands"; closer than he comes by singing to civil rights workers in Greenwood, Mississippi, at the start of his career.

What the blues encompasses is summed up succinctly in Paul Oliver's book *Conversation With The Blues*:

> The narrative and folk tales, the telling of "lies" or competitive tall tales, the healthily obscene "putting in the dozens", the long and witty "toasts" and the epigrammatic rhyming couplets which enliven the conversation of folk negro and Harlem hipster alike, have their reflections in the blues. They are evident in the earthy vulgarity, the unexpected and paradoxical images, the appeal of unlikely metaphors, the endless story that makes all blues one ...

For all this, Dylan's work shows an affinity, and it is often blatant and forceful. He has absorbed its characteristics into his thinking and thereby his vocabulary. It is, thus, an affinity that testifies to Dylan's comprehension of black American history, of the links between that history and contemporary dilemmas and of the pertinence of black folk music for the serious contemporary artist. Paul Oliver reminds us that there are sizeable drawbacks to relying on the blues as a form that will reveal much about the society that produced it: but Dylan's knowledge is assuredly a more internal force than could be claimed for the sort of reliance that Oliver has in mind.

Another point made by Oliver is worth noting here too: namely, that

> ... if the blues, like any folk art or indeed almost any art form, is illuminating in terms of a whole group it is still sung and played by individuals ... the individual tends to become submerged ... [and even] when the assessment of the major figures is made, the minor blues singer is forgotten.

To listen to much of Dylan's work—which, since his break with "protest", has in every sense put a consistent emphasis on the importance of the individual rather than the mass—is to feel that Dylan has not forgotten the minor blues singer at all. One guesses that he has listened to the minor figures wherever the somewhat random process of recording folk artists has allowed. He must have learnt and assimilated experience from the older songs and the older singers—singers who, in some cases, have been "discovered" or "re-discovered" in recent years. Mississippi John Hurt is one example, Mance Lipscomb another.

Lipscomb was "discovered" in July 1960 by Mack McCormick and Chris Strachwitz and recorded—for the first time—a few weeks later in his two-room cabin. Dylan met Lipscomb at about this period, and we can get an idea of the aura of the man, and thus a hint of the insights he could have given Dylan, from the description of Lipscomb, and a transcribed conversational fragment, in Paul Oliver's book. He was a

> Texas sharecropper and songster with a reputation that extends widely in Grimes, Washington and Brazos counties ... A man of great dignity and natural culture ... a veritable storehouse of blues, ballads and songs of more than half a century ... He was born on April 9th, 1895.

This is Mance Lipscomb talking (the spelling is as in Oliver's transcript):

> I been playin' the git-tar now 'bout forty-nine years, and then I started out by myself, just heard it and learned it. Ear music. ... My pa was a fiddler; he was an old perfessional fiddler. All my people can play some kind of music. Well, my daddy ... he played way back in olden days. You know, he played at breakdowns, waltzes, shottishes and all like that and music just come from me. ... Papa were playing for dances out, for white folks and coloured. He played Missouri Waltz, Casey Jones, just anything you name he played it like I'm playin'. He was just a self player until I was big enough to play behind him, then we two played together ... "Sugar Babe" was the first piece I learned, when I was a li'l boy about thirteen years old. Reason I know this so good, I got a whippin' about it. Come out of the cotton-patch to get some water and I was up at the house playin' the git-tar and my mother came in; whopped me 'cause I didn't come back—I was playin' the git-tar:

> > Sugar babe I'm tired of you,
> > Aint your honey but the way you do,
> > Sugar babe, it's all over now. ...

Such a man must have been an invaluable contact for Dylan—the one a black Texan with a personal repertoire stretching back to 1908, the other a white Minnesotan would-be artist of the whole American people born in 1941. Not only could Dylan have gained a knowledge ready to work for him but also, in a specific and personalized testimony, a feeling for the intimacy of connection of words and music in the expression of a spirit and a theme.

> Song, speech and music are frequently one in the blues ... the piano, guitar, even harmonica is a complement to the voice. Though he may play instrumental solos, the most characteristic blues artist sings through both voice and instrument(s). (Paul Oliver)

How striking is the pertinence of that passage to Dylan's work. Dylan plays piano, guitar and harmonica—three of the commonest blues instruments—plays instrumental solos on each and emphatically uses each as a complement to his voice.

This is evident even in such a "white" protest song as *The Lonesome Death Of Hattie Carroll*, where, in the final refrain, the irregular strum of the guitar rises and falls, quickens and slows again, conveying the heartbeats of the narrator, while the harmonica phrases between the vocal lines act as graphs of his anger, shame and sympathy.

Because of the continuous increase in the influence black and white folk musics have had on each other; because of the common experiences of the depression period (an ingredient in American history made particularly relevant by the persecution shown today of both black and white militants in the U.S.A.); because of the influence of Guthrie on Dylan;[10] and because Dylan has imbibed a characteristic part of black American culture—for all these reasons, it is logical enough that even a recording like *The Lonesome Death Of Hattie Carroll* should show the meeting of white and black traditions in Dylan's art.

The huge instance in Dylan's work where this fusion shows vividly its creative force is in his wide-ranging, flexible, recurrent treatment of the classic Railroad Theme.

Just as the heroic-outlaw-of-the-West myth was, despite having European antecedents, significantly the product of the frontier social situation, so too the railroadmen, the hobo and the railroad itself became folk heroes as a result of environmental circumstances. The railroad meant, or was at least seen to mean, Freedom, Opportunity, Rebirth. It became, as Guthrie's autobiography serves to emphasize, a duo-racial symbol and experience. It is only natural and appropriate that a duo-racial consciousness is required to deal with such a theme in modern folk art. Dylan applies just such a consciousness to his focus.

It isn't altogether possible, however, to isolate or point to specific pieces of vocabulary or whatever and say there, precisely there, is the black ingredient; and that it is an ingredient—subservient to the art as a whole—argues against the value of any projected isolation of that sort. In his songs explicitly "about" contemporary America—the protest songs, in the main—one of the aims is, as Mellers suggests, to express the relation of the spirit of the young white outcast to that of the alienated Negro. In Dylan's later work his encompassing of black traditions serves more subtly to enhance the expression of many different perceptions.

Musically, of course, this is often obvious. Beyond examples like the one already cited—*Hattie Carroll*—in which part of the impact comes from a blues-derived feeling for voice, words and instruments as complements, there are plenty of examples in Dylan's work of songs with the conventional 3-line, 12-bar verse structure. Others use similar structures to similar effect.

One such song is the outstanding *Pledging My Time,* from the "Blonde On Blonde" album.

> Well they sent for the ambulance, and one was sent
> Somebody got lucky, but it was an accident
> Now I'm pledging my time to you
> Hopin' you'll come through, too.

In that verse the black influence is strong. It goes beyond the music —the coiled insistence of guitar, harmonica, drums and voice— and beyond that characteristic bending to "ambulance" in the pronunciation. There is also the curious ominous quality of those first two lines. They recall dramatically those stories of the legendary Beale Street in the Memphis of the '30s, where Saturday night razor fights between blind-drunk blacks were so frequent that a fleet of ambulances waited like taxis at one end of the street. Killer ambulances, apparently, with drivers who made sure that if you weren't dead when they got to you, you were finished before they'd finished their night's work. (As these stories have blown up into

59

myth, they provide a curious corollary to the stories about hospitals and doctors, and particularly surgeons, widely current in nineteenth-century England—and passed into upper- and middle-class consciousness by terrifying children's nannies. The subject is aired in George Orwell's grim essay, "How The Poor Die".)

But it is Dylan's treatment of the Railroad Theme that merits a closer consideration. If it is a standard American symbol of freedom, the railroad also represents "home" for the professional tramp of the dust-bowl years; the railroad symbolizes other things too, from the real as well as from the dream world. The traditional black folk song which includes these lines:

> When a woman blue, she hang her little head an' cry,
> When a man get blue, he grab that train an' ride

—makes the railroad a symbol of masculine social virility. Dylan, singing in the 1960s, emancipates contemporary woman. The song is *It Takes A Lot To Laugh, It Takes A Train To Cry*:

> Don't the moon look good, mama, shinin' through the trees?
> Don't the brakeman look good, mama, flagging down the double-E's!
> Don't the sun look good goin' down over the sea—
> Don't my gal look fine when she's comin' after me! . . .

(These lines are an adaptation of several things—including parts of Presley's version of *Milk Cow Blues Boogie* (see Chapter 4) and from an older—I think—blues song, which runs:

> Don't the clouds look lonesome 'cross the deep blue sea
> Don't the clouds look lonesome 'cross the deep blue sea
> Don't my gal look good when she's comin' after me

—but the Dylan version in *It Takes A Lot To Laugh, It Takes A Train To Cry* is also adapted from his own earlier song *Rocks and Gravel* (unreleased):

> Don't the clouds look lonesome shinin' across the sea
> Don't the clouds look lonesome shinin' across the sea
> Don't my gal look good when she's comin' after me.

And Dylan often does this—often preserves a phrase and, with

60

perhaps some alteration, uses it again in a later song. In his unreleased Civil Rights song *Aint Gonna Grieve*, he uses "notify your next of kin" which, almost unchanged, crops up years later in his *This Wheel's On Fire*. The verse of *Just Like Tom Thumb's Blues* which deals with "my best friend my doctor"—who "won't even say what it is I got" is revisited in another song of the same time, the unreleased *Barbed Wire Fence*:

> The Arabian doctor comes in 'n' gives me a shot
> But he wouldn't tell me what it was that I got.

And the whole of the *Outlaw Blues* verse beginning "I got my dark sunglasses" is contained also in an unreleased song of Dylan's called *Going Down South*.

In this context it was funny that in *Rolling Stone*'s interview with Dylan in 1969, Jann Wenner used the phrase "unload my head" and Dylan, who had used that phrase in his *From A Buick 6*, remarked on how good it sounded and said he'd have to write a song with that phrase in it.

Paradoxically, the repetitive framework helps what is a notable economy in the evocation of a railroad feeling in those four lines. In the music—of which the vocal tone and phrasing are parts—the drums and piano suggest not only the rattle of the train, and, as such, a measure of its speed and mechanic vitality, but also the elation of the traveller who identifies with the locomotive's performance. The lyric's economy on adjectives and emphasis of nouns—the moon, the sun, the brakeman, the trees, the sea, "my gal"—makes for an exciting balance between the romantic and the concrete. Symbol and reality are fused.

This fusion, in context, recalls a passage from one of those autobiographical Dylan poems which get into print from time to time on the back of LP covers and in underground magazines. This particular poem was published in the sixth issue of the English magazine *Circuit*.

> An' my first idol was Hank Williams
> For he sang about the railroad lines
> An' the iron bars an' rattlin' wheels
> Left no doubt that they were real ...
> An' I'll walk my road somewhere between
> The unseen green an' the jet black train

I quote that only to amplify the point that Dylan can not only give the railroad the importance a hard-travellin' hobo might give it but can also use it as an axis round which to spin his ideas of what is real and thus pursue his quest for the concrete.

The railroad appears in many other songs—*Freight Train Blues* has been mentioned already in this chapter—and in several an essential ingredient is the railroad's importance where some fundamental choice is involved, related to the real or the true. In the poem just quoted from, the "iron bars an' rattlin' wheels" provide a yardstick, albeit simplistic, of reality, against which are contrasted smoother kinds of beauty—the nightingale sound of Joan Baez's voice is an instance he gives—and against which is balanced Dylan's consciousness of "the unseen green". In *Tonight I'll Be Staying Here With You* the choice is between two life-styles, with the railroad as the symbol of the one Dylan at last renounces. It calls to him on behalf of the "keep travelling" spirit and it loses to new-found love:

> I find it so difficult to leave—
>
> I can hear that whistle blowin'
> I see that station-master too . . .
> 'Cause tonight I'll be staying here with you.

He hears, but this time, at last, he doesn't follow.

In direct contrast, there is Dylan's first-album adaptation of the traditional *Man Of Constant Sorrow*, which equally relates to this particular choice. In this song, he wants the girl but cannot have her. He has travelled a long way to make the attempt to win her, and so the railroad becomes the symbol of a nomadic no-man's-land:

> Through this open world I'm about to ramble
> Through ice and snow, sleet and rain
> I'm about to ride that mornin' railroad
> P'raps I'll die on that train

With this, of course, Dylan has come away from the concrete —despite the "realism" of that wintry weather—and into the realms of romance. There are no inwardly felt iron bars or rattlin' wheels impinging here. We might almost hear, in the background, atmospheric echoes of the Joan Baez voice; the wheels might be

62

singing to her. What could be more splendid, granted the imagined death-wish, than dying on that train?

Even though *Bob Dylan's Dream,* with all its ponderous nostalgia, is launched with these lines—

> While riding on a train goin' west
> I fell asleep for to take my rest
> I dreamed a dream ...

—Dylan never quite returns to the dream mood given us by the *Man of Constant Sorrow* railroad. There is a parallel of sorts on the "Blonde On Blonde" album, in the surrealistic symbolism of *Absolutely Sweet Marie,* but the mood is very different. The solemnity is replaced by a good-natured if double-edged mockery:

> Well your railroad gate, you know I just can't jump it
> Sometimes it gets so hard, you see
> I'm just sitting here beating on my trumpet
> With all these promises you left for me
> But where are you tonight, sweet Marie? ...
>
> And now I stand here lookin' at your yellow railroad
> In the ruins of your balcony ...

but the symbol there, though used at both the beginning and the end of the song, is incidental. It is not a song that has much to do with trains.

The romance returns, but more respectably than in *Bob Dylan's Dream,* or even *Man of Constant Sorrow,* in another part of *It Takes A Lot To Laugh, It Takes A Train To Cry,* where the narrator grows lyrically expansive:

> Well I ride on the mailtrain baby; can't buy a thrill
> Well I've been up all night, leanin' on the windowsill
> Well if I die on top of the hill—
> Well if I don' make it, you know my baby will.

That last line provides the ballast, taking the railroad romance away from narcissism and into a wider context—that of a more selfless and universal celebration of life. The goal here is to "make it", not to die in glory on the train (although paradoxically, that conjectured dying "on top of the hill" brings in by allusion a

63

picture of history's most celebrated martyrdom, that of Christ on the Cross on Calvary).

Such celebration of life is, naturally, the business of any artist, but the use of the railroad theme, as of the highway theme, is the province very largely of the folk artist.[11] Dylan is more than a folk artist—his creative insight and integrity set him beyond that sphere—but his work has been gorged on the folk culture of America. It has provided a basis for his creativity, has literally been fundamental. In both senses, folk music is behind him.

NOTES

[1] Blind Lemon Jefferson: a great Negro blues singer, also a guitarist and composer, born in the 1890s in Texas, about 80 miles south of Dallas, where he was a player contemporary with Lonnie Johnson. He shaped the Texas blues and put it on record, though his recording career was, typically, very short (1926–1930). He was the main blues influence on Leadbelly and, therefore, through Leadbelly, an important tutor to many, many others. He wrote the line

I'm standin' here wonderin' will a matchbox hol' my clothes

which crops up twenty-five years after Jefferson's death in Carl Perkins' song *Matchbox* and again, around the same time as Dylan's arrival in New York, in Sam Cooke's *Somebody Have Mercy*.

[2] Guthrie travelled around a lot with Leadbelly, Sonny Terry and Cisco Houston during the Second World War. They recorded a number of things together, including a Leadbelly song, *We Shall Be Free*, on which Dylan based his own *I Shall Be Free* and *I Shall Be Free No. 10*. Part of the Leadbelly song runs as follows:

I was down in the henhouse on my knees
Thought I heard a chicken sneeze
It was only a rooster saying his prayers
Thanking his God for the pullets upstairs.

Dylan sings, among much else of precisely the same tone;

Well I took me a woman late last night
I was three-fourths drunk, she looked all right
Till she started peelin' off her onion-gook
She took off her wig said how do I look? ...

The tune is the same all through the three songs. Not that this par-

64

ticular debt is all Dylan owes to the men he mentions in his tribute to Guthrie. Leadbelly must have impinged on him a good deal—and in doing so must have passed on much that he himself learnt from Blind Lemon Jefferson. Sonny Terry's harmonica-work has influenced practically everyone. Guthrie's influence on Dylan is rather different. He is deriving from Guthrie in hammering on the strings in *Song To Woody* and it is Guthrie who gives him his talking-blues format; but basically Guthrie had nothing to teach anyone musically. His tremendous impact on modern American folk music has come from his words, and indeed from his exemplary life. Certainly his influence on Dylan is as much moral as cultural in origin.

[3]Interestingly, this alteration of tense is paralleled in a much later piece of work, the brilliant *All Along The Watchtower,* which gives another, and a very sinister, hint of imminent finale: "All along the watchtower/Princes kept the view/While all the women came and went/Their foot-servants too . . .' In Eliot's *Prufrock,* "all the women come and go". For Dylan, the continuous present is an illusion.

[4]Lasting, well-known traditional Yankee songs include—many remaining quite close to their English antecedents—*The Erie Canal; The Bay of Mexico; The Foggy Dew; Weary of the Railway; Katy Cruel;* and of course *Yankee Doodle.*

[5]This "live" version has to be one of the greatest pieces of underground music ever put on record. It pushes the *Blonde On Blonde* vision of chaos to an apocalyptic conclusion. It is the ultimate statement of pure anarchy—the genuine monument after which Hendrix always strove in vain. It's more than unfortunate that it can't be available in stereo, and that it is less listened to than most Dylan rock. There is, in mono, though, a bootleg album of one of Dylan's 1966 British tour performances, one of the two Albert Hall concerts —and the whole thing is unsurpassable. The strong audience hostility, which builds to a highly-charged confrontation situation, is also clear on the record, so that it reveals very eloquently the quality of Dylan's artistic integrity.

[6]It is all too easy to oversimplify questions of cultural isolation in the Appalachian mountains. On the one hand we have the clear evidence of its survival up to the time of the First World War (see the reference to Cecil Sharpe in Chapter 3); on the other hand, there is this note by Paul Oliver, which is offered in his invaluable book *The Story Of The Blues*: "Although the Appalachians divide North Carolina from Tennessee, the mountains provide no physical barrier and . . . numerous roads . . . break across them which . . . circulating singers used. Highway 70 was the most popular, linking the Atlantic coast by way of Raleigh, Ashville and Knoxville with Nashville and Memphis."

[7]i.e. the beaver-trapping mountain-men, who married Red Indian squaws and whose history precedes that of the Oregon and California trails. Lomax (to whom, by now, my indebtedness must be embarrassingly obvious to those familiar with his writing) provides a graphic picture of one such early pioneer "beating on his rock-hard belly with huge fists, shaking the mirror with his rhythm" as he lay drunk on a bar-room floor on his annual spree in the big city, St. Louis.

[8]A fine example, this, of the hillbilly traditions of grammar construction. Dylan's multiple negatives in this line are a direct inheritance from those traditions.

[9]If, incidentally, that use of the word "stranger" seems puzzling at first, it is because the logic of the song and Dylan's myth lead us to assume he applies the word to himself as narrator; whereas in fact we should take the "stranger" as being the spell-binding woman. Then there is no puzzle.

[10]Guthrie's impact on Dylan was not only direct—it also came via Ramblin' Jack Elliott, whom Dylan met and befriended early on in his time in New York City in the very early sixties. Ramblin' Jack Elliott was the singer-guitarist of whom Guthrie once remarked, "He sounds more like me than I do."

[11]Like railroads, highways (and indeed some rivers, particularly the Mississippi, which runs from Dylan's one-time home-town of Duluth down the 1,700 miles to the Gulf of Mexico) are main arteries in the body of American folk culture. It is the folk-spokesman, the Preacher Casy, in Dylan who relishes lines like "I know this highway like I know my hand" (From *Highway 51 Blues* on the album "Bob Dylan").

3

Dylan and the English Literary Tradition

PART ONE

We talk nowadays as though the relationship between ...
[words and music] ... constituted a problem; even as though
there were a natural antipathy between them which composer
and poet must overcome as best they may. Yet the separation
of the two arts is comparatively recent, and the link between
them would seem to be rooted deep in human nature.

Wilfred Mellers, critic, composer, professor.

The folk tradition ... the English literary tradition ... it sounds
like pigeon-holing but everything connects. A very intricate chain
links the two and runs from pre-Aelfredian England through to
contemporary America.

Because we have forgotten this, we find it hard to accept Dylan
as a serious artist. He has chosen a medium we are unused to
taking seriously: an inseparable mixture of music and words—and
we grew up finding this a cheap and trivial formula. Thank you
Gilbert and Sullivan, Gershwin and Porter.

We don't think back very far. We don't look back beyond the
Elizabethan Age to the time when troubadours were an important
part of our culture, when that culture was orally-dominated and
when sophisticated art was the same kind as the heritage "of
the people".

If Marshall McLuhan is right, if our electric technology is
pushing us forward into another orally-dominated age, then it
shouldn't be surprising to find a serious artist once again at work
in the medium Dylan has chosen. Nor should it astonish us that
such an artist can have re-forged the links between folk and
sophisticated culture.

Dylan's work needs this wide historical context. It is no good just looking at it against a background of Coca Cola and "mod-a-go-go stretch-elastic pants": no good making vague references to kids in the '50s having increased spending-power, or their cousins in the '60s getting tired of the stars and stripes. To go back further, beyond Presley, Guthrie or Ginsberg, and see Dylan's art also in relation to the English literary tradition, makes more sense than simply to fool about with a few sociological guesses about what's made America tick for the last fifteen years.

Those who feel, like Nik Cohn, that the significance of anyone with an electric guitar can be summed up as "Awopbopaloobpop Alopbamboom!" had better skip straight to Chapter Four.

It isn't true that songs must be trivial, that words and music together need to be opera before they can claim to be art.

It is only comparatively recently, too, that folk and sophisticated culture have been separate. The gulf was not complete in England until the emergence of the Augustans, with their classicists and coffee-house smart-sets, although it had started with Chaucer, who brought to dominance an East Midlands dialect which became what we call "standard English".

With only a few exceptions, pre-Elizabethan poetry was "of the people". Pre-Aelfredian poetry was all vernacular and all, in essence, orally disciplined, including "Beowulf". It was sung, and its development was the responsibility of its singers; and so, roughly, things continued until the Norman Conquest. And in the long run, the English absorbed the Normans and the English language rose in importance.

The poetical literature which grew with it was again emphatically "of the people" from Orm's *Ormulum* to Langland's *Vision of Piers Plowman* in 1362. *Piers Plowman* might now be the province of University English Departments, but in its own time it appealed to everyone. Written in the Old English manner, in alliterative verse, it had an equal impact on those who wanted a reform of the Church and those labourers and serfs to whom Wat Tyler offered himself as a symbol of progress and hope.

Throughout the virgin fifteenth century the divisive power of Chaucer's influence was fought by the ingredients of English life which worked towards keeping up the old cultural unity. In this transitional period, the ballad, lays and so on, blossomed along-side a renewed concern with classical literature. So the Elizabethan age that followed grew out of a cultural turmoil never equalled before or since, until our own times. Folk culture was intimately and creatively linked with literary culture in the age that has given us an unmatched richness of artistic achievement.

The links are clear enough in Shakespeare. He might have amused the cockneys and the refined with his rustic caricatures—Bottom doing battle with Pyramus and Thisbe—yet in his poetry he builds upon rural thought and metaphor, upon imagery springing naturally from a traditionally agricultural society. And so do the best of his contemporaries. As drama abandoned these folk foundations, and country communities went under to puritanism, so that drama declined. Hardly coincidence.

All English literature lost out as a result, and the more recent onslaught of the Industrial Revolution made the loss irretrievable. As F. R. Leavis describes it, what was involved was

> not merely an idiomatic raciness of speech, expressing a strong vitality, but an art of social living, with its mature habits of valuation. We must be aware of idealizing, but the fact is plain. There would have been no Shakespeare ... if ... with all its disadvantages by present standards, there had not been, living in the daily life of the people, a positive culture which has disappeared.

At this stage in the narrative, enter John Bunyan, precursor in achievement of Bob Dylan. Although he was the worst, the least Miltonic, kind of puritan, epitomizing narrow sectarianism, Bunyan restored the strengths of popular culture to mainstream literary culture after the two had gone their largely separate ways. He was thus Elizabethan in spirit, and he helped stave off the disappearance Leavis laments.

Granted the new conditions, it is reasonable to say that what Bunyan did then, Dylan has done again: put the dynamics of folk culture back into sophisticated art, exalting the one to the level of the other's greatness.

The parallel between the two writers is worth pursuing: and to do so, it has to be said that *Pilgrim's Progress* is, in the best sense, a classic. Overriding its reductive intention—the disease of Calvinism trying to lacerate life with the stick of hell-fire, it offers an enriching humanitarianism.

Its humanity comes across with that Biblical dignity of

expression which graces the language of all folk culture. Bunyan's work is a reminder of the powerful influence of the various English-language translations of the Bible, from Wyclif's version to the Authorized of 1611—an influence that still operates on folk idiom both in England and America, as, indeed, Dylan's work testifies. The Authorized version has been the most important: has been, for hundreds of years, the countryman's only book. In imagery and rhythm, it is popular, not classical; it harks back to and reflects the language of medieval England.

Bunyan therefore harks back also to the language of medieval England—and so does Dylan. It is not mere coincidence—it is a question of common roots: shared cultural history. The Bible's linguistic influence is clear in all the kinds of American folk music dealt with in the previous chapter which have affected Dylan's work.

As if to prove the point, Cecil Sharpe discovered the popular culture Bunyan represented, not fossilized but vitally alive, in the remoter valleys of the Southern Appalachians during the First World War. And if anyone doubts that this has impinged on Dylan, the guitar-work on his *Ballad Of Hollis Brown* should alone prove the point.

Bunyan, then, is very much Dylan's forebear; and, as the external evidence would suggest, there are many and noticeable similarities in the rhythm of language in their work. Isn't this, for example, instantly recognizable as a Dylan line (say, from the "John Wesley Harding" LP)?

Pray who are your kindred there, if a man may be so bold?

But it is not Bob Dylan, it is Christian in *Pilgrim's Progress*. And doesn't this comply almost exactly in rhythm and dignity of tone?:

Oh what dear daughter beneath the sun could treat a father so:
To wait upon him hand and foot and always answer no?

Thus Dylan's *Tears Of Rage*. (It hardly contradicts the general drift of these remarks, either, that the lines just quoted evoke so obviously—and succinctly—the plight of King Lear.)

What *Tears Of Rage* also illustrates, as do many other Dylan songs, is its creator's concern for salvation. In terms of the para-

70

llels with Bunyan, this is the nearest to a merely coincidental one: and yet even here, coincidence is perhaps not the right word.

"Salvation" exposes universal predicaments which no serious writer ignores. Only the ideal behind the term has changed as succeeding philosophies have shifted it from generation to generation. Consequently, Dylan's idea of it is far from Bunyan's—though it is noticeably not very different from Lawrence's. When Bunyan was writing, of course, God existed. To his contemporary pamphleteers, salvation was a narrowly Christian matter (either you got there or you didn't) and it was a wider thing to Bunyan himself in spite of, not because of, his Calvinism. Since then, God has been through many changes, all reducing His omnipotence. He has been through a career as Watchmaker Extraordinary in a Newtonian world—a career already made redundant by David Hume by the time that Paley crystallized it—and on through Victorian loss of faith ("Oh God, if there is a God, Save my soul, if I have a soul!") to twentieth-century oblivion and beyond. And now perhaps we think ourselves too plagued and helpless easily to countenance that God is really dead. We identify with the tortured vision of the medieval Hieronymus Bosch. There is serious anguish behind our trivia—hence the power of a book like *Catch 22* and the widespread quotation from a lapel-badge: "God Is Not Dead, He Just Doesn't Want To Get Involved".

What comes to mind on the impulse of Dylan's concern for salvation is a consciousness, modern yet universal, of how spiritual sickness damages the individual psyche. It is a delicate thing, unspecific: a religious concern for life that has nothing to do with theology. And in this sense, a Laurentian consciousness. Dylan points to this by projecting himself as spiritually healthy in a world that is patently not so; and confirming a sense of need, he attributes a similar quality to the women his songs celebrate:

> My love she speaks like silence,
> Without ideals or violence,
> She doesn't have to say she's faithful
> Yet she's true like ice, like fire.

There is more involved in that "faithful" than a pop-writer would be conscious of, and the clarifying "like ice, like fire" suggests (with succinct understatement) just how much more. Again, the echo is of Lawrence: Lawrence deploring the merely lovable and

71

trying to restore the elemental, asking us to go beyond a simplistic use of our senses, to be more real. Part of Lawrence's poem "Elemental" runs:

> Why don't people leave off being lovable
> or thinking they are lovable, or wanting to be lovable,
> and be a bit elemental instead? ...
>
> I wish men would get back their balance among the elements
> and be a bit more fiery, as incapable of telling lies
> as fire is.

Dylan's "she's true" plainly encompasses all this. Being true involves being true to yourself.

This sense of elemental tension comes up again and again in Dylan's work. In *Gates of Eden* we are given this image: "With a candle lit into the sun/Though its glow is waxed and black" and in *It's All Over Now, Baby Blue* there comes the powerful "Crying like a fire in the sun".

All this search for the quintessential man comes into an intelligent concern for salvation, a concern Dylan stands by in much of his work. It is there in *Don't Think Twice, It's All Right* in the simple line (it is almost just a passing remark): "Gave her my heart but she wanted my soul" and in his tender, appreciative *To Ramona*:

> Your cracked country lips I still wish to kiss
> As to be by the strength of your skin,
> Your magnetic movements still capture the minutes I'm
> in ...

That "strength" is felt by him, it implies a given moral strength, a Laurentian awareness of the real derived from an alertness of the physical senses.

There is, incidentally, a little-heeded (because officially unreleased) Dylan recording—*Let Me Die In My Footsteps*—which, in its exclamatory life-affirmation and its forthright, simple sincerity, is very reminiscent of Lawrence also (if on a lower level than the resemblance noted above):

> I will not go down under the ground
> Because somebody tells me that death's comin' around ...
> The meaning of life has been lost in the wind;

And some people thinkin' that the end is close by
Instead of learning to live they are learning to die.
Let me die in my footsteps before I go down under the
    ground.

(That is also notable in being one of the very few Dylan songs that is at its most effective in *poem* form. Just as with Lawrence's short poems, it demands an abrasive, conversational—almost a declamatory—delivery. The tone establishes that required delivery —which is enough. The Greenwich Village aura imposed by the song's tune only detracts from the freshness of the lyric.)

Through the abrasive intelligence of work invested with such values, Dylan has changed a generation—has made it more sensitive to what is enhancing and what is impoverishing. Not that he has preached such values, or ever assumed the sage's (or the idol's) responsibility for his audience. He has not posed as a doctor at the sick-bed of society, but rather has been like some lithe and striking faun glimpsed outside the window, radiating spiritual health. It is as much as the artist can do; it will always be the politicians who pretend to wear the stethoscope, always the dead who overtly lead the dying. Dylan's art is music and words, not music and messages.

It is to "words" I now return. I was tracing the historical links between, among other things, the language of folk culture and of literature. The creative links are worth examining too.

Why is it that there is such a marked similarity of impulse between idiom and poetic expression? How come the "uneducated" countryman, whose life has been traditionally agricultural and whose vocabulary is limited, apparently carelessly produces those terse, ellipsed phrases which "educated" people find unreachably admirable and evocative? Why is it that the unschooled Englishman or American with a rural background is closer to the poet than are most "educated" men?

I found the answers to these questions, and many a missing link thrown in as well, in an essay written by Adrian Bell[1] and published nearly forty years ago. It's an exciting essay (at least, it excited me; like *John Wesley Harding,* it opens many a door). Bell argues:

To understand how language is still reborn out of tradition in the unlettered mind ... it is necessary to be immersed in the

73

life until one thinks as well as talks, in local usage. The country-man kindles as he speaks, assumes the authority of one rooted in his life, and that emotional quickening is the same in essence as the artist's—creative. In the glow of it he coins words. Linguistically, there is a kind of half-light in his brain, and on the impulse of an emotion, words get confused with one another and fused into something new—a new shade of meaning is expressed ... [and the result is] not traditional words, but words born of momentary need out of tradition.

Bell concludes:

The countryman's speech is only roundabout to that superficial view which regards a poem as going a long way round to say what could be conveyed in a few words. Sustainedly, the emotional and muscular content of his idiom is almost equal to that of poetry, *for he possesses the same instinct by which the poet places words in striking propinquity: the urgency of his feeling causing his mind to leap intermediate associations, coining many a "quaint" phrase, imaginatively just, though superficially bizarre.*

That's immensely revealing, I think. There is that phrase "almost equal to poetry" which stays in the mind—because isn't it exactly the half-praising half-damning judgement that the work of a really good folk artist, a Guthrie, inevitably receives? Thus such work is locked forever within the labyrinth of its popular roots and fails to reach the notice of a literary public. Or much of a musical public, for that matter. Yet Bell's "almost", coming after his other observations, shows again, I think, how natural and logical it is that a Dylan figure, like Bunyan before him, should have broken through the barriers to achieve recognized greatness by making the cultural mainstream from a folk source.

More than this, doesn't the section quoted above in italics give a striking insight, in effect, into the kind of poetry on the "Highway 61 Revisited" and "Blonde On Blonde" LPs? It can't provide anything like a total explanation—it can take no account of the non-folk part of Dylan's background and work, no account of his sophisticated manipulation of language, with its complex surrealistic technique—but it makes clear that the words on these albums do relate to what is normally agreed to be his folk song repertoire.

74

It also gets us a lot further than most alternative accounts. It avoids (and exposes the emptiness of) the easy judgement of "obscurity"—the judgement so often levelled at Dylan's mid-sixties work. It's ironic that while this "obscurity" is so properly explained by attention to the creative impulse which makes for folk idiom, it should have been the folk purists who most vociferously condemned this section of Dylan's output.

Bell's account also offers encouragement against the other theory so frequently applied to the albums of '65 and '66—the theory that you can only understand their songs with a thorough and first-hand experiencing of the drugs scene, man, because that's all they're about. Balls to that.

There is another aspect of this general inquiry, which up to now has merely been stumbled against from time to time. That is: what has followed the "positive culture" that Leavis says has disappeared? What has been the aftermath, for folk culture, of the twentieth-century acceleration in industrial technology? Are there any "folk" left? What has happened to the countryman's life, daily and communal, now that the traditionally agricultural society is all but extinct in England and is in America locked in incongruous partnership with a mechanical hierarchy of insecticide-spray aircraft, pylon totem-poles, giant TV screens and the linguistic tricks of Madison Avenue?

Bell's essay deals with a part of this theme, though with fewer of the changes that have occurred this century, simply because he was writing in the early 1930s. Nevertheless, his observations are interesting. He traces the decline of the "uneducated" countryman in England, and writes of the young men:

The first taste of education and standard English has had the effect of making them acutely self-conscious. They realize (and agricultural depression helps this) not that they stand supreme in a fundamental way of life but that they are the last left on a sinking ship. No one decries civilization who has not experienced it ad nauseam. Modernity offers dim but infinite possibilities to the young countryman if only he can rid his boots of this impeding clay. Pylons, petrol pumps and other "defacements" are to him symbols of a noble power. The motor-bus, motor-bicycle, wireless, are that power's beckonings. But he is late, he is held hapless in a ruining countryside, everyone else is laughing at him, he feels . . . The old men had their defence. They knew what they were. But he can't stay where they are. The contentment of it is gone. . . .

And so Bell comes to argue that we

must go to America for a modern counterpart of the old idiomatic vigour of common speech. American slang may be ugly and unpleasant, but it has the fascination of abounding vitality, hectic and spurious though that may be. It presupposes knowledge of a thousand sophistications, of intimacy with the life of a modern city, just as the traditional idiom presupposed a familiarity with nature and the processes of agriculture.

Bell falls down, and thus oversimplifies, I think, in underestimating the staying-power of the old life, in England and America. In England, many of the "young countrymen" of 1933 held on in their agricultural villages and are still there today—in "uneducated" middle age—with, despite their TV sets, their inventive idiom by no means extinct. It is under pressure but it is not yet ruined. In America, agricultural living has hung on also, so that there is still no coast-to-coast city idiom of the kind Bell plainly envisaged.

Yet Scott Fitzgerald was able, as early as 1925, to write to his publisher (from Paris, mind you) that

. . . the American peasant as "real" material scarcely exists. He is scarcely 10% of the population, isn't bound to the soil at all . . . and, if [he] has any sensitivity whatever (except a most sentimental conception of himself, which our writers persistently shut their eyes to), he is in the towns before he's twenty.

That too is oversimplified; but in Guthrie's dazzling autobiography, *Bound for Glory*, and in the story of the blues—which is the story of an exodus from down-home to Chicago—we have the more complex truth: and it does not basically contradict Fitzgerald's view.

Dylan himself touches on this migration process in his beautiful *To Ramona*:

I can see you are torn between staying and returning
Back to the south . . .

and as Thomas Wolfe said, you can't go home again.

What remains, as much in England as America, is an incredible hotch-potch of environmental influence. If it were otherwise, there would be no "purist" folk movement, except in the museums, and no problem in defining what today's folk music can be.

A part, then, of McLuhan's America has already arrived. His theories fill out the hotch-potch so that we can understand it not as a simple, melodramatic silhouette in the shape of industrial encroachment but as a newly three-dimensional change in the environment of countryman and city lad alike.

McLuhan is right in the simple observation that you can't shut out sounds, ideas or other people once they are globally broadcast. Not even the Southern Appalachian valley-dweller can today have an insulated, self-expanding culture. Among the 1970s Okies, the language of even the oldest men and women must now be intruded upon by the language of *Time* magazine. Their traditional music must now be under pressure from the Andy Williams Show. To broadcast to the English nation as a BBC announcer or newsreader, you have to have a voice that shows no trace of regional accent, while the ideal of "standard English" runs rampant through Britain's state-run schools.

Everywhere in the West, minority cultures are being tossed together and mixed with, on the one hand, lumpen uniformity and on the other, what passes as the *haute culture* of our age, so that whatever our class and whatever our geographic centre, we have—and the process accelerates all the time—more in common with one another, more shared experience, than the men and women of any generation since the heyday of the Elizabethan Age in England. Full circle. And this wheel's on fire—we are caught up in a kind of vulgar, neurotic renaissance. Hail the return, as McLuhan insists, to oral primacy.

Small wonder that Dylan should select—or rather, find himself at home in—an artistic medium not merely literary but involving a return to a medieval interdependence of words and music. It would be tantamount to playing Canute to maintain that serious poetry, merely by virtue of its "seriousness", must continue as a slim-volumed affair, shying away from other openings, other forms.

This kind of separatism, which calls itself purity, may well disappear, partly because intuitively the artist will not be disposed to maintain it and partly because its public is disappearing. The viability of media other than books is obvious enough from such a statistic as Aidan Chambers offers, in his survey "The Reluctant Reader". He maintains that 60% of the children leaving school in Britain in 1969 will never pick up a book again: 60%. "Popular songs", said Dylan, in 1965, "are the only art form that describes the temper of the times ... That's where the people hang out. It's not in books; it's not on the stage; it's not in the galleries." We are turning the West into a ghetto—and who has time to read sonnets in a ghetto?

In the meantime, the uprooting confusion is in spate. The artist who doesn't try for "originality" as something in limbo, but who uses re-creatively the heritage imbibed with his native air, must find himself, today, not with a clearly-defined ethnic background, but with a totally kaleidoscopic one ("collidescopic" is McLuhan's word).

It is, of course, this situation that gives the impulse to contemporary surrealism and to much of what people call, in Dylan, "druggy music". You don't need to take drugs to be confused— though they do help, sometimes, to see you through. If Dylan had written *Mixed-Up Confusion* not in '62 but in '65, people would have claimed it as a drug-song, and been wrong.

Dylan's position inside the kaleidoscope is clear. A middle-class trader's son, and Jewish, from a series of small mid-western towns—Duluth, Sioux Falls, Hibbing and Gallup, New Mexico— and then from the University of Minnesota, he has had a perfectly natural exposure to innumerable winds of culture. The Mississippi River flows down from Minnesota, through Iowa, Missouri, Arkansas and Louisiana—flows 1,700 miles to the Gulf of Mexico. For Dylan, Highway 61 leads to the dust-bowled '30s, Kerouac and Kant, Chuck Berry's neon-California and Eliot's wasteland simultaneously.

Not that McLuhan's global village can ever come about, as he sees it, 100%. Some aspects of the total bombardment of information and influence in this electric epoch will always be more formative and important to people than others. Variation in impingement will still be moulded by local differences. Some memories are less delible than others. The grapes of wrath leave an aftertaste that peaceful memories do not, both for the men from those areas and those times, and for their children. Dylan, partly raised on the dust-bowl aftermath ("My name it aint nothin'/My age it means less/The country I come from/Is called the Mid-West") was unlikely, for instance, while witnessing the death of Hibbing,

78

to have been equally affected by the invading electric message that he was in the Pepsi Generation.

But present-day confusion is less reductive than future uniformity. Increasing centralization is well advanced, moving as rapidly as Stalin moved his workers to the industrializing cities of the USSR: and the inevitable consequences are obvious. John Steinbeck set out, at the beginning of the '60s, to search for America. His conclusions are set down in *Travels With Charley*, and they include the following observations:

> ... regional speech is in the process of disappearing, not gone but going. Forty years of radio and twenty years of television must have this impact. Communication must destroy localness ... speech becomes standardized, perhaps better English than we have ever used. Just as our bread, mixed and baked, packaged and sold without benefit of accident or human frailty, is uniformly good and uniformly tasteless, so will our speech become one speech ... no region can hold out for long against the highway, the high-tension line, and the national television.

Plenty of people can be optimistic about this. Some things, at the moment, look not bad. Dylan told *Rolling Stone* magazine that "people are making music. That's a good sign. There are certainly more people around making music than there was when I was growing up, I know that."

Let it be admitted also that the traditional agricultural life now in its death-throes has had its unpalatable features. They are at their worst now, now that the life is threatened. Walk long-haired through a small East Texas community and you'll get beaten up by cornered rat-men, bitter and uncomprehending. And when the threats weren't there, traditional rural living was poverty-pinched, demanding and possessive.

Now that actors, movie-stars even, have finally started to think, Rod Steiger can be optimistic, too, about the passing of regional, rural living—though from rather a different perspective. He told the *Guardian*:

> Transportation is bringing us more together than thousands of idealists ever have ... We're all citizens of the world, brothers and sisters under the skin, not because of idealism, but because jumbo-jets are going to take us all over by the thousand.

The myth of all of us, millionaires, miners and the unemployed, all tripping round together up in the sky, is interesting—and was, in effect, exploded long ago by Matthew Arnold, eminent Victorian. What is the good, asked Arnold, of those trains whizzing from Islington to Camberwell with letters three times a day, if all they can tell the inhabitants of dismal, illiberal Camberwell is that it's dismal and illiberal in Islington as well?

But you can take a wide view without showing, as Steiger does, such callous disregard for economic realities and the quality of life. Steinbeck certainly does so, again in *Travels With Charley*. He provides a suitable comment with which to finish accounting for the importance of folk heritage in Dylan's work:

> What are roots and how long have we had them? If our species has existed for a couple of million years, what is its history? Our remote ancestors followed the game, moved with the food supply, and fled from evil weather ... Only when agriculture came into practice—and that's not very long ago in terms of the whole history—did a place achieve meaning and value and permanence. But land is a tangible, and tangibles have a way of getting into a few hands ... Roots were in ownership of land, in tangible and immovable possessions. In this view we are a restless species with a very short history of roots, and those not widely distributed. Perhaps we have overrated roots as a psychic need.

If Dylan has grown in part from folk roots—psychically needed or not—and created art of universal greatness, so too the culture he has added to has had its effect on his contribution. The English literary tradition is continued in Dylan's work, continued in both senses, and it is possible to see its influence in that work. The second part of the present chapter tackles this theme.

PART TWO

"It's all bin done before—
It's all bin written in a book"
—from Dylan's *Too Much of Nothing*

I can't remember anyone ever asking Dylan about his reading

habits, so I must do things the proper way and judge his literary background from the evidence not of the man but of his work. That work seems to me to contain many recollections of major English poets. I have mentioned D. H. Lawrence already, if insufficiently; I have not yet dealt at all with the others—with Donne or Blake or Browning or Eliot. (Eliot, of course, is American, not English, but I include him here because, like Henry James, he gave himself to Old World high culture, rather than, like Hemingway, shying away from it.)

That Dylan's work sometimes calls John Donne to mind actually says little, I think, about Dylan, but serves largely to reinforce a sense of Donne's modernity, which is the modernity of the Metaphysical Poets generally. This is not the place, therefore, to develop a case around Donne in any detail. Nonetheless, some points may be worth making before passing on to Dylan in relation to Blake.

Donne's modernity stems partly from a directness of statement so well represented in his famous opening lines: "For Godsake hold your tongue, and let me love"; Now thou hast lov'd me one whole day"; "Oh do not die, for I shall hate/All women so when thou art gone"; and one of Dylan's contributions has been to reintroduce such directness to white popular music. (Black music, even in its pop-orientated forms, has always had a *double-entendre* device so crude as to become directness, effectively, as '50s records like the Penguins' *Baby Let Me Bang Your Box* illustrate, though that quality of directness is hardly Metaphysical.)

Isn't the Donne immediacy—directness balanced by intelligent discretion—at work here? :

> Go 'way from my window
> Leave at your own chosen speed

(the song is *It Aint Me Babe*). And here? :

> You got a lot o' nerve, to say you are my friend

(*Positively 4th Street*). And here? :

> Ramona come closer, shut softly
> Your watery eyes

(*To Ramona*).

What these and others share with Donne is actually more than plain directness—more than the conversational tone. More, even, than the measuredness both writers communicate, which takes its power from the sense that intellect is engaged in the communicating. Common to both is the bond between the passion and the rhythm.

It was another poet, Coleridge, who pointed this out in Donne's case. He wrote: "To read Dryden, Pope etc., you need only count syllables; but to read Donne you must measure Time, and discover the time of each word by the sense of Passion."

That must go down as an equally useful approach to Dylan's metre: although it needs to be stressed as always that with Dylan, the music is equally central in determining rhythmic pattern. It is because the music *is* so central that so much of what is great in Dylan's work, as it comes across from the records, seems rather less impressive when consigned to the printed page. I remember, years ago now, an attempt on BBC Television to read *Gates Of Eden* as "pure" poetry—which failed utterly. You just can't wrench away half the medium and expect the other half to stand alone. But Coleridge's point is proved by songs like *The Lonesome Death Of Hattie Carroll*—or, come to that, *Like A Rolling Stone*. The vibrant and intricate changes of rhythm in each occur through the investment of different words with differing degrees of feeling. In *Hattie Carroll* the guitar-work enforces this relationship. It acts as a musical graph of Dylan's heartbeats. The drumming on *Like A Rolling Stone* does the same. (A much earlier, almost didactic, example is the drumming on Presley's original recording of *Hound Dog*.)

A final point in relation to Donne is this. Donne's tricksiness appeals to our habit of expending the intellect on trivia—and Dylan is not exempt from this, as songs from *I Shall Be Free No. 10* through to *Million Dollar Bash* transparently show.

Donne in this sense suits our times very well. It takes a serious man to be funny; it takes a sizeable mind to write satisfying minor love-songs. Donne would have made a great pop song-writer for this reason. He couldn't have written pure teenybop stuff, any more than Dylan would choose to. He couldn't have done *Sugar Sugar* or *I Heard It Through The Grapevine* or *My Fair Lady*, which is music for teenybop senility. But he could have done excellent tricksy little things for people like, say, Jackie de Shannon.

A line from Donne's *The Good-Morrow*, for instance, would, adapted slightly, make a perfect Jackie de Shannon title: *You*

Make One Little Room An Everywhere. It should be remembered, too, in this context, that the famous pop line "catch a falling star" originates with Donne, not Perry Como.

In particular, the openings of two Donne poems are perfectly fitted to the best of pop. One is from *Song* and runs:

> Sweetest love, I do not goe
> For wearinesse of thee,
> Nor in hope the world can show
> A fitter Love for mee ...

which would do very nicely for Dylan—or the Band, or Mick Jagger.

The other John Donne opening which would make intelligent, delicate, strong, tricksy pop is from his poem *The Triple Foole*:

> I am two fooles, I know,
> For loving, and for saying so
> In whining poetry ...

That shows perfectly the kind of conscious flirtation with ideas and nonsense that Dylan has exploited so well. It's in the same class as *Peggy Day*, with its

> Love to spend the night with Peggy Day

or as *Open The Door Richard*[2]:

> ... one must always flush out his house
> If he don't expect to be housing flushes

Perhaps the Dylan song most involved in this kind of tricksiness is *4th Time Around*, from "Blonde On Blonde", with its incredible stretched-out metaphors of sexual innuendo culminating in the rebounding pun on "crutch".[3]

Going on to William Blake, I turn first (taking the ridiculous before the sublime) to A. J. Weberman. Weberman calls himself the world's only living Dylanologist, presides over a kind of Dylan museum of unreleased tape-recordings, posters, magazine-articles and, I imagine, Bobby Dylan T-shirts, and gave up college to do so. He was sitting there in college and suddenly it came to him. "Well fuck this shit, man," he claims to have said to himself. "Interpreting Dylan is a hundred times more interesting than going to school so I dropped out of school and became a Dylanologist full time ... I really pushed my brain and I began to get some insight into Dylan." So now he is writing, or has written (in two volumes) a book.

Weberman plays detective. He sniffs through files, keeps an ear to the ground for useful rumours and combs Dylan's output for coded messages. Example: when Dylan uses the word "lady" he means "oligarchy". So pushing our brains and letting insight dawn, we have *Lay, Oligarchy, Lay, Sad-Eyed Oligarchy of the Lowlands* and so on.

I bring this in here because there is an excellent reply to Weberman's position in an article by Greil Marcus (once the best of America's rock critics, in my opinion) and because the reply Marcus offers brings in, and usefully, William Blake. The article, called "Let The Record Play Itself" appeared in the San Francisco *Express-Times* (no date).

Marcus explains the existence of Webermanesque interpretations by saying that people apparently have a need to know

if Dylan is a transvestite or on heroin or stubbed his toe buying beer; and they want to convince themselves that Dylan is ... wonderfully obscure and ambiguous, so that they won't have to feel insecure about listening to someone who did, after all, play all that really loud music that got in the way of the words. The game is still going on ... *As I Went Out One Morning*, a song in which Tom Paine guest stars, is about a dinner Dylan attended years ago, at which he was presented with the Tom Paine Award by the Emergency Civil Liberties Committee. Dylan, during his acceptance speech, said something about how he might understand how Lee Harvey Oswald felt, and the audience booed. This interpretation makes Dylan a real interesting guy. He waits for years to get a chance to get back at an unfriendly audience, and all Tom Paine means to him is the bad memory of an award dinner. Poor Tom Paine. The fellow who came up with this job [Weberman] has said: "I consider Bob Dylan America's greatest poet." Well, naturally; why should such a mind waste his time on a lesser figure? It's not just that such

84

terms are pointless ... but is this sort of thing—the Tom Paine Award Dinner Revenge—is this what makes a great poet?

Poetry, music, songs, stories, are all part of that realm of creation that deepens our lives and can endow our lives with a special kind of grace, tension, perhaps with beauty and splendor. Meaning has many levels—one might meet the artist himself on one of those levels, find friends on another, reach a fine solitude in the light of another man's creation on yet another level. That kind of power in art might be scary—it might be sure enough to survive interpretation and the enforcement of the particular ... Take these lines from *London* by William Blake:

> But most thro' midnight streets I hear
> How the youthful Harlot's curse
> Blasts the newborn infant's tear
> And blights with plagues the Marriage hearse.

Now what that "means", it was once explained to me, is that a prostitute got syphilis, gave birth to a deformed child, the father of which also died of the disease ... That can all be confirmed by balancing and referring the images in the verse—but is it necessary to grasp that ... in order to feel the weight and power of Blake's vision of London? Blake's words transcend the situation about which he's writing.

Likewise, says Marcus, with Dylan:

One will never "understand" *Just Like A Woman* by proving, logically, that is it about transvestites or Britain (Queen Mary and the fog) even if, by some chance, the song "really is about" such things. Art has powers of its own. "Never trust the artist, Trust the tale", wrote D. H. Lawrence.

It isn't surprising that Marcus invokes Blake when alluding to the meaning of "meaning" in poetry. This is partly because Blake's words are his own much more emphatically than with other poets one can readily call to mind.

Blake fought off the vagueness and tiredness of meaning that common social usage imposes on words, by simply refusing to recognize that vagueness. His own thought didn't succumb to it, so his writing disregards it. And then again, he concentrated his thought. A great deal of intellect is telescoped (and is used in the process of telescoping) into very few lines in his poetry.

It is hard to get anything much from Blake without a corresponding effort of concentration in one's reading. Consider the riveting and forging of exact vocabulary in even a prose passage such as this:

> Where any view of money exists, art cannot be carried on, but war only, by pretences to the two impossibilities, Chastity and Abstinence, gods of the heathen ...

And yet, if Blake's words are in this way his own, don't his poems belong actually to the reader?

> And did those feet in ancient time
> Walk upon England's mountains green?
> And was the holy Lamb of God
> On England's pleasant pastures seen?
>
> And did the Countenance Divine
> Shine forth upon our clouded hills?
> And was Jerusalem builded here
> Among these dark Satanic Mills?
>
> Bring me my Bow of burning gold:
> Bring me my Arrows of desire:
> Bring me my Spear: O clouds unfold!
> Bring me my Chariot of fire.
>
> I will not cease from Mental Fight,
> Nor shall my Sword sleep in my hand
> Till we have built Jerusalem
> In England's green and pleasant Land.

That is a hymn, in England. The scholarship of F. W. Bateson, on the other hand, emerged in 1950 with an interpretation so different as to be ironic. Blake wrote it, Bateson established, as an anti-ecclesiastical manifesto. The altars of Anglican churches were the "dark Satanic Mills" that clouded men's vision of spiritual reality and polluted the sanctity of man's desires.[4]

But what about the hymn? What about the meaning almost everyone except Bateson and Blake himself has given that poem?

We have had D. H. Lawrence's answer: never trust the artist, trust the tale.

Our own tendency to side with scholarship in this instance—because we feel more sympathy for an anti-ecclesiastical manifesto than for a Church of England hymn—is misleading. Reader-response, uncluttered insight, normally yields more than scholarly research. A poem gets written because it says what a prose statement of intention on the author's part could never convey.

The Blakeian influence on Dylan is apparent first as a question of "thought": that is, in a labour of thought which achieves an economy of language, by its concentration, and a tone almost of disinterestedness about what is actually experienced with intense emotion by the writer. In Blake we see this, for instance, in *The Sick Rose*. In Dylan we see it, though less powerfully, in the make-up of the "John Wesley Harding" album (especially on *I Dreamed I Saw St. Augustine*) and in other individual songs throughout his repertoire. It is there, for example, in a song already looked at, *Love Minus Zero/No Limit*. That song, in fact, refers to the same theme as *The Sick Rose*: the theme of possessiveness destroying love.

Blake's short poem comes from the *Songs of Experience* and runs as follows:

> O Rose, thou art sick!
> The invisible worm
> That flies in the night,
> In the howling storm,
> Has found out thy bed
> Of crimson joy:
> And his dark secret love
> Does thy life destroy.

Dylan deals with this same theme by positing an antithetical consciousness—an awareness of what a love that is not like a sick rose needs for survival:

> My love she speaks like silence
> Without ideals or violence
> She doesn't have to say she's faithful
> Yet she's true like ice, like fire

The awareness I mention is conveyed by Dylan confronting the listener with a series of contrasts: the contrast between "without ideals" and "(without) violence"—both of which colour that "silence"; and the contrast, noted in an earlier context, between the tired, socially dulled "faithful" and "true" and the qualifying, regenerative "like ice, like fire".

As if thrown at these quick-firing contrasts, the listener is himself thrown into thought: he must flex his mental limbs or drown; and so, with the effort of swimming, he becomes conscious of the values Dylan conveys in the song, and aware that they are the values of health in love. Blakeian values, put across with Blakeian economy.

The last stanza of the song invokes the "tyger" of Blake's most famous poem. The tyger (like ice, like fire) is elemental; naked life. And Dylan's tyger is a raven:

> The wind howls like a hammer
> The night blows raining
> My love she's like some raven
> At my window with a broken wing.

The ultimate and immediate effect of the first two lines there is to invigorate. In the first, this is achieved by juxtaposing the wind's sound and sheer physical force—a feat of concentrated language that rivals anything in English poetry. In the second, the sense of a corresponding release of energy comes, in the words, from telescoping the wind's activity with the rain's; and it is enforced in the music by a half-staccato rhythm:

and this is strengthened, paradoxically, by the redressing *softness* (and openness) in Dylan's voice.

The energy of that line carries over—beyond the pause created by its own cadence—to invest the "raven" image with an associated litheness. And so we are carried to the potent centre of the song. On the surface, the woman in the song is admired and respected, and the voice plays a part in emphasizing this; but the fundamental thing is why she is so highly valued, what wins this respect and admiration—and "she's like some raven" confirms the answer that has been implicit throughout the song.

If the "raven" corresponds to Blake's tyger, it corresponds also to D. H. Lawrence's "Snake" and Coleridge's albatross. It represents the spiritually noble, ensymbolled in physical perfection. (So in the Dylan song, the "raven" is a symbol within a symbol.)

Coleridge's albatross is violated by the base thoughtlessness of human approach; Lawrence's snake suffers at the bidding of similar instincts (and Lawrence, whose fault as a poet is also a strength sometimes, an over-explicitness, even puts in the line "And I thought of the Albatross"). But Blake keeps a respectful, awe-filled distance from his tyger; and Dylan's technique is similar: he makes it clear that he likewise knows his place. The awe felt for his "raven's" nobility is indicated, lightly and subtly enough, by that word "some": "like some raven" suggests the half-bewildered sense of privilege experienced, as no apparently exchangeable word could do.

But the "raven" has a broken wing, has been brought down, so that, though it might seem almost unbelievable (and this impression is enforced by the temporary nature of a "a broken wing": it will heal) the mortal artist can pay his tributes from a position of equality, can walk appreciatively among the gods. The "raven" is at his window. Each can give strength to the other, if human possessiveness does not intrude, nor the urge to destroy. And the artist's fine awareness of this, as it makes itself felt, gives the song its tension, its underlying concrete power.

Very much like Blake's *Sick Rose*, the brevity of *Love Minus Zero/No Limit* belies its importance. It is light, delicate, poised; yet it handles intensely-felt emotional experience, experience distilled by thought, so that what we are offered has neither an obtrusive atmosphere of intense feeling—none, as Leavis said of Blake, "of the Shelleyan 'I feel, I suffer, I yearn' "—nor an obtrusive suggestion of how much intellect has gone into its making.

One might apply that contrast of Blake and Shelley to one of the essential differences between Dylan and another poet-singer, Leonard Cohen. Cohen in any case often paddles in the maudlin, but an associated weakness in his work is exactly that Shelleyan

quality of saying, as it were, "Look at me: God! I'm sensitive!"
A fundamental strength of Dylan's sensitivity is to avoid calling
attention to itself.

There is another way in which Dylan's work is faithful to
Blakeian characteristics: that is, in the eruption of the occasional
written gesture of mockery, aimed at a hostile public.

The existence of such gestures, hints, of course, at similarities
between the two artists' circumstances as much as between their
work; and indeed, reading T. S. Eliot's description of Blake's
background and way of life, one is reminded of Dylan's responses
to circumstance. ("William Blake" (1920), published in *Selected
Essays by T. S. Eliot* (Faber & Faber, 1963).)

When Eliot writes that Blake had nothing to distract him from,
or corrupt, his interests, one thinks of the pressures on Dylan—
the film *Don't Look Back* exposed their enormity—and of how
little he has allowed them to interfere with his preoccupations.
"I'm not interested in myself as a performer," said Dylan in
1966. "Performers are people who perform for other people.
Unlike actors, I know what I'm saying. It's very simple in my
mind. It doesn't matter what kind of audience reaction this whole
thing gets. What happens on stage is straight. It doesn't expect any
reward or fines from any kind of outside agitators ... [It] would
exist whether anybody was looking or not." And when Eliot tells
us that Blake approached everything with a mind unclouded by
current opinions, we can profitably reflect on how little of Dylan's
variegated achievement has been shadowed by the clouds of other
people's ideas. Dylan has had to reject other people's ideas of
what singing should be, what songwriting formulae dictate, what
the pseudo-ethnic togetherness of his early Greenwich Village
patrons demanded, and more besides. There is the additional
testimony of his determined move over to what others labelled
Folk-Rock, then Acid-Rock; his adroit retreat from all outside
affairs from late '66 until nearly two years later; and his (infuriating to others) residence in New York State while an acid-rock/
psychedelic scene he had played an unwitting part in founding
played on and on into hopeless narcissistic decadence in California.

A final similarity of predicament between Dylan and Blake is
their sharing of the desire to fight off accusations of abnormality.
Blake found it astonishing and perplexing that people should have
considered him and his work deliberately puzzling and peculiar;

90

Dylan told *Playboy*, in their mammoth interview with him in 1966:
"... people actually have the gall to think that I have some kind
of fantastic imagination. It gets very lonesome."

It isn't surprising that this commonly-felt sense of isolation
provokes similar face-pulling defiance in Blake and Dylan. As
a result, Blake produced his *Island In The Moon* and Dylan wrote
waspish liner-notes on two of his album-covers, "Highway 61
Revisited" and "John Wesley Harding". They share striking
convergences of tone and technique. The extract that follows is
from *Island In The Moon*:

> ... in a great hurry, Inflammable Gass the Wind-finder enter'd.
> They seem'd to rise & salute each other. Etruscan Column &
> Inflammable Gass fix'd their eyes on each other; their tongues
> went in question and answer, but their thoughts were otherwise
> employ'd. "I don't like his eyes," said Etruscan Column. "He's
> a foolish puppy," said Inflammable Gass, smiling on him. The
> 3 Philosophers—the Cynic smiling, the Epicurian seeming study-
> ing the flame of the candle, & the Pythagorean playing with
> the cat—listen'd with open mouths ... Then Quid call'd upon
> Obtuse Angle for a song, & he, wiping his face & looking on
> the corner of the ceiling, sang: To be or not to be/Of great
> capacity/Like Sir Isaac Newton,/Or Locke, or Doctor South ...

And from the sleeve of Dylan's "Highway 61 Revisited":

> Savage Rose & Openly are bravely blowing kisses to the Jade
> Hexagram-Carnaby Street & to all of the mysterious juveniles &
> the Cream Judge is writing a book on the true meaning of a
> pear—last year, he wrote one on famous dogs of the Civil War
> & now he has false teeth and no children ... when the Cream
> met Savage Rose & Openly, he was introduced to them by
> none other than Lifelessness—Lifelessness is the Great Enemy
> & always wears a hipguard—he is very hipguard ... Lifeless-
> ness said when introducing everybody "go save the world" &
> "involvement! that's the issue" & things like that & Savage
> Rose winked at Openly & the Cream went off with his arm in a
> sling singing "so much for yesterday" ... the clown appears—
> puts a gag over Autumn's mouth & says "there are two kinds of
> people—simple people & normal people" this usually gets a
> big laugh from the sandpit & White Heap sneezes—passes out

& wakes up & rips open Autumn's gag & says "What do you mean you're Autumn and without you there'd be no Spring! you fool! without Spring, there'd be no you! what do you think of that ???." then Savage Rose & Openly come by & kick him in the brains & colour him pink for being a phony philosopher—then the clown comes by ... & some college kid who's read all about Nietzsche comes by & says "Nietzsche never wore an umpire's suit" & Paul says "You wanna buy some clothes" & then Rose & John come out of the bar & they're going up to Harlem ...

Manifest as these similarities are, they represent, of course, only peripheral aspects of Blake's and Dylan's work. Both passages are attractive for the same reasons: because of their facility, their zest, and so on. But in the end, they are not all that important, either in themselves or as keys to more difficult and central works.

When you consider in relation to Blake what *is* a difficult and central work of Dylan's, you come inevitably to *The Gates of Eden*. The purposive force of what is palpably Blakeian impinges in every verse. It is the major Dylan song that is most like Blake, and like the most characteristic Blake at that. It begins with this:

> Of war and peace the truth just twists
> Its curfew gull it glides
> Upon four-legged forest clouds
> The cowboy angel rides
> With his candle lit into the sun
> Though its glow is waxed in black
> All except when 'neath the trees of Eden.

And after seven others comes this concluding verse:

> At dawn my lover comes to me
> And tells me of her dreams
> With no attempts to shovel the glimpse
> Into the ditch of what each one means;
> At times I think there are no words but these
> To tell what's true
> And there are no truths outside the gates of Eden.

In the whole, we have what Eliot, talking of Blake, calls naked vision.

It is very tempting simply to stare, to take nothing away but the dream-pictures—make no attempt to shovel the glimpse. That line and the one that follows it make a powerful argument against analysis: powerful because of the image they commandeer. Yet even as you identify that source of power, analysis is already under way. (And perhaps it's relevant here to say that a part of Dylan's supposed antagonism towards analysis springs not from his pessimism as to its results but from a fault in his attitude, or at least in his defence-equipment, which is the same as Dickens complained of in Thackeray—namely, that he makes a pretence of under-valuing his art, which is not particularly good for the art he holds in trust.)

The general themes of *Gates of Eden* could not be more Blakeian; and nor could their treatment. Yet when you try to state those themes, how vague you need to be. It appears hardly possible to go beyond contending that Dylan is treating of balances of opposites—of material wealth and spiritual; of earthly reality and the imaginatively real; of the body and soul; of false gods and true vision; of self-gratification and salvation; of mortal ambitions and the celestial city; of sins and forgiveness; of evil and good.

Not only are these Blake's themes, but they receive directly comparable handling. Both artists address themselves "not to common sense, but to individual senses." For Blake, as Max Plowman phrased it, "all things existed in Eternity ... All things had external existence, and their manifestation in Time was a subjective sensory impression ... and what he desired to do was to restore to the minds of men the continuous consciousness of infinity which he believed rationalism—or the tyranny of the reasoning over the poetic faculty—had largely obliterated ... He spoke of 'seeing the Eternal which is always present to the wise'; and said that 'if the doors of perception were cleansed, everything would appear to man as it is, infinite!'" (*An Introduction to the Study of Blake*, Max Plowman, Frank Cass, 2nd Edition, 1967).

Gates of Eden is certainly an attempt to focus attention on that "continuous consciousness of infinity", an attempt to point through the doors of perception; and Dylan's vision takes in our world, a world which largely fails to see "the Eternal which is always present to the wise".

Dylan tries to harmonize with (it is the Blakeian use of the

93

phrase, meaning to come level with) songs the lonesome sparrow sings: the sparrow flying, humbly enough, between the earth and the heavens, passing between and observing equally, the Time-trapped foolish and the real, the infinite. The vision evokes this balance of flight, this tracking between opposites.

(Perhaps I'm appropriating the sparrow to an extent here. In the context, it must shoulder—if sparrows have shoulders—its Biblical responsibilities. Not a bird valued or admired by society, it is thereby more easily possible for its sense of proportion to remain intact. Its salvation need not involve the difficulties of the proverbial camel negotiating the needle).

This evocation of balance is very neatly enforced by the contrasts completed in every verse of the song:

> ... he weeps to wicked birds of prey
> Who pick up on his breadcrumb sins.
> There are no sins inside the gates of Eden

and:

> men wholly totally free
> To do anything they wish to do but die

and:

> ... the princess and the prince discuss
> What's real and what is not

and many more. Friends and other strangers, the glimpse and the ditch, a savage soldier who merely complains, the candle cradled into the sun.

This elaborate establishing of opposite poles has its corollary in the frequent internal rhymes, which lend weight to the underlying duality of everything presented. Waxed and black; all in all can only fall; Aladdin and his lamp; relationships of ownership; the foreign sun it squints upon; wholly totally free; no attempts to shovel the glimpse. (There is another such rhyme which comes across from the voice, though it is not apparent in the words on the page. On the first line of the seventh verse, that "of" rhymes with the final syllable of "experience".)

Not only do the contrasts referred to enforce a sense of the ever-present balance the song establishes: they also clarify its

94

nature. The glimpse and the ditch focus the gulf between the perceptions of Reason and of the poetic faculty; the incongruity of prince and princess discussing "reality" calls to mind the same dichotomy.

I can't claim it's all crystal-clear. There is plenty that seems, to me at least, irrevocably obscure. The third verse, for instance, certainly evades me. It isn't that nothing of it impinges. There is a great deal of power in its last three lines: a power that has to do with the visual imagery at that point, with the dream-picture.

> Upon the beach where hound-dogs bay
> At ships with tattooed sails,
> Heading for the gates of Eden.

That word "sails" impersonates the verb more than the noun, producing the movement of a huge black fleet sailing. Somehow there is a powerful accompanying sense of silence, and finally a pure dramatic force given by the combination of that silence with the purposive, inevitable momentum of "Heading, for, the gates, of Eden." This dramatic impact is electrified by the interplay of words and tune. With stunning sureness of touch, that "Heading for", introduced with a switch to a more economic rhythm, stays on the same musical note as "sails" and so darkens the sense of purposiveness already noted.

Yet the rest of the verse fails to elicit much response, beyond a sneaking desire to ask the kind of questions that Weberman— remember Weberman?—might ask. Who is the deafened, shoeless hunter? Is it an event, or normality, for hounds to sit on beaches baying out to sea? Are the hounds coyotes and the sea therefore really a desert? Is the soldier Buffy St. Marie's Universal Soldier, whose ostrich-act is to say, well, I'm just doing my job, and who is answerable to the politicians—shoeless hunters in that they do their fighting vicariously? And if so, could the baying hounds be the callous American franchise—the Great Silent Majority baying for the blood of those who frighten them, those with vision: pirates, ships with tattooed sails.

And it's no good if you want to ask that sort of question: it's obscure because it only holds your interest on the surface. Its power is infirmly argumentative, not poetic, and so it doesn't convince. The poetic force lies in that part of the song which doesn't encourage questions but gives the imagination and the emotions palpable answers, yielding insights of poetic reality whether they remain as dream-pictures or not.

More than enough of *Gates of Eden* does that, but one should not say too little about its flaws. They seem to me large ones, but wholly of the kind cited above: that is to say, there are parts of the song which try to sustain themselves merely by argument—they lack poetic power.

The fourth verse, in particular, strikes me as utterly lacking in what one demands of a serious creative artist. It has argument, it has technique, but beyond that only facility. "Side-saddle on the Golden Calf" is appealing, but the appeal wears off; its attraction belongs really to short-cut oratory.

Yet this is niggardly reservation in the face of the total achievement. The song as a whole accommodates infinite re-playing. It is effectively reminiscent of Blake; but it ranks as a major achievement, and gets its Blakeian stature, on its own merits. It has every distinction of great poetry, flawed but indestructible.

Gates of Eden crops up again—to the extent that its form is the Dramatic Monologue—when we come down a little nearer to earth to consider Bob Dylan and Robert Browning together.

Notes Towards A Definition: the dramatic monologue differs from the soliloquy, to which it superficially approximates, in starting with an already established perspective, instead of searching for one as it runs its course. It looks outwards, so that self-revelation appears incidental. It takes the form of a one-sided conversation—half of a dialogue in which the imagined other participant gets only an implicit hearing. It is an open-ended excerpt from the mind of the speaker: it has, in Robert Langbaum's words, ". . . no necessary beginning and end but only arbitrary limits, limits which do not cut the action off from the events that precede and follow, but shade into those events, suggesting as much as possible of the speaker's whole life and experience".

The unity of the form is its singleness of viewpoint: there is none of the inward search for such a viewpoint that characterizes the soliloquy and gives that form its very different purpose and possibilities.

Browning mastered, as no one before him, this form, the dramatic monologue. Dylan has used it as no one else since.

Not that the similarity ends there. This is Browning (from *Up At A Villa—Down In The City*):

> Look, two and two go the priests, then the monks with
>   cowls and sandals
> And the penitents dressed in white shirts, a-holding the
>   yellow candles
> One, he carries a flag up straight, and another a cross with
>   handles,
> And the Duke's guard brings up the rear, for the better
>   prevention of scandals.

This is Dylan (from *Subterranean Homesick Blues*):

> Better jump down a manhole
> Light y'self a candle,
> Don't wear sandals,
> Try to avoid the scandals
> Don't wanna be a bum
> Y' better chew gum
> The pump don't work
> 'Cause the vandals
> Took the handles.

Obviously, the similarities there are spectacular—but there is more that needs saying than just that.

When Browning uses such rhyme-scenes, G. K. Chesterton dismisses them as "only mathematical triumphs, not triumphs of any kind of assonance". When Dylan writes like that, Ewen McColl pulls a face. Both "critics" miss the point. The Browning piece works because the rhyme's preposterousness is consciously embraced as part of the irony. Dylan's works similarly. You can't make the effort of rhyming "manhole" with "candle" and then pile up sandals, scandals, vandals and handles in such proximity without being deliberate about it. In Dylan's music this purposiveness is complemented by the clipped concentration on four neighbouring notes—a concentrated musical "monotony" that very neatly associates itself with the lyric idea of gum-chewing, so that the deadpan element of delivery is double-barrelled.

There is, anyhow, more in the comparison of those two passages than the startling coincidence in rhyming words. If you read out the Browning verse in Bob Dylan's "Blonde On Blonde" voice (relishing Dylanesque words like "penitent") you find them perfectly compatible. The brand of irony exhibited is common to both of them.

Elsewhere, this shows up in equally dramatic similarities of technique. Part of Browning's *Bishop Blougram's Apology* runs as follows:

> You Cigadibs, who, thirty years of age
> Write stately for *Blackwood's Magazine*
> Believe you see two points in Hamlet's soul
> Unseized by the Germans yet ...

In *Ballad of a Thin Man* Dylan sings:

> You've been with the professors and they've all liked your
>   looks
> With great lawyers you have discussed lepers and crooks
> You've bin through all of F. Scott Fitzgerald's books
> You're very well read, it's well known;
> But something is happening here and you don't know what
>   it is,
> Do you, Mr. Jones?

These two examples of mockery, adopting almost the same tone of voice—the difference being merely that the Bishop has to sound middle-aged and the Dylan persona sounds younger—become identical in tone when addressing their silent interlocutors. You, Cigadibs. Do you, Mr. Jones?

Not only do the techniques resemble each other—and strongly enough to add to the impression that Dylan has looked acquisitively at Robert Browning's work. They are put to comparable uses. Both attack the complacency which makes men use their intellects as blindfolds. Norman Mailer says that people smoke cigarettes to distance themselves from experience; Browning and Dylan maintain that burning up with the theoretical has the same effect. Bishop Blougram reproves Cigadibs for not being alive to the real world; Dylan posits the artificial safeness of vicarious living.

And the same song extends his attack:

> You have many contacts
> Among the lumberjacks
> To get you facts
> When someone attacks
> Your imagination

98

("Mathematical" rhymes again, too!)
  The same theme is echoed in Dylan's *Tombstone Blues*:

> Now I wish I could write you a melody so plain
> That could hold you, dear lady, from going insane
> That could ease you, and cool you, and cease the pain
> Of your useless and pointless knowledge,

and perhaps also in *Temporary Like Achilles*:

> I'm trying to read your portrait
> But I'm helpless like a rich man's child . . .

and again, with a different focus, in *Desolation Row*:

> Her profession's her religion,
> Her sin is her lifelessness

When the irony of Browning, as well as of Dylan, turns to this theme of life versus nullity of experience, the results are comparable more than once. Here is Browning again:

> Lord so-and-so—his coat bedropped with wax
> All Peter's chains about his waist, his back
> Brave with the needlework of Noodledom—
> Believes!

Here is Dylan (again from *Desolation Row*):

> And Ezra Pound and T. S. Eliot
> Fighting in the Captain's tower,
> While calypso singers laugh at them
> And fishermen hold flowers
> Between the windows of the sea
> Where lovely mermaids flow
> And nobody has to think too much
> About Desolation Row

and Browning again:

> you know physics, something of geology,
> Mathematics are your pastime; souls shall rise in their
>   degree;
> Butterflies may dread extinction,—you'll not die, it cannot
>   be!

In Dylan's *Desolation Row* we have a classic utilization of the dramatic monologue form, with its exposition of how one mind sees the world around it, so that to listen to the song is like watching a film shot entirely from one camera-angle, an angle that would not be our own. But what may consequently appear fantastic is real. Implicitly throughout the song, and explicitly here at the end, Dylan argues the sanity of his "perverse" perspective:

> Right now I can't read too good
> Don't send me no more letters, no:
> Not unless you mail them from
> Desolation Row.

In this, Dylan's use of the dramatic conforms to Browning's use of it. There are, however, interesting differences in the scope of the form in the hands of the two artists.

Browning usually identifies the narrator and his environment explicitly; Dylan often fills in these details only implicitly—frequently using a belated introduction of his persona's position to achieve a particular effect. Thus in *Desolation Row* it is only in the final verse that the persona dwells on his own position at all, and it is sprung on the listener that the whole song has been communicating on a person-to-person, and intensely personal, level:

> You asked me how I was doing:
> Was that some kind of joke?

And as we come upon this deliberately held-back switch from an apparently general polemical dream to the personal pressing involvement of "you", "me" and "I", the urgency and power of the vision Dylan offers is effectively magnified.

In *Gates Of Eden* the technique is the same. The last stanza so fixes the perspective that the rest of the song is thrown back upon us, with a demand for an immediate reassessment. The end of the song gives us the narrator's reflection that

> At times I think there are no words
> But these to tell what's true
> And there are no truths outside the gates of Eden.

and, quoting Steve MacDonogh's comments,

100

we are brought back to the starting-point of the monologue where

> The truth just twists
> Its curfew gull just glides.

... [and we] are made to examine what has gone before, the mention of the speaker's lover—providing the dramatic location of the song—bringing us back to a more concrete ... level of understanding.

Another difference in the use to which Browning and Dylan put the dramatic monologue is that whereas Browning projects varied fictional characters, Dylan, like other modern poets, projects himself. This is one reason why—as, in fact, with F. Scott Fitzgerald, whose fictional heroes were largely himself from the unfortunate Anthony Patch to the unfortunate Mr. Hobby—it is exceptionally difficult, and not necessarily worth trying for, to distinguish the work from the man. (When Shakespeare writes "... when I love thee not, Chaos is come again," we link that "I" and the "me" first to Dylan sings "Honey I want you", or even "... carry yourself back to me unspoiled," we link the "I" and the "me" first to Dylan himself. He projects his personal in his artistic self.)

There is a consequent further divergence between Browning's conventions and Dylan's. With Browning, the silent interlocutor is not merely silent but actually unnecessary. A mere tip of the hat to Victorian expectations. In contrast, Dylan's "silent" interlocutor is not merely eloquent in helping to draw out the narrator's mood and predicament, but in many cases has a felt presence the exploration of which is central to the song's purpose.

In his songs to women, where they are the "silent" ones, the portrayal of their characters is a main ingredient. On "Blonde On Blonde", for example, the image of a particular woman is deliberately established by the one-sided dialogue in *Most Likely You Go Your Way And I'll Go Mine*:

> You say my kisses are not like his
> But this time I'm gonna tell you why that is
> I'm gonna let you pass
> Yes and I'll go last

By attributing to the woman the clichéd thought exposed in that

101

first line, this "exchange" shows itself as much concerned to colour in the woman as the narrator himself.

The same emphasis of purpose is apparent in many other songs —in *4th Time Around*, where two women are portrayed in this extraordinarily implying way; in *One Of Us Must Know* (*Sooner Or Later*); *Leopard-Skin Pill-Box Hat*; *I'll Be Your Baby Tonight* to some extent; and perhaps most of all in *Positively 4th Street*:

> You see me on the street,
> You always act surprised;
> You say How are You—Good Luck!
> But you don't mean it
> When you know as well as me
> You'd rather see me paralysed;
> Why don't you just come out once and scream it?

The effect, in this passage, doesn't just—or even mainly—come from the "How are you?" and the "Good luck!" that the woman is permitted to actually say: a considerable proportion of his portrayal comes from that masterfully irregular last line. Its length and pent-up cadence half-echo, half-mimic the scream she won't reveal: effectively, we see it in her eyes, hear it in her head, and we can see her standing there, features fighting off contortion, across the street.

In all these songs, we see the women's faces, as we never do with Browning's Cigadibs.

Abandoning the dramatic monologue at this suitable juncture, it has to be said that there are two other notable corridors between Dylan's work and Robert Browning's. The first is their equal relish for the blatantly grotesque.

Chesterton, thinking of Behemoth in the book of Job, wrote that '... the notion of the hippopotamus as a household pet is curiously in the spirit of the humour of Browning.' It has the appeal of incongruity, and this scatters itself throughout Browning's work, in rhymes, names, ludicrous alliteration (that 'needle-work of Noodledom') and in a puckish garlanding together of temperamental incompatibles, as in *The Cardinal and the Dog*. In this short poem, the Cardinal lies on his death-bed at Verona and cries out aloud to try to stop "a black Dog of vast bigness, eyes flaming" from jumping all over the sheets.

It is an area of humour Dylan enjoys as fully. His sense of the

102

grotesque continually invades his visions both of carefree living ("Saddle me up a big white goose/Tie me on her and turn her loose") and of Apocalypse.

There is the common circus imagery—camels, clowns, freaks, masked faces, organ-grinders, dwarfs and "the phantom of the opera": plus physically normal people with their trousers down, from the President of the United States to Dylan himself: "They asked me for some collateral an' I pulled down my pants."

There is also a celebration of the incongruous in Dylan's work that echoes Browning as much as anyone. *Leopard-Skin Pill-Box Hat* devotes itself to this mood. It isn't only the panache of, say, "You know it balances on your head just like a mattress balances on a bottle of wine" sung with appropriate top-heaviness (Chaplin on a tightrope) as just one line within a formal 3-line, 12-bar framework. It's also the obvious pleasure taken in Dylan—prophet, visionary, seer—singing a whole song about someone's ridiculous hat.

This same mood, Dylan as Puck, also figures beguilingly in songs like *Million Dollar Bash*—where a Browning-like alliterative lunacy is much in evidence. The needlework of Noodledom lives!:

> Well that big dumb blonde
> With her wheel gorged
> And Turtle, that friend of theirs
> With his cheques all forged
> And his cheeks in a chunk
> With his cheese in the cash
> They're all gonna meet
> At that Million Dollar Bash

Serenading the ludicrous is, with more restraint and subtlety, a major ingredient in the brilliant *The Drifter's Escape*, from "John Wesley Harding". It is both here, in the idea of the attendant and the nurse crying out in chorus and in the inanity of that chorus itself:

> 'Oh stop that cursèd jury,"
> Cried the attendant and the nurse
> "The trial was bad enou-u-u-ugh
> But this is ten times worse!"

(which captures perfectly the vagary of Browning) and at the end, where the "explanation" of the drifter's escape is absurdly fortuitous in the same way as Shakespeare's famous device for getting a character in *A Winter's Tale* off the stage—"Exit pursued by a bear":

> Just then a bolt of lightning
> Struck the courthouse out of shape
> And while everybody knelt to pray
> The drifter did escape.

There is, finally, a much more serious feature of Dylan's work that reaches back to Browning—to Browning the archetypal Victorian in experiencing (like Dorothea Brooke in George Eliot's *Middlemarch*) "aspiration without an object". Experiencing, that is, religious ardour without being able to focus it on traditional Christianity. Unable to worship God, George Eliot consecrated Duty. Faced with the same predicament, Browning realized Love.

As Houghton explains it in his fine re-assessment of the period, *The Victorian Frame of Mind*:

> In an age of transition in which crucial problems, both practical and theoretical, exercised the thinking mind at the expense of the sensibility, and in which baffled thought so often issued in a feeling of impotence and a mood of despair, the thinker could find in love a resolution of psychological tensions, and a religion ... to take the place of Christianity.

The first hint of this process at work in Dylan comes at the end of the "John Wesley Harding" album, where the agonized search for a more noble America ends in "Close your eyes, close the door".

Browning substitutes for Christianity a conception of fulfilment which demands that intellect and feeling be fused and interdependent—and this conception Dylan shares. In *Men And Women* Browning writes: "Where the heart is, let the brain lie also"— which could well be a Dylan aphorism. In Browning's *Paracelsus* the hero embodies knowledge and Aprile embodies love. Paracelsus tells Aprile:

> ... We must never part.
> Are we not halves of one dissevered world
> Whom this strange chance unites once more?

Part? never!
Till thou the lover, knows; and I, the knower
Love—until both are saved.

The same idea of partnership colours all of Dylan's love songs. He addresses his lovers intelligently, demanding the engagement of their intellects, and the strength of his feeling, in such addresses, can be gauged by his openness in doing so.

The mutual exploration of Bishop Blougram and Cigadibs mixes thought and emotion just as Paracelsus mixes with Aprile; and it is a characteristic mixture in Dylan's appraisals and "dialogues". Dylan's addresses to women always seem to deal in a combined judgement on emotional and intellectual worth ("You just want to be on the side that's winning")—partly because honesty in emotion is dependent on a lack of dishonesty in thought. When Dylan admires, he admires both intellect and feeling (*She Belongs To Me*); when he denigrates, both are scorned (*Positively 4th Street*).

In the context of this elevation of love, Houghton's account is enlightening in terms of the whole tone of the "Nashville Skyline" album. Add to that account the upshot of that quotation from Paracelsus—he ends his speech on the word "saved"—and lines like these become clear:

One more night.
I will wait for the light.

"Nashville Skyline" admits the failure of "John Wesley Harding's" attempt to find psychic salvation in the myths of a bygone America, back in that continent's uncorrupted past. That quest has failed and the Dylan of "Nashville Skyline" has re-directed his search towards fulfilment through love. As with the Victorians, that way lies salvation. "Love is all there is".

(The poets of nineteenth-century England share something else with Dylan and his contemporaries: the use of drugs. I don't know whether Browning used opium (or, like the eminently respectable Sherlock Holmes, cocaine), but his wife, at least, took both morphine and opium on regular prescription, and it is well enough known that the earlier Romantics turned on a good deal: and this does provide an obvious theme for comparison with an artist like Dylan today. The fieldwork on the Romantics in this respect has been done by Alethea Hayter's now-famous book *Opium And The Romantic Imagination* (Faber) and more than one commentator has provided some speculative comparing of that era with our own in a drugs context, including Kenneth Allsop in a piece in *Encounter* magazine called "The Technicolor Wasteland".)

There is another Victorian whom Dylan's work occasionally recalls —and though he hardly counts as being centrally of the English Literary Tradition, he counts as a very typical Victorian—namely, Lewis Carroll. (And one might claim that this point is not entirely disconnected from that raised in the note above—since the adventures of Alice can so easily be construed as drugs trips. The Alice of "In Wonderland" is on soft drugs—she hallucinates a white bunny-rabbit and it all flows on from there, through walls and into gardens, while the caterpillar she meets, of course, sits on a mushroom smoking a hookah. The Alice of "Through The Looking Glass", seven years older—is on hard stuff. She really has to struggle—all that clambering up on to the mantelpiece—to get her kicks.)

If, for instance, a substantial portion of Dylan's *The Drifter's Escape* seems to remind one vaguely of the pack-of-cards trial scene in "Alice", this is principally because it echoes the knowingly preposterous tone (and the metre) of many of the Lewis Carroll verses. The Dylan lines begin with this:

> Well the judge he cast his robe aside
> A tear came to his eye
> "You'd fail to understand," he said
> "Why must you even try?"

The tune fits this:

> How doth the little crocodile
>   Improve his shining tail
> And pour the waters of the Nile
>   On every golden scale!

and there is, between the two, a partial sharing of tone. The judge and the crocodile are seen in very much the same way. Again, there is a resemblance between the Dylan song and this (from *The Lobster Quadrille*):

> "What matters it how far we go?" his scaly friend
> replied.
> "There is another shore, you know, upon the other
> side ..."

where again, the Dylan tune fits as if purpose-built—as indeed it does the verses read as "evidence" in the card-pack trial; and it's easy to imagine Dylan singing this one (especially the second line):

> He sent them word I had not gone
> (We know it to be true):
> If she should push the matter on
> What would become of you?

Resemblance extends also through much of the famous *Walrus And The Carpenter* poem; and finally, while the song about Tweedledum and Tweedledee ends with these lines:

> Just then flew down a monstrous crow
> As black as a tar-barrel
> Which frightened both the heroes so
> They quite forgot their quarrel

the Dylan song ends like this:

> Just then a bolt of lightning
> Struck the courthouse out of shape
> And while everybody knelt to pray
> The drifter did escape.

As, now, for affiliations with Eliot, well, the finely chiselled language of Dylan owes something emphatic to the tutoring of Eliot's early poetry; but the first thing to be said is this: Folk-Rock is Dylan's *Prufrock*.

With it, Dylan—like Eliot in 1917—was alone in answering the demands of the times for a new poetry.

"Prufrock" threw away "the canons of the poetical" and made

nonsense of the distinction between "seriousness" and "levity" in art. He broke the rules laid down by tradition as to what the language of poetry should be. Folk-rock has broken the rules again, and with similar results (even to the early hostility of academics to Eliot being echoed in the initial response to "the electric Dylan").

It uses "pop" as opposed to "serious" music, and marries it to fresh language, including much slang and entailing a full use of the double-meanings and double-imagery of cult terms—especially drug terms. (For example, "railroad" is used to mean railroad but also to mean the vein into which heroin, etc., is injected.) The result is that it offers "poetry that freely expresses a modern sensibility, the ... modes of experience of one fully alive in his own age". That description was written nearly forty years ago, to cover Eliot's early work. It is every bit as accurate a comment on "Highway 61 Revisited" and "Blonde On Blonde".

The other affiliations between Dylan and Eliot stem from this. There is the attempt to turn formlessness into form itself. *The Waste Land* tries it openly; Dylan's attempts are usually checked by his allegiance to regular verses—a musical check on his lyrics. But though they may be regular, the verses of a song like *Subterranean Homesick Blues* are hardly conventional—and the departure from convention reflects the attempt to interpret the formlessness of the age. "I accept chaos," Dylan wrote on the album cover of "Bringing It All Back Home": "I am not sure whether it accepts me."

Allied with the formlessness is the uprooting, urbanizing process dealt with elsewhere in this chapter—and so Dylan shares with Eliot the use of urban imagery and the expression of urban disillusion.

Eliot first developed this in poems like *Preludes* (from the "Prufrock" collection):

> The morning comes to consciousness
> Of faint stale smells of beer
> From the sawdust-trampled street
> With all its muddy feet that press
> To early coffee-stands.

Dylan begins his *Visions Of Johanna* with:

Aint it just like the night
To play tricks when you're tryin' to be so quiet
We sit here stranded
We're all doin' our best to deny it ...
In this room the heat-pipes just cough
The country music station plays soft
But there's nothing
Really nothing to turn off

Yet only occasionally do you catch, in Eliot, the feeling of warmness towards language that is a Dylan trademark and which, in the context of urban disillusion, gives an added complexity and force to Dylan's work.

Not surprisingly, it is only in his early work that you come across a passage of Eliot's that Dylan might have written. An instance can be found in an early poem *Rhapsody on a Windy Night*. Dylan could have written some of this:

Along the reaches of the street. ...
Every street lamp that I pass
Beats like a fatalistic drum,
And through the spaces of the dark
Midnight shakes the memory
As a madman shakes a dead geranium.

... The street-lamp said, "Regard that woman
Who hesitates toward you in the light of the door
Which opens on her like a grin.
You see the border of her dress
Is torn and stained with sand ..."

That leaves no doubt about the influence of Eliot on Dylan. It's plainly a source of direct strength, carrying the tutor's message: chisel your language. And Dylan has certainly done it:

He sits in your room, his tomb
With a fist full of tacks
Preoccupied with his vengeance
Cursing the dead that can't answer him back
You know that he has no intentions
Of looking your way
Unless it's to say that he needs you
To test his inventions

109

(from *Can You Please Crawl Out Your Window*).
Again:

> The wind howls like a hammer
> The night blows raining
> My love she's like some raven
> At my window with a broken wing.

(from *Love Minus Zero/No Limit*).
Or again—and here bringing in Eliot's use of allusion:

> Yonder stands your orphan with his gun,
> Crying like a fire in the sun.
> Look out, the saints are coming through
> And it's all over now, Baby Blue.
> The highway is for gamblers, better use your sense.
> Take what you have gathered from coincidence.
> The vagabond who's rapping at your door
> Is standing in the clothes that you once wore:
> Strike another match, go.
> Start anew;
> And it's all over now, Baby Blue.

That this influence has been direct is in any case confirmed by Dylan's allusions to Eliot's phrases. That oddly-presented "geranium" crops up again in *Sad-Eyed Lady of the Lowlands*; in *Visions of Johanna*, there are echoes of *The Waste Land*'s handful of dust: Marie holds a handful of rain, "tempting you to defy it".

> In the room the women come and go
> Talking of Michelanglo

writes Eliot: Dylan's *All Along The Watchtower* changes the tense:

> While all the women came and went
> Bare-foot servants too.

This kind of obtuse allusion-making is, of course, a game that Eliot himself perfected. In the third section of *The Waste Land*, for instance, he writes:

> To Carthage then I came
> Burning burning burning burning

which, subtly enough for most of us, quotes from St. Augustine's *Confessions*:

> To Carthage then I came, where a cauldron of
> unholy loves sang all about mine ears ...

and indeed in Dylan's *The Wicked Messenger*, the hero comes from Eli—like the boy Samuel to the Israelites at Shiloh—and just appears one day with a note in his hand, which reads: "The soles of my feet, I swear they're burning." It is no coincidence that Dylan's song *I Dreamed I Saw St. Augustine* is so faithful to the spirit of the Augustine Eliot evocation.

The clearest of Dylan's cross-references to Eliot occurs in the penultimate verse of *Desolation Row* (a title, of course, not unlike *The Waste Land*)—the verse that does more than simply mention Eliot specifically:

> And Ezra Pound and T. S. Eliot
> Fighting in the captain's tower ...
> Between the windows of the sea
> Where lovely mermaids flow
> And nobody has to think too much about
> Desolation Row.

That song has two endings (one, in the final verse, is there to introduce a new perspective, as was cited in the earlier section on Dylan and Browning). One is in those lines just quoted: and it parallels the ending of "The Love Song Of J. Alfred Prufrock":

> We have lingered in the chambers of the sea
> By sea-girls wreathed with seaweed red and brown
> Till human voices wake us, and we drown.

Same imagery, same contrast, same argument.

There is a final point that needs making in relation to Eliot's impressing Dylan: that it's greatly to Dylan's own credit that such influence has been in every respect creative.

If Eliot was superb linguistically, he was a moral death's-head (as his attacks on Lawrence—even to refusing Lawrence an obituary in his "Criterion"—well illustrate).

The Waste Land has left a mark on many poets, but usually a bad one. "It has", as R. T. Jones wrote (*Eboracum 5*, 1966) "taught ... poets to avoid false 'poetical' feelings ... and [made

111

it] disastrously easy to mock—habitually—any real feelings one may encounter."

The poem has, not unfairly, been taken as a "full justification for not living". Its tone, after all, is often not the ironical detachment it claims to be, but "an insidious mockery, going with a life-denying habit". The "impersonality of great poetry" that Leavis and others point to is, in Eliot, frequently not impersonality at all —it is a forced personal spleen, reductive twice over: once in intruding in the poem, lessening the artistic sincerity, and once in that its personality is so unpleasant.

For all his annotated allusions to innumerable cultures, Eliot recalls first the spidery sourness of his own over-educated contemporaries. The young man carbuncular, the footman sitting on Aunt Helen's dining-table with the second housemaid on his knees— the forced sordidness of Eliot's glimpse (it can't be called vision) is the same in tone as the scene at the end of Aldous Huxley's *Point Counterpoint*, where two unpersonable adults play games together in the bath.

In another sense also, Eliot's affiliations with his contemporaries detract from the value of his work. Eliot is old-fashioned. His greyness seems less to focus a state of the human soul than the particular social drabness of his own environment in the years between the two world wars in England. He always radiates "the wireless":

I grow old ... I grow old ...
I shall wear the bottoms of my trousers rolled

He points at a shabby gentility but would like to preserve the gentility-element. He only wants to be rid of the shabbiness.

That brand of disillusion is gone; and is redundant in Eliot's poetry because he made it inseparable from the symptoms offered of it/with it—the taking of toast and tea (the dated archaism of that "taking of"), the stained coffeespoons, the damp souls of housemaids. It is, for this reason, as irrelevant in vision as (if more accurate than) 1950s cinematic "realism".

That Dylan is unlikely to date in the same way comes from the simple, undeniable fact that his poetry does not provide "a full justification for not living" or communicate "a life-denying habit". Dylan's warmth of language is only one symptom of this. He is also, simply, more open to real feelings than Eliot—and such feelings are plainly more universal than a stylized disillusion which is married to its own symptoms and divorced, by self-consciousness and the false prudence of a Casaubon, from passion and openness.

Baudelaire deals in urban imagery, yet his work is still fresh. Open emotion is essential to his vision: and in this at least Dylan is nearer to Baudelaire than to Eliot (although those who find that, compared to "Blonde On Blonde" or even "Nashville Skyline", the "John Wesley Harding" album has an off-putting ascetism, would effectively be saying that there at least, Dylan was not so much close to Baudelaire as to his "soulless" equivalent, Gautier).

NOTES

[1] "English Tradition and Idiom", Volume II, *Scrutiny* magazine, 1933; reprinted in *Selections From Scrutiny* No. 2, Cambridge University Press, 1968.

[2] The sheet-music gives the title as *Open The Door Homer* which, although the name Homer gets no mention in the song, is just as likely a title: indeed just the sort of disparity Dylan enjoys creating.

[3] This song is much more closely dealt with in Chapter 6.

[4] You don't need the scholarship, actually. You don't have to go far through even the best-known work of Blake to get at a clearer statement of his views on the debilitating effects in institutionalized religion. "The Garden of Love" is representative:

> I went to the Garden of Love/And saw what I never had seen:
> A Chapel was built in the midst,/Where I used to play on the green.
> And the gates of this Chapel were shut,/And "Thou Shalt Not" writ over the door;
> So I turn'd to the Garden of Love/That so many sweet flowers bore;
> And I saw it was filled with graves,/And tomb-stones where flowers should be;
> And Priests in black gowns were walking their rounds
> And binding with briars my joys and desires.

4

Dylan, Pop and the Rock Revolution

"You might make it on your own but you don't make it with this band: you're fired," said Bobby Vee to Bob Dylan, who had, till that moment, been his pianist for a while.

1: IT WAS ROCK-A-DAY JOHNNY SINGIN' TELL YOUR MA, TELL YOUR PA, OUR LOVE'S A-GONNA GROW WAH WAH ...

Pop history isn't about a social phenomenon. Who cares whether Nik Cohn's ancestors ripped up cinema seats for Bill Haley, or whether that was storming bastilles of post-war tedium? The sociological approach gets you nowhere: the music is what matters.

So Bill Haley is utterly unimportant. His influence was nil because his musical value was nil. He failed to make it because his music was boring and his voice was about as riveting as a dishcloth. People only remember him because he was so inept— and he wasn't even indisputably the first. Johnny Otis claimed his band had been playing rock 'n' roll music since 1948. He may be right. What *is* true is that when rock took off, it wasn't thanks to Otis or Bill Haley.

Rock happened as a strange appealing mixture of "race" and country music. Mix Fats Domino with Hank Williams and you get the beginnings of rock 'n' roll. (In fact, that very combination occurred. The song *Jambalaya* uses creole language but was written by Hank Williams; Fats Domino includes it in his every performance.)

But rock took off *en masse* for Whites because of Elvis Presley. Without Presley, Bill Haley's thing would have been a nine-day blunder, like The Twist, and just as false; without Haley, Elvis would still have been a massive original talent. It simply wasn't

114

Haley in 1955 that mattered, it was Presley in 1956—and even the Billboard charts bear this out.

Rock Around The Clock topped the U.S. Hot 100 in '55, only to be followed for the rest of that year by appalling Mitch Miller, the Four Aces, the saccharine piano of Roger Williams and the saccharine gravel of Tennessee Ernie Ford. 1956 began just as comfortably, with Dean Martin. Then—the false craze exposed —Kay Starr climbed up there with her peekaboo *Rock 'n' Roll Waltz*, just as Frank Sinatra and Ella Fitzgerald were to yawn in on the Twist craze in 1962, crooning in the coffin-nails. After Kay Starr, it was naturally back to dinner-suits with the Nelson Riddle Orchestra and Les Baxter.

And that would have been that, but for *Heartbreak Hotel*, Presley's second single but his first nation-wide release. It owed as much to Bill Haley as Dylan owes to Ringo Starr, and on its own, it transformed the U.S. charts and more besides. (The No. Ones that succeeded it that year were *Hound Dog* and *Don't Be Cruel*, both by Presley, the Platters' *My Prayer* and back to Elvis for *Love Me Tender*.) Popular music was forced to notice that the Second World War had come and gone. The give-me-the-moonlight régime was vanquished.[1]

Presley became the prototype: rock 'n' roll was made in his image.

In England, to begin with, Tommy Steele was supposed to be an Elvis: and in his attempts he focused on one of the changes that happened when popular music went pop. Before, you had to enunciate—every word had to be heard, though why that should have been the case is difficult to imagine, not only because the words so carefully delivered weren't generally worth any attention. It's quite impossible, after all, to distinguish words sung in opera, so that it hardly matters whether an opera is performed in English, Italian or Urdu. With pop, language regained its operatic function. The meaning of words, as a general rule, mattered less than their sounds, and the voice became an instrument. The grown-ups who laughed at Presley's "mumbling" didn't understand. It was actually nice to have part of the record where you didn't know what you were singing when you sang along with it. I still can't make out all the words on lots of '50s records that I know, as records, very well. For instance, in *Let's Jump The Broomstick*, by Brenda Lee, there is what sounds to me like this:

Gonna Alabama
Getcha-catcha-kamma

Who needs to translate?—it's perfectly satisfying left like that.

(This revised usage of words was another Presley innovation: on Bill Haley's records, you can hear every word, from "one o'clock" right through to "twelve o'clock rock".)

So there was Tommy Steele, back in England in 1957, trying to be Elvis Presley and therefore very consciously slurring the words. Only Tommy Steele did it, of course, like any Cockney novice would, by leaving out all the consonants. It sounded, on his smash hit *Singing The Blues*, like this:

Weeeeeeeeeeeeeeeeeeeeellllll—
I never felt more like a-singin' the blues
CoIe'uroraIe'uoozz
Your love, dear

And this showed up the whole gigantic difference between American and British pop. The best of the American stars had music that grew out of their own local roots, ethnic and limited though these may have been. They picked up genuine skills and techniques unselfconsciously. Their English equivalents always had to imitate. Pop had nothing to do with fol-de-rol-round-the-maypole music—which was fossilized in any case—so the British rock stars had nothing behind them. They had to learn, and so they had to copy. Tommy Steele was hardly from the same world as Elvis Presley: he was the archetypal cheery Cockney, from a decent British slum, whose musical heritage was *Knays Ap Muvvah Braan*, and who sang with a guitar strictly for laughs (at first) when on leave from the Merchant Navy.

Yet Elvis he tried to be, and sang *Hound Dog* on the first British TV pop show—"6.5 Special"—to prove it. And to do him justice, he probably didn't do it too badly, considering: and certainly by 1959, when his popularity was on the wane with teenage audiences, he'd learnt to sing rock quite well. His versions of Ritchie Valens' *Come On Let's Go* and Freddie Cannon's *Tallahassie Lassie* still appeal, to me at least.

Steele was superseded in Britain principally by Cliff Richard, as "6.5 Special" was superseded by Jack Good's "Oh Boy!". (It's fashionable to hail Jack Good as a visionary, a pop genius from

116

way back when, but really the only way his show stood out powerfully from the BBC's diffident "6.5 Special" was that Jack Good's studio was dark and trained a spotlight on the performer. Apart from that it was a copy. Lord Rockingham's XI, with their infuriating *Hoots Mon*, equalled asthmatic old Don Lang and his so-called Frantic Five.)

Cliff Richard was like Brigitte Bardot—or rather, like Bardot pretending to be Presley. He had a baby-doll face and pouted a lot. His hair was black, which made him sexier than Tommy Steele straight away, and he had long sideburns (or "sideboards", as they were often called in England). He wore black shirts and white ties, which gave a little bit of teddy-boy toughness to his image. He wasn't very good at the songs, and his early rock records are hopeless (though this was partly the Shadows' fault). In fact Cliff was so bad that he has consistently improved. All the other big names of the pop '50s have declined in power and artistry; Cliff Richard has grown better and better at timing and phrasing and control. He ends with the advantage of having had no skill to start with, no basic exciting ingredient to get stale and tired over the years.

The other male solo stars, or would-be stars, who emerged in Britain tended not only to imitate Presley but also to take on names designed to suggest his attributes: Marty Wilde, Billy Fury, Duffy Power, Vince Eager; and later, Robb Storme and, with more subtlety, Lance Fortune and Johnny Gentle.

Yet no matter how hard they copied, they never learnt. As Nik Cohn said, the gulf between America and Britain showed at its widest when Elvis Presley became God and Tommy Steele made it to the London Palladium instead. Duffy Power, Vince Eager and Messrs. Fortune and Storme never really made it anywhere much; Billy Fury gave up imitating Presley and imitated Eddie Cochran instead; and Marty Wilde, the only truly good one, killed his career with too much TV. After "Oh Boy!" Marty agreed to be link-man on a show called "Boy Meets Girls"—so he lost the benefits of the darkened studio and had to talk and introduce people week after week. He couldn't, understandably, survive the familiarity. You wouldn't have caught Col. Parker letting Elvis touch that kind of thing.

Later, in Britain, it was Mick Jagger who became Elvis Presley: cynical, rude, ruthless, sulky, insinuating, stylish; but he remoulded the formula, he didn't just re-work it. But back in the early days of rock, even the British people most unlike Presley were shaped by his influence. People fell for Laurie London—as in America they fell for Frankie Lymon—because unconsciously they wanted Elvis Presley castrated. And finally, the fact that in England the aim was to set up an equivalent for everyone shows in itself the extent of Presley's impact.

In America, Ricky Nelson was pushed as a replacement Presley when Elvis went into the Army. Gene Vincent tried it too; so did the very underrated Conway Twitty. Twitty must have been very badly managed, because after his first hit, the million-selling *It's Only Make-Believe*, he went into a rapid and constant decline in popularity—and yet he cut many, many good records, from *Is A Bluebird Blue?* through a great *C'est Si Bon* to the masterly *I Hope I Think I Wish*.

But Presley was not a suffocating influence in America—he got a lot of sounds and a lot of people started on things that weren't just copies of his own work or image. Duane Eddy said that "none of us would have got anywhere without Elvis", and Duane Eddy didn't sound at all like Elvis Presley, except in the coincidence of toughness.

The Americans not only had other things to offer; they were also very much smarter than the British, and a lot more independent-minded.

Partly, this was because they had vital popular musics to draw on, and partly it was because pop in America was never handled through one monopolistic institution.

In America, local radio-stations shaped the pop environment; in Britain, everything was obstructed, diluted, mishandled and misdispensed by BBC Radio, which had no idea what pop music was, didn't know how long it would last, didn't like or approve of it—and so hardly bothered to adapt to its demands. Radio Luxembourg, the only alternative lifeline, was little better. Reception was terrible, it was evenings only, and the DJs were mostly the same old men: Jack Jackson, Sam Costa, Pete Murray, plus younger, greasier people who tried to convert you to mainstream jazz. David Gell—an incredibly suitable name—had a show where either the title or the slogan was "Music For Sophisticats". Imagine what that was like.

In one way Luxembourg really was better than the BBC: it wasn't at the mercy of the infamous Musicians' Union. The BBC was its hapless lackey, and fell in with its insistence that teenagers couldn't hear pop on the radio without listening at the same time to elderly orchestras and "combos" which were politely said to perform "live".

Variety was also inbuilt for U.S. pop and effectively excluded from its British equivalent because of the record-company situation. In America, there were myriad small companies attuned to local communities and able to breathe because of local radio. By 1961, there were over 6,000 independent labels in America, and consequently hundreds of pop artists got auditioned, recorded, played and popularized who, regardless of their talent, would not have stood a chance in Britain. There, records were in the hands of The Big Four—Decca, E.M.I., Pye and Philips. It would be hard to say which was the most blinkered, slow-moving and unimaginative. It was more or less the same old monopoly story. They watched each other slavishly, and so exacerbated the imitation process. To imitate was always safer than to innovate, and playing things safe was all they knew. Their reactions to The Beatles showed this well. Decca rejected them because they didn't sound quite like anyone else around at the time. Eventually, E.M.I. risked them because hell, what can you lose when you don't have to pay an orchestra for the session? Then bless my soul, people were buying their records!—maybe Eden Kane and Helen Shapiro aren't the right sounds any more! So all the recording managers rushed up to Liverpool—funny place, Liverpool: in the provinces, y'know—to sign up groups like The Beatles. And since they didn't really understand what The Beatles were like, they had to sign up more or less everybody.

But they remained apprehensive about that name, "The Beatles". How could you copy that? You couldn't call your new group "The Slugs", surely? Could you? So they copied the other Epstein names instead or left them with the names they'd used in Liverpool. These, after all, were safe enough, since they were themselves just copies of American-sounding names. Danny & The Juniors begat Gerry & The Pacemakers, Gerry & The Pacemakers begat a hundred more. Hurriedly-discovered London groups too, and Manchester groups, and Birmingham groups—the more the merrier. Brian Poole & The Tremeloes?—meet Carl Wayne & The Vikings.

Today, more uniformity has crept across America too, for not entirely dissimilar reasons. The major record-companies handle

119

the major stars, and group names again are much like each other. In the old days everyone was Rubin & The Jets; now try Turquoise Abortion. Yet America still offers vastly more variety.

In any case, you have to single out the BBC, because of its hold over Britain's air-waves, as the worst uniformity-machine of all in pop. Any monopoly makes for mediocrity, decision by committee, the dictation of an imaginary consensus, appeasement, dilution, the deathly compromises of trying to please all tastes and yet dictate those tastes at the same time: and all this works against the individual, the genuinely new, the imaginative and the delicate.[2]

It also results in the imposition of an arbitrary censorship which always proves itself amoral. When "Sergeant Pepper's Lonely Hearts' Club Band" came out, the BBC banned the last track (which happened to be the best, but that didn't matter) because of the line "I'd love to turn you on". The Beatles have really gone too far, said a spokesman, as if—and this was the typical Corporation attitude—the Beatles were rather cheeky children who had failed to behave in accordance with the obvious rules governing pop, as laid down by the BBC itself. But that was a long time ago. These days, "turn you on" is perfectly acceptable: and so the BBC has a jingle (good idea, jingles—clever of the pirate stations to have thought of them!) which runs: "Radio O-one, really turns you on—". No doubt they call that progress.

So in the '50s and early '60s, American pop was quite a contrast. Even at its most imitative, it had far more variety than British. After Presley, teenage artists sprang up from all over the States, ready and able to revamp almost every form of previous popular music. Not just rockers trying for Presley's toughness and energy but also younger, smoother crooners; younger, sweeter Miss Americas; younger countryish talents; and a good many truly individual voices who saw their chance and took it.

The best of the rockers are already legends: Little Richard (black and beautiful); Chuck Berry (coffee-coloured and mean); and Jerry Lee Lewis (white). The many others included Buddy Knox (white and briefly) and Lloyd Price (black and briefly).

Then there were the revamped crooning stars. Suddenly it was Tab Hunter with *Young Love* instead of Eddie Fisher with *Oh My Papa*. And Pat Boone. And Paul Anka, who never rocked and who was really just a juvenile Pat Boone plus a little sex. Ricky Nelson was pretty all-American too, and was joined by Frankie

Avalon and Fabian, and later by Brian Hyland, Bobby Vinton and a good many more.

As for the sweet Miss Americas, well in 1957 it had been Debbie Reynolds with *Tammy*; later it was Connie Francis and Connie Stevens, Annette Funicello and Shelley Fabares.

Countryfied pop changed from Jo Stafford's *Buttons And Bows* —"And French perfume that rocks the room/And I'm all yours in buttons and bows"—to the equally lugubrious sounds of Jim Reeves and Jack Scott. Yet that's not a fair way to put it. Nashville country music produced some of the best pop of all time. It wasn't just made of things like *Ballad of Davy Crockett*, *Sixteen Tons* and the Kingston Trio's *Tom Dooley*. Nor was it just Jimmie Rodgers' *Honey-Comb*. Nashville produced the great Everly Brothers, who first made it big back in 1957 and who still sound good today—despite all their desperate attempts of the late '60s to not sound like The Everly Brothers.

Country pop also provided Don Gibson, John D. Loudermilk, Chet Atkins, Floyd Cramer, Hank Locklin, Patsy Cline and Skeeter Davis—as well as Johnny Cash and Marty Robbins.

Also from the '50s in America came a number of people who started off in one thing and slid successfully over into other spheres. Neil Sedaka, ex-classical pianist, was one. He started as a sub-pubic rocker and ended with the best, most exciting teeny-bop sound there was. He moved from *Ring-A-Rockin'* and the amazing *I Go Ape* through to *Calendar Girl* and *Breaking Up Is Hard To Do*. Brenda Lee changed a lot too. She began recording very young and very raw, producing *Let's Jump The Broomstick* and then the great *Sweet Nuthins* (which was, to add a little fact to all this value-judgement, the last record issued on 78rpm wax in England, except for a tedious Tiny Tim gimmick-issue ten years afterwards). Then she moved through exquisite ballads which were still essentially pop. More recently, the pop has gone out of her voice and out of her ambition too, so that today she's just a second-rate night-club singer back in the world of Cole Porter. That's been the Bobby Darin story too. He started with *Rock Island Line* and *Splish Splash*, rushed on through *Mack The Knife/La Mer/Clementine/Lazy River* to eventual limbo among the smoothie Sinatra-scholars. So now he makes boring albums full of *A Nightingale Sang In Berkeley Square*: and he wanted to be a legend by the time he was 25.

Late '50s America also promoted a number of groups which found sounds of their own and which developed these well and independently. The Platters were first. Later came The Crickets, Fleetwoods, Coasters, Teddy Bears, Danny & The Juniors, Dion & The Belmonts, and the Drifters. And finally, there were the odd individual voices—with talents as original in their own ways as Presley's talent was. Sam Cooke, who was very popular but never popular enough, especially in Britain; Ritchie Valens, who died; Chuck Berry, who was immensely clever; Duane Eddy, who couldn't last but who made hits that still sound good; and the very great Buddy Holly.

Holly's voice, iridescing through *It Doesn't Matter Any More*, lingered all through the summer of '59. It was the record that pinned down the year, just as "Blonde On Blonde" was to pin down 1966–67. And alongside it that autumn clustered the variegated sounds and images of the pop America which had flowered in the aftermath of Elvis' earlier impact.

By March 24th, 1960, when Sgt. Presley was discharged from the U.S. Army, there really was a whole scene going, and a scene of mixed-up confusion at that. Names in the British charts in the first two weeks of Presley's return included Lonnie Donegan and Perry Como, Jimmy Jones and Max Bygraves, Johnny & The Hurricanes and Anthony Newley, Jim Reeves and Bobby Darin, Bobby Rydell and Marv Johnson, Adam Faith and the Everlys, Jack Scott and, yes, Fats Domino.

At this point, enter Bob Dylan. Some time the previous year he'd been playing harmonica in a Central City, Colorado stripjoint, and by this time he must have reached New York City, guitar at the ready and still listening to everything. By this time too he must have soaked up all the cumulative residue of skills—in lyric-writing as well as in the music—of Presley, Chuck Berry and Domino.

The myth has been created that 1960 was an all-time low in pop, which would suggest that there was nothing much for Dylan to gather from it; would suggest that he'd have had to go back to early rock giants for his pop education. But the myth is a lie. 1960 wasn't the best year ever, that's for sure, but it introduced some beautiful sounds—a situation that held all through '61 and '62 as well. The only thing missing was a genuine trend. All the good things were disconnected; separate end-products of the earlier

122

rock years. This very disconnectedness made for unprecedented variety: so not only had Dylan grown up through the early years but he also had, at the start of his own career, a great deal happening in pop worth picking up on.

Even the bad sounds could/should have been instructive, and it's true that there were plenty of those. The list that follows is in no special order: it's just an attempt to reassemble some of the appalling sounds and people—the particularly shitty things—that go a long way to justifying the myth that 1960-62 were the barren years.

British cover versions: Trad Jazz and, in particular, Mr. Acker Bilk, Kenny Ball and Terry Lightfoot; piano party records; the overloading of the charts by mainstream bores like Sinatra, Ella Fitzgerald, Shirley Bassey, Johnny Mathis, Johnny Dankworth and Matt Munro; Anthony Newley; *Sailor*, not only by Petula Clark but by Anne Shelton as well; *Footsteps* by Steve Lawrence; John Leyton and the songs of Johnny Worth; Helen Shapiro; The Shadows at full strength—if "strength" is not too grand a term for it; *Muskrat*, the only seriously bad Everlys record ever; Craig Douglas and Frankie Vaughan singing Gene McDaniels numbers; *Mama* by Connie Francis; the Allisons; *Exodus* by Ferrante & Teicher; the singing debut of Hayley Mills; *Big Bad John*; The Tornados' *Telstar*; British Comedy records and *Love Is Like a Violin*, by Ken Dodd.

I think that list omits the mediocre; I've tried, at any rate, to just include the really terrible. And it's quite a list. Of course, a lot of it deals with British things, very few of which could have got through to Dylan, but I could hardly have left them out. The state of British pop then was abominable, and it's salutary to be reminded of the details.

Always, though, it works out somehow that when anything noticeably grim is happening in pop, it's only there to counteract something equally good. So what were the good things that happened in 1960-62—the things that invalidate the myth of pre-Beatles infertility?

The first thing to say, and which Nik Cohn conveniently forgets about, is that '60-61 was actually the year that some rock came back. Gene Vincent with *Pistol Packin' Mama*; Eddie Cochran with *Cut Across Shorty*; and Brenda Lee with *Sweet Nuthins*. Connie Francis tried it on *Robot Man*; Ricky Nelson tried it, with blaring saxes, on *I Got My Eyes On You* (*And I Like What I See*). The Piltdown Men arrived; U.S. Bonds came along with *New Orleans* and *Quarter To Three*; and Freddie Cannon did *The Urge*. The Everly Brothers did *Lucille*; Jerry Lee Lewis came back with a classic version of *What'd I Say*; Presley himself did *Little Sister, A Mess of Blues* and *I Feel So Bad*. Del Shannon at least made a gallant attempt on his second hit, *Hats Off To Larry*, and they issued a great but doctored Buddy Holly rocker, *Baby I Don't Care*.

Apart from this unchristened rock revival, on came a super-abundance of sounds that were newer, maybe cleverer, and which certainly stick in the mind. They don't need looking up—they're not just facts or statistics—they're well remembered to this day.

Blues singer Bobby Bland made it with *Let The Little Girl Dance*. Floyd Cramer started something with *On The Rebound*—something that came to final fruition on Dylan's "Nashville Sky-line" track, *Tell Me That It Isn't True*. The Ventures did *Perfidia* and Johnny & The Hurricanes did their *Rockin' Goose*. Duane Eddy went from *Shazam* through to *Dance With The Guitar Man*. A man called Troy Shondell cut a record called *This Time*. Clarence Frogman Henry was around, and making truly delightful concert appearances as well as the records *But I Do*, *You Always Hurt The One You Love*, *Ain t Got No Home*, *Lonely Street* and a great, great flop called *A Little Too Much* (not the Ricky Nelson song). Roy Orbison arrived, with grace and elegance and a voice that could not fail—the prototype voice for Dylan's *Will Ye Go, Lassie, I Forgot More* and part at least of *Lay, Lady, Lay*. Ray Charles balanced nicely between soul and a bowl of slop. The Marcels did *Blue Moon* and Ernie K. Doe did *Mother-In-Law*. Dion found his *Runaround Sue* sound and Neil Sedaka found *Breakin' Up Is Hard To Do*. The Everly Brothers were better than ever, with *Cathy's Clown*, *Nashville Blues* and *Stick With Me Baby/Temptation*.

Tamla-Motown was young enough to be refreshing, as on *Please Mr. Postman* by The Marvelettes and Mary Wells' *My Guy*. Phil Spector came along like Armageddon with The Crystals, Bob B. Soxx & The Blue Jeans and later The Ronettes. The Tokens did *The Lion Sleeps Tonight*, and *B'Wa Nina*—both so bad they were good. Little Eva emerged, and so did Bruce Chanel. Presley made his beautiful *Surrender*. Paul Anka came back with *Love Me*

Warm And Tender, and Sam Cooke sang *Nothing Can Change This Love*. There was *Monster Mash* by Bobby Boris Pickett & The Crypt-Kickers, and there was Walter Brennan (!) with *Old Rivers/The Epic Of John H. Glenn*—a double-sided classic if ever there was one.

Add to all that the arrival of the Four Seasons, Jay & The Americans, the Shirelles' *Will You Love Me Tomorrow*—a minor breakthrough—and *Tell Him* by The Exciters. Then add *I Sold My Heart To The Junkman* by the Blue-Belles, and *I'm Blue* by the Ikettes. *Letter Full Of Tears* by Gladys Knight & The Pips. *Snap Your Fingers* by (the American) Joe Henderson. The Contours' *Do You Love Me* and the Isleys' *Twist And Shout*. Ketty Lester's *Love Letters* and Claude King's wonderful *Wolverton Mountain*. The devastating *What's A Matter Baby?* by a satanic Timi Yuro; and perhaps the very greatest of the lot, one minute twenty-eight seconds' worth of *Stay*, by Maurice Williams & The Zodiacs.

(Plenty of material there for Where Are They Now? investigations. Where is Maurice Williams? I really wish I knew.)

Far from being bad years, plainly, 1960–62 were very rich, and very diversified.

The dominant influence, if there was one, was the search for a new duo-racial RnB-type music. Lots of the vocal groups were looking for that, and in England at least it was accepted that these Americans had found it. So Billy Fury moved on to Phase Three: not Presley, not Eddie Cochran, but by covering *Letter Full Of Tears* he became a mixture of processed cheese and Gladys Knight & The Pips. A complex sound, and to go with it, rumours that he wrote strange and secret poetry no one was allowed to read. Decca were obviously quite proud of the new sound they'd given him—so Lyn Cornell, an ex-back-up singer from Jack Good's "Oh Boy!" TV show, covered *I Sold My Heart To The Junkman*, and Liverpool's Beryl Marsden covered Barbara George's *I Know*.

Underscoring developments at the time of this RnB quest there was, as usual, a corresponding country strength. It was there behind most of the rock revival records; it was there for Floyd Cramer; Ray Charles mixed it with his soul-singing. *Blue Moon* and *You Always Hurt The One You Love* are sort of country songs. The Everlys were from Country country and relied heavily

125

on the songs of the Bryants—which included their *Nashville Blues*. The Walter Brennan record hammed it up, but the Claude King record put heavy accent back into perspective. And Roy Orbison emerged, like Presley and Johnny Cash before him, after a less successful start on the Memphis label, Sun. Long after *Only The Lonely* and the move to Monument Records, he was still singing country songs on albums, including the much-recorded *All I Have To Do Is Dream*.

So altogether there was plenty happening for Dylan to notice, react to, pick up on: his pop education didn't need to have finished—couldn't have finished—in the 'fifties.

2: EVERYTHING'S BIN RETURNED WHICH WAS OWED PART 1:

What Dylan did gain from the years up to '59 were lessons learnt from Fats Domino and Chuck Berry, Elvis Presley and Buddy Holly: relatively specific things from highly distinctive artists.

Fats Domino taught white pop fans about idiosyncratic flexibility in lyrics—particularly in rhymes—through odd emphasis (a Dylan trick) and odd pronunciation. In Domino's *Good Hearted Man* he manages, by his accent and his disregard for consonants, to make the word "man" rhyme with "ashamed"—no mean feat. He put out a record called *Rockin' Bicycle* but he sang it "Rockin' Bi-sic-l", and the words of that song are interesting too, in a simple but individualistic way.

There's plenty of evidence in Dylan's work of Domino's oddities of emphasis. For instance, in *Absolutely Sweet Marie*:

> Well I waited for you when I was halfsick
> Yes I waited for you when you hated me
> Well I wai-ee-ded for you inside of the frozen traffic
> When ya knew I had some other place to be:

Domino also comes up, maybe accidentally, with the pathetic use of bathos, which again is something that Dylan has used. I can't remember the title but there is a Domino song which includes this amazing couplet:

> Her hands were soft as cotton
> Her face could never be forgotten.

126

From Chuck Berry, Dylan learnt a lot more. Berry was ahead of his time.

Berry offered an urban slang-sophistication slicker than any city blues man before him. He offered a bold and captivating use of cars, planes, highways, refrigerators and skyscrapers, and also the accompanying details: seat-belts, bus-conductors, ginger ale and terminal-gates. And he brought all this into his love songs. He put love in an everyday metropolis, fast and cluttered, as no one had done before him. In Chuck Berry's cities, real people—individuals —struggled and fretted and gave vent to ironic perceptions. And it was all so controlled, so admirably neat. This is the first verse of his great song *Nadine*:

> As I got on a city bus and found a vacant seat
> I thought I saw my future bride walking up the street
> I shouted to the driver "Hey Conductor! you must
> Slow down! I think I see her, please let me off this bus."

In *Maybellene* he manages to cram in three car-names in as many lines:

> As I was motivatin' over the hill
> I saw Maybellene in a Coup de Ville
> A Cadillac a-rollin' on the open road
> Nothin' will outrun my V8 Ford

and in *You Never Can Tell* every couplet has a special kind of wit and economy:

> They bought a souped-up Jidney, 'was a cherry red '63,
> They drove it down to New Orleans to celebrate their
>   anniversary. . . .

Chuck Berry also specialized in place-names, as no one before him or since has done. He releases the power of romance in each one, and thereby flies with relish through a part of the American dream. Place-names are scattered around like syllables in songs like *Back In The U.S.A.*, *Sweet Little Sixteen* and *The Promised Land*.

The last of these is the story of the poor-boy from Virginia who makes it to success-land, California—although we never discover what he really finds there. The song mentions lots and lots of place-names in passing, or rather, while the poor-boy's passing

127

through, and a corresponding number of methods of transport. "And that hound broke down an' left us all stranded in downtown Birmingham." It ends up like this:

> ... come down easy,
> Taxi to the terminal-zone;
> Cut your engines an' cool your wings
> An' let me make it to the telephone:
> "Los Angeles, give me Norfolk, Virginia,
> Try Waterford 1009,
> Tell the folks back home this is the promised land calling
> An' the poor-boy's on the line!"

Who else could take up two lines of a song in giving the operator the number?

He humanizes the operator as well, of course, by the licence involved in explaining his message to her. Dylan is probably conscious of turning this on its head when he uses the telephone to emphasize isolation in *Talkin' World War Three Blues*.

> So I called up the operator of time
> Just to hear a voice of some kind
> "When you hear the beep it will be three o'clock."
> She said that for over an hour
> And I hung up.

The urban slickness, precision and irony are there in many Dylan songs, including *On The Road Again*—which could almost be *You Never Can Tell* turning sour, with its wild domestic detail. And Dylan uses the same Berry qualities on *From a Buick 6*, *Highway 61 Revisited*, *Memphis Blues Again*, *Bob Dylan's 115th Dream*, *Visions of Johanna* and so on.

The corresponding musical influence is even more widespread. Chuck Berry's distinctive, driving cameos, tight-knit and self-sufficient, inspired most of the rock side of Dylan's "Bringing It All Back Home" and much of "Highway 61" and many other unreleased cuts, including, in slow-motion, *Barbed Wire Fence*.

Dylan also took over Berry's manipulation of objects and the details and adman phrases that surround them. There are plenty of equivalents of that "souped-up ... cherry-red '53" in Dylan's rock songs: and, for example, in *4th Time Around* and *It's Alright Ma, I'm Only Bleeding*.

128

Dylan doesn't go in for the massed place-names which Berry parades so generously, although there is one song—less characteristic than just interesting—which crams in all the following names (it's an unreleased song called *Wanted Man*): California, Buffalo, Kansas City, Ohio, Mississippi, Cheyenne, Colorado, "Georgia by the sea" (!), El Paso, Juarez (used again later at the beginning of *Just Like Tom Thumb's Blues*), Shreveport, Abeline, Albuquerque, Syracuse, Tallahassee and Baton Rouge.

It's also true that Dylan could never have written a song like *Tombstone Blues* without Chuck Berry; and nor could *Subterranean Homesick Blues* have come into being without him, either in its musical format or its words. It needed Berry's *Too Much Monkey Business* first.[3]

The Berry song's technique is to pile up disconnected ideas, building up—like a list—the pressures that are on the story's narrator, and suggesting their unreasonableness by their phrased sharpness and their multiplicity. This is done fairly straightforwardly, but the simplicity adds to the effect. It's by no means artless. The last verse runs:

> Workin' in the fillin' station
> Too many tasks
> Wipe the windows
> Check the tyres
> Check the oil
> Dollar gas?!

Dylan, taking this up, makes it serve in a far more complex capacity. He widens the context and the predicament of the man under pressure. Chuck Berry might have a nasty job but Dylan has to fight off the whole of society:

> Ah, get born, keep warm,
> Short pants, romance, learn to dance,
> Get dressed, get blessed,
> Try to be a success,
> Please her, please him, buy gifts,
> Don't steal, don't lift,
> Twenty years of schoolin' an' they put you on the day shift
> Look out kid . . .

Obviously, despite the differences in scope, you couldn't have had

T–SDM–E

the one without the other. (Mick Jagger, incidentally, used the same technique and idea for what is arguably the Stones' best single ever, the wild, gargantuan *Get Off My Cloud*).

Lastly, Chuck Berry—like Little Richard—indulged a sort of consciously-laughing and highly effective quirk which made for line-endings on little words that prose would never emphasize. They don't just work as fill-ins: they help define the mood and add to the individuality of the songs. There's a totally characteristic example, which could have come from either Little Richard or Chuck Berry, in the Credence Clearwater tribute-song *Travellin' Band* where the rhyming line after "hotel" is "oh well". Dylan picks up on this too. He doesn't use it in quite the same way, ever, and the most interesting examples are where he modifies its function most, in two of his narrative funny-songs, *Motorpsycho Nitemare* and *The Ballad of Frankie Lee and Judas Priest*:

> He said he's gonna kill (*pause*)
> Me if I don't get out the door in ten seconds flat

and

> For sixteen nights and days he raved
> But on the seventeenth he burst (*pause!*)
> Into the arms of Judas Priest

All this said, it's important to recall, I think, that Berry was pioneering all this at a time when most people were either saying "Rock, baby, rock", or "I love you when you do the—".

We forget just how stultified most pop lyrics were. We say, rather automatically, yes of course they were inane—but we tend to forget the extent of the inanity. Consider this lyric, to a song called *I Love You Still*, put on around 1961 by the man who discovered the Dixie-Cups, Joe Jones (& His Orchestra):

> You know I love you
> I always will
> You are the one I love
> I love you still

> You know I need you
> I always will
> You are the one I love
> I love you still.

130

That was the complete lyric. (The music wasn't too mind-blowing either.)

If Dylan learnt a lot from Chuck Berry, who stood out in splendid contrast to the Joe Jones/Dixie-Cups kind of thing, he learnt a lot also from Elvis Presley.

As everyone must know, Presley came from Tupelo, Mississippi, where he was born poor in the 1930s and moved to Memphis with his mother and unemployed father when he was 13; later he got a job driving a truck. (There's a very nice Dylan allusion to this, delivered in a tough, Presley voice, on the unreleased tape cut with The Band between "Blonde On Blonde" and "John Wesley Harding": "Goin' down t' Tennessee! get me a truck or somethin'".

Very much a Southerner, Presley said Yes Ma'am, No Sir to hostile press reporters, was inward with a simple gospelly religion (via The First Assembly Church of God) and was in love with the voice of Mahalia Jackson. Close your eyes while she sings The Lord's Prayer in *Jazz On A Summer's Day* and you could oh so nearly be listening to Presley. And like a good Southerner, Elvis loved home-cooking and ball-games and the rest. There's a certain autobiographical aptness in the lyric of a 1969 Presley recording *You're Wearing That Loved On Look!*

> Baby if you never loved me
> Then Bonnie an' Clyde loved the law
> Birds can't fly an' I don' like apple pie
> An' trees don't grow down in Arkansas.

So Presley had the formula for rock 'n' roll within him: a natural upbringing on blues and country music in its living environment. His first record, issued by Sun for distribution only in the Memphis area, was Arthur Big Boy Crudup's blues *That's All Right Mama*, sung with a kind of subdued freneticism that sounds hillbilly, amateurish and absolutely genuine. The change to *Heartbreak Hotel* is a large but a logical one.

Strangely, it is hard to find anywhere attempts to discuss Presley's music. For Tony Palmer, for instance, Presley is just Cadillacs, suits of gold, mansions, cigar-butts and money. And his music? "Well," Mr. Palmer concludes, "who cares about that?" The consensus strikes again and the *Observer*-reader can

131

feel safe—he's been told there is nothing he doesn't understand. It isn't true.

The legend does not provide all of the answers—Presley's real importance is in his records—his music.

From '56 to '60, that music was fine. The Poor Southern White made good, the prophet of rock, the sexual threat to bourgeois virginity, the pop equivalent of Brando in *The Wild One*, the untouchable and inaccessible prototype superstar: all this was maintained by the records, not the reporters. And when he had gone plastic and the Beatles were screamed at instead, the failure, correspondingly, was in Presley's music, not in his image. Had his output 1962–64 been up to his pre-Army standard, then the Beatles might have got no further than those wonderful 1961 American groups like Maurice Williams and the Zodiacs, Cathy Jean and the Room-Mates, Nino and the Ebb-Tides. The gap was open for Beatlemania not because of Presley's age (he was younger than Dylan is now) or because kids were tired of solo stars but because something drastic had happened to his music.

What was it that had gone out of Presley's work? All the sex; all that curious amalgam of insinuation and bluntness which Presley had introduced to pop and which Jagger was picking up on; all the pregnant charisma that had, from the very beginning, more than compensated for the false posturing of everything in the pre-Dylan years; all the therapeutic role-distancing humour; an impeccable control in a strong voice that understood (rare thing then) nuance; and an avowing, ever-present nobility.

When he started, the two most important things in his music were lack of inhibition, and sex. Lack of inhibition is very important. Adolescents admired him because he could be socially unacceptable and get away with it, on stage and on record and in the mind, even if not more than once on the Ed Sullivan TV Show. Sullivan was right, by his own lights, to take Presley's hips out of camera-range: they were being rude. And certainly a lot of teen-singers who came after him were to discover that getting up on a stage and yelling WAAAAAAAAHHHHH! ! ! is like exposing yourself in public without being stigmatized.

Sexually, Presley offered a new world, at any rate to whites, and offered it with a blunt statement of interests. There was none of the sycophantic "dating" appeal that was the context of the most of the '50s stars, recorded love-affairs. *At The Hop, Teenager In Love,*

Lonely Boy: these were the typical titles of the time—but not for Elvis. His titles suited the black labels that announced them (just as in England Cliff Richard suited the flat green of the old Columbia label).

Trouble, I Got Stung, Jailhouse Rock, Paralysed, King Creole —these all fitted the various significant elements that made Presley a unique, thrusting and ominous force. He embodied an untapped violence—consider that prophetic, pre-Townsend line, "He don't stop playin' till his guitar breaks"—that a song like *Trouble* made explicit. As for the kind of hard bravado that *Jailhouse Rock* merged with ecstasy, you only have to compare it to the Jeff Beck version, on the "Beckola" album, to see what made Presley a giant. *Jailhouse Rock* is a direct descendant of *Hound Dog*, where the voice seems to rage like King Kong in chains.

Of course, lots of rock stars tried to be aggressive and masculine. Lots, too, made love to the stage microphone—Gene Vincent most endearingly: but only Elvis Presley projected himself so well that he seemed often to be bearing down sexually on the listener.

This comes across best in the love songs. Here, he offered the constant implication of prior sexual experience and a corresponding cynicism which others could never bring off.

> Hey babe—I aint askin' much o' you
> No n-no n-no n-no no baby—aint askin' much o' you:
> Just a big-uh big-uh hunk of love will do.

That, for example, came across in 1959 as freshly candid, its message the forerunner of that line from Dylan's *If You Gotta Go, Go Now:* "It's not that I'm askin' for anything you never gave before." The two extracts share the same ambiguity, the same ostensible politeness. Obviously, the mindless virginity-assumptions of others were as far away from late-'50s Elvis as from mid-'60s Dylan.

It was certainly a unique stance at the time—unique, at least, in reaching the mass of white middle-class adolescents. Black pop naturally insinuated also, but more as a series of in-jokes than as a manifesto for white libido.

Even the likes of Chuck Berry, a black star with broad duo-racial appeal, cut innumerable maudlin slow-shuffles where all the words seemed to say, roughly:

133

Can I carry your books home from school, darlin'
Cos gee—you're lookin' good.

And think of the other white heart-throbs. Take Rick (then Ricky) Nelson's forte:

I hate to face yr dad
Too bad
I know he's gonna be mad
It's late ...
Hope this won't be our last date;

or take the mournful, sexless world of Eddie Cochran (though admittedly these lines are classics, encapsulating most of pre-Dylan pop America):

Six hot-dogs oughta be just right
After such a wonderful night ...

Presley, in contrast, got down to the eternal verities of passion underlying the middle-class Saturday night:

If you wanna be loved, baby you gotta love me too
Cos I aint for no one-sided love affair:

Well a fair exchange aint no robbery
An' the whole world knows that it's true ...

And Presley's cynicism had such pungency—it provided, over the years, a sharp, concerted attack on the two-faced conventions which were imposed on the children of the '50s.

Why make me plead
For something you need?

How much of an attack the characteristic Presley songs constituted is hard to recall in the context of contemporary rock music, but if you think back to the other niceties operative in the '50s pop world, Presley's achievement is again striking. At the time, for instance, even sweating was taboo. Presley alone ripped off these petticoats of the undiscussible. He shocked and thrilled because his lyrics talked about his body:

One little peck on the back of my neck
'n I break out in a cold cold sweat ...

134

This kind of point takes some appreciating, but that second line was pretty daring then—and more than compensated for rarely-used phrases of the "one little peck" variety. And his delivery gave a stylishness and authority to these open, soliciting songs which was utterly lacking in the other rock artists. Not just by sneers but by his pent-up tremble in the bass notes, the sudden full-throated rasps and the almost confessional, mellow country moans, Presley was saying "I'm over eighteen, I'm clean, let's fuck" not only years before the acid-rock groupies but a full six years before John and Paul were wanting to hold your hand. Millions of eager seven-teen-year-olds, weary of the Fabian-style pudge-next-door who only did want to hold their hands, could respond a good deal more honestly when Elvis sang *Stuck On You*, *Treat Me Nice* and *Baby Lets Play House*.

Not surprisingly, considering the time-span of Presley's ascendance, there were other songs which, if quoted carefully, could give an opposite picture—a picture of Presley as effete and, like all the Bobby Vees and Vintons, sycophantic. *Girl of My Best Friend* is a good example:

> What if she got real mad and told him so?:
> I could never face either one again . . .

But first, the delivery was never remotely effete, and even at his most melodic (which he was never afraid to be anyway and which he always carried off without false delicacy) there was a saving power. And second, such examples were simply untypical of what Presley stood for. In the same way, the sensitive unisex aura of Buddy Holly—who avoided plasticity in an opposite way to Pres-ley—was sometimes absent from his work yet remained its distinctive feature. *Annie's Bin A-Workin' On The Midnight Shift* is an exception in the Holly repertoire, not an archetype.

A final point on Presley's sexuality. It is true that the pre-rock chart-toppers and radio-favourites, the night-club stars whose idea of perfection was a Cole Porter song and the Nelson Riddle Orchestra, dealt with sex too—but never, never with passion. Physical contact, desire, sexual aspiration always come across from Sinatra, Torme, Fitzgerald, Tony Bennett and the rest as a kind of world-weary joke that goes with old age. The standard it's-one-in-the-morning-and-we're-pretty-smooth treatments of *I've Got You*

Under My Skin, Night and Day, etc., could easily be addressed to a can of flat beer.

Against this lifeless background, Presley's initial impact coast-to-coast in America and in Britain also, was holocaustic. Yet lack of inhibition, sex and the voice to carry it was not all that he offered. He also gave out a fair share of the vital humour which goes with the best hard-line rock and which Fats Domino, Chuck Berry and Little Richard used very well.

This kind of humour shows itself aware of outside values and of the inextricable mixture of the important and the trivial, the real and the stylized in the pop medium. And if you go back now to the original Presley recordings, the pungency and freshness of this humour still hits home. Think of the self-awareness of Elvis, polite Southern boy with grafted-on rebel image, pounding out this:

> Ah sure would be delighted with your com-pan-y:
> Come on an' do the Jailhouse Rock with me ...

Or less subtle flashes such as this:

> If you can't find a partner use a wooden chair
> And let's rock

Or:

> She wore a clingin' dress that fit so tight
> She couldn't sit down so we danced all night

Or (this one funnier in retrospect, I admit):

> Well there aint nothin' wrong with the long-haired music
> Like Brahms, Beethoven and Bach,
> But I was raised with a guitar in ma hand
> An' I was born to rock. Well ......

Or finally:

> Samson tol' Delilah—Delilah say Yeah?—
> Keep yo' cotton-pickin' fingers out ma curly hair
> Oh yeah, ever since the world began
> Hard-Headed Woman bin the thorn in the side of man.

And yes, the deliberate yet essentially unselfconscious Negro reference in that last example indicates how inward, how fundamental a strength, is Presley's understanding of the blues. Its idiom comes in naturally enough.

Mess of Blues; *One Night*; *That's All Right Mama*; *Reconsider Baby* (a Lowell Fulson song); *Blueberry Hill*; *Anyplace Is Paradise*; *Lawdy Miss Clawdy*; *It Feels So Right*; *Heartbreak Hotel*; listen to any of these today and the claim that Presley is a great white blues singer (albeit a commercial one) is hard to deny. And that he brought all this before a vast, non-specialist white audience in the drab Eisenhower era was a really explosive achievement.

Some of these tracks still sound undiminished in quality. *Heartbreak Hotel* still sounds strangely ahead of its time, even now, despite all the white blues-slanted artists who have emerged (and been hailed as so progressive) in recent years. Indeed, many of these owe as much to Presley as the early rock copiers did. Canned Heat, for instance, sounds like the child of a white *Tobacco Road*, and any white *Tobacco Road* sounds like a bad imitation of *Heartbreak Hotel*, which Presley recorded fifteen years ago. And *Lawdy Miss Clawdy* remains a vital, exciting classic, sufficiently accurate and unadulterated to make the best of Tamla-Motown-Stax sound like the Black & White Minstrel Show.

Presley's voice had nobility—a clear, charismatic rarity to which a generation rallied and felt uplifted in hoping to protect: just as another generation intensely desires to protect the man whose voice lights up *I Threw It All Away*.

There are many other links between the two. In the first place, Dylan would have heard at least part of his old blues material second-hand through Presley. Elvis' *Milkcow Blues Boogie* is an old song by Kokomo Arnold—not a well-known name, I'd guess, up in Minnesota—who was born in Lovejoy, Georgia, in 1901. Perhaps also it was adapting the Elvis version of that song which provided part of the lyric for Dylan's *It Takes A Lot To Laugh, It Takes A Train To Cry*.

Similarly, Dylan's lyric and tune on *One More Night* are heavily reminiscent of Elvis' record of *Blue Moon Of Kentucky. That's All Right, Mama*, Presley's first record, is down there in the Bob Dylan songbook. The piano-work on Dylan's *Mixed-Up Confusion* owes a lot to the spirit of that on *Lawdy Miss Clawdy*; and the clear allusion to Floyd Cramer's piano-style on the end of *Tell Me That It Isn't True* is an allusion to a style much associated with Elvis and his RCA Victor studios at Nashville.

137

The opening lines of *Lay, Lady, Lay* are doing what Presley has stood for all along. Dylan may be sexier (and his sexuality somehow brings in his intelligence) and therefore better at it, but it's the same kind of ennobled overture that comes across in a hundred Elvis songs:

> Lay, lady, lay—
> Lay across ma big brass be-ed

and altogether the immaculate soulfulness of *I Threw It All Away* is like Presley's great *Is It So Strange?*.

A smaller but none the less indicative parallel can be found between an Elvis record mentioned, *Milkcow Blues Boogie*, and *Dylan's 115th Dream*. Both cuts begin and then stop and start again; Elvis says "Hold it fellas!" and Dylan replaces this with "Hey, wait a minute fellas!" And that is not the only Dylan amendment of a Presley line. In the much later Elvis song *Cotton Candy Land* there is this pre-packed glycerine line: "We'll ride upon a big white swan"; and Dylan revisits it with suitable irreverence—in his knowingly gauche *Country Pie*—to "Saddle me up a big white goose!" (Bathos, no less).

There are many take-offs of Elvis slipped into Dylan's work—but it's significant of the considerable value of Presley's influence that they are never so much take-offs as tributes. Presley is melodramatic, and Dylan mocks that, mocks the exaggeration, but always he does it with a smile that confesses he can't help falling for Presley, that he notices the good things just as keenly. These take-offs/tributes include the end, musically, of *Peggy Day*:

> *ting, ting, ta-ba-ba* Love to, *ba ba-ba-ba ba,*
> Spend the night *ba-ba-ba-ba-ba-ba-bam,*
> With Peggy Da-ay—*ba-am, ba-am, ba-am, ba-am-ba-ba-am!*

Elvis' songs often really do end like this, right from his very early *I Got A Woman* through to *Beach Boy Blues, Steppin' Out Of Line* and *Rock-a-Hula Baby*.

Dylan doesn't stop there. On the unreleased acetate of *The Mighty Quinn*, which is very different from the "Self Portrait" version, the Dylan voice is deliberately near to the Presley voice of *Trouble*. And there are two versions of *Nothing Was Delivered* on that acetate which evoke the Presley world. The one with the heavy piano-backing is a finely measured acknowledgement of

Elvis' handling of Domino's *Blueberry Hill*; the version with Dylan's monologue is a wide-open laugh at Presley's monologue posturing on *That's When Your Heartaches Begin*, *I'm Yours*, *Are You Lonesome Tonight* and, again, *Trouble*. On the last of these especially, Elvis "talks tough", like a kind of upstart Lee Marvin:

> I don' look f' trouble but I
> Never ran
> I don' take no orders from
> No kinda man

and Dylan simply makes the hollowness transparent by using the same bravado on weaker lines. Elvis stands there as if all-powerful, delivering the goods; Dylan comes on like a swindled consumer to talk from positions of weakness:

> Now you must, you must provide some answers
> For what you sell has not bin received
> And the sooner you come up with those answers
> You know the sooner you can leave.

Five or six years ago, when Dylan was held to be the absolute opposite, the antithesis, of Presley, it would have been, if not actually heretical, at least controversial to argue that Dylan could owe Elvis anything. Now, despite the lack of commentary published on his recordings, recognition is growing for what Presley has achieved. I have grown up with his records, I have always believed in him—so it's hard for me to judge whether somebody largely unfamiliar with his output could, on going through it attentively now, understand its greatness enough to get a glow like I get from it. It's probably too late for that—the clichés and artifice that are a discountable part of it to me must almost certainly be too obtrusive for new listeners to cope with except on a few classic tracks. If that is the case it's a major barrier to appreciating what Dylan has got from Presley—because there's more to that appreciation than I have managed to convey. But it's there in the music.

For different reasons it's even harder to write anything useful about Buddy Holly. Nik Cohn is quite mad to suggest he had no talent. He had more personal talent, more charisma and more potential than anyone except Presley. Even on his very early recordings, where the studio sound, the arrangements and the type of song featured all drew heavily on Presley's earliest Sun cuts, you could not but be aware of a very different talent feeling its way and testing its strengths. By the time he was having hits, he not only had a distinctive sound but also an integrity and an inquiring interest in country music and city blues. The famous Holly sound is on songs like *That'll Be The Day* (Version 2: and it's instructive to compare it to the earlier, unstable version); *Peggy Sue*; *Heartbreak*; *Every Day*; *Listen To Me*; *Tell Me How* and so on. Maybe his later ones are the best, with their slightly mellower sound—in particular, *Peggy Sue Got Married*; *That's What They Say*; *What To Do*; and the truly immortal record that was his latest release at the time of his death, *Raining In My Heart* coupled with Paul Anka's composition *It Doesn't Matter Any More*.

Holly's voice transcends the limits set by the words of his songs. *What To Do*, transcribed on to the printed page, may be fatuous and trite:

> What to do
> Now that she doesn't want me
> That's what lonesome means
> What to do—
>
> The record-hops and all the
> Happy times we had;
> The soda-shops, the walks to school
> Now make me sad, oh!
>
> What to do
> I know my heartache's showin'
> Still not knowin'
> What to do

but on the record, Holly's voice moulds it, lights it up, so that it becomes a good deal more than trite—more even than acceptable sentimentality. I can't say in what way he achieves this, and the achievement itself is, at the centre, elusive—but every time that record plays, magic comes across (and it is not just throwing me back to age-fourteen-when-life-seemed-easy-etc.-etc.) I am sure it will still come across when I am sixty-four. Artistically, Holly hasn't died, and never will. In some ways he is/was better than

140

Presley—his voice at its best was the first artistic permanence, the first universal statement ever made by pop music.

Holly died, if anyone doesn't know it, with Ritchie Valens in 1959, in a chartered single-engined plane which crashed in the snow in the early hours of February 3rd, on its way to North Dakota. The last things studio-recorded before his death were in some ways a little cold. Titles were *True Love Ways* and *Moondreams*, and they were very mellow indeed. (One of them even used an aspidistra saxophone sound.) But if there's a hint that he might have been already slacking off into popular balladland, the evidence of his musical interests belies it. He cut the only white commercial blues that could even touch Presley's best, *Lawdy Miss Clawdy*: the song was called *Mailman, Bring Me No More Blues*. He could handle Bo Diddley and Chuck Berry too, not just competently but adding something of his own in a way that showed rare understanding. *Bo Diddley* and *Brown-Eyed Handsome Man* make the point with a kind of raw panache.

As for the music on his own songs, it's riddled with the clichés of the time, but, he handled these clichés with intelligence enough to show that had he lived he would have readily discarded them. People talk automatically about the Claptons of this world as "the great guitarists"; I think there's a sense in which Holly was a great guitarist, boxed in by the restrictions of convention in his time. If he had lived ...

Greil Marcus said that Buddy Holly would have joined Dylan for a duet on, say, *I Don't Believe You*. That sounds true to me, and true in part because of the similarities that exist in any case between the two singers.

They were both small, delicate-looking people, yet they both gave out a big sound—which gives them a certain resemblance in image. To call it little-boy-lost is too simple, but on stage there was a suggestion that both of them were lost in their own worlds of loudness—except that that implies wrongly that they weren't in control of the sound. Little-boy-uncorrupted seems a slightly less clumsy tag.

Control is the second point of resemblance. It's a thing that was missing altogether from rock when the British beat-group boom got going in 1964. One of the main things that marked out such groups from the solo stars they replaced was that a loose, ramshackle sound was considered good enough and a rather erratic vocal technique came into vogue. Suddenly, singers weren't sure where they were throwing their voices and didn't care which notes, if any, they were going to catch. Many of the solo stars had known exactly what their voices were doing—even when they were ripping it up. Little Richard was wild, but he was always in control. Presley had this same sort of precision. So did the Everlys and Jackie Wilson—especially on his classic *Reet Petite* (1956).

Buddy Holly had it too. Control in Holly was a special thing, tantamount to integrity—a precision demanded by artistic considerations, which was one of the things that made for his greatness. Dylan learnt a lot about such considerations, I would say, directly from Buddy Holly. There are times when both of them appear not to have this control, times when bits of phrasing sound at first hearing like bad mistakes, but they never are. The wild swoop-up/hiccup at the end of the title-phrase in Holly's *Tell Me How* is an example; and Dylan provides others in *Times They Are A-Changin'* and, among others, *Drifter's Escape*. The oddities are not mistakes, they're far more right than the expected alternative bits that don't appear. A few more playings and they both prove their points. The control and precision were perfect after all, and when that realization dawns, both artists have taught you something.

You can trace the effects of this teaching, as Holly gave it to Dylan, right down to similarities of timing, phrasing, emphasis, pronunciation. Greil Marcus, as usual, has dealt very well with this. "Dylan and Holly", he wrote in *Rolling Stone* (June 28th, 1969), "share a clipped staccato delivery that communicates a sly sense of cool, almost teenage masculinity", and he cites Buddy Holly's performance on *Annie's Bin A-Workin' On The Midnight Shift*. There, says Marcus, "the phrasing is simply what we know as pure Dylan"—

> If she tells you she wants to use the caahhh!
> Never explains what she wants it faaahhh!

Marcus goes on from there to make another but a connected point, in discussing some of the home-tape-recordings of Holly's voice which were released, after his death, with backing-tracks added:

Sometimes, these ancient cuts provide a real sense of what

142

rock 'n' roll might have become had Holly lived. The same shock of recognition that knocked out the audiences at the Fillmore West when The Band ... lit into Little Richard, takes place, with the same song, when the ghost of Buddy Holly is joined by the Fireballs for *Slippin' And Slidin'* ... An agile, humorous vocal is carried by a band that knows all the tricks. They break it open with the Everly Brothers' own seductive intro, constantly switching, musically, from song to song, while Holly ties it together. The guitarist actually sounds like Robbie Robertson, throwing in bright little patterns around the constant whoosh of the cymbals ... it's certainly one of the best things Buddy Holly ever did.

The same "shock of recognition" is there when Marcus first suggests the Holly-Dylan duet that would have happened if Holly had lived. There must be a good deal of similarity that is perhaps too intangible to document in order for that idea to strike home so sharply. Obviously, the *Annie's Bin A-Workin'* resemblance is tangible enough—and we have it on innumerable Dylan tracks from *I Want You* to *On The Road Again* and from *Absolutely Sweet Marie* back to *When The Ship Comes In*. The last of these may seem a strange choice, but Buddy Holly could have sung *When The Ship Comes In*. It has all the right tensions, all the polarities of high and low notes, rushes and lapses, that Holly alone among the pre-Dylan stars could easily control.

That brings home another fusion of delivery: an intangible additive in the voices. Both Dylan and Holly suggest a level of emotion at work below the words, way out beyond the scope of the lyric. Holly shows it incredibly well on, for example, *True Love Ways,* and Dylan uses it everywhere.

In the end, perhaps the best way to encompass what Dylan has done via Holly is to say that Dylan, really, has replaced him. You could say, without undue exaggeration, that Dylan has replaced Nashville too. He has put all it stands for into a handful of songs. He has pinned down the best of Nashville single-handed —it is all there at the end of "John Wesley Harding" and on the following album, "Nashville Skyline".

I've been considering the major influence on Dylan's pop/rock music, and it's tempting to carry on through his countrified output, the material just mentioned, from exactly the same perspective—dealing in "influences". When you hear a song like his *I'll Be Your Baby Tonight* (from "John Wesley Harding"), the temptation is to say, ah yes, Hank Williams—and yet switch straight from the Dylan song to any Hank Williams album and the strong and derivative resemblance you imagined just vanishes. *I'll Be Your Baby Tonight* isn't really like Hank Williams at all.

The answer is that the perspective is all wrong. Dylan owes a lot, not to Hank Williams (or anyone else) in particular, but simply to Nashville; and it isn't influence so much as stimulus. Dylan hears Don Gibson bring something close to perfection, in its own small way, with *Sea Of Heartbreak*; Dylan hears Jerry Lee Lewis break into extraordinary lyrical piano-work on beautifully poised performances of songs like *Cold Cold Heart*, *Your Cheating Heart*, *Together Again* and *How's My Ex Treating You*; Dylan hears and befriends Johnny Cash (whose self-penned number, *Understand Your Man*, forms the basis of the tune for *Don't Think Twice, It's All Right*); Dylan hears Flatt & Scruggs, Patsy Cline, Jack Scott, Marty Robbins and a hundred others, with and without international "names"—all exploring different paths but from the same prolific headquarters. So Nashville provides the stimulus of example, and Dylan, with "Nashville Skyline", decides to commit himself to a country music album. The result is stunning because he sees through to basics in whatever he tackles: that's why he's brilliant at whatever he tries. So he turns out an album unrivalled in country music, an album so precisely right, so faithfully lifelike and yet so alive, that it almost makes the rest of Nashville redundant.[4]

In its own right, that's a major achievement—yet in the full context of what Dylan, as an artist, has done, it is only of minor importance. Country music just isn't that valuable. A one-man Nashville has so much less to offer than the Dylan of "Highway 61" to "John Wesley Harding".

But all the influences, including Nashville, have helped Dylan produce great work; and in turn Dylan has made it possible for a revolution to take place in rock music. But before examining that there is another aspect of Dylan worth dealing with in the context of the old pop as much as the new rock: that is, not Dylan the artist but Dylan the star.

3. WHO'S GONNA THROW THAT MINSTREL BOY A COIN?

Dylan is the greatest rock'n'roll star in the world. Partly, of course, this is because he's the best rock writer and singer and performer there has ever been; but partly—and the two aren't by any means totally distinguishable—it's because he's become an idol, a superstar.

There are certain strategies which dictate impressively whether "star material" makes it to legend status. One such successful strategy is to build up your rarity value. You reach a point when it is fatal to appear too often, when the occasional rumour is more effective than frequent hard news, when it's better to only release one record a year than attempt a three-monthly assault on the charts, when it's best not to talk at all to the outside world, when it's necessary to shun the company of other celebrities, wise to turn down huge money offers, and above all essential to avoid the TV medium.

This starts out as a simple show-biz rule—"always leave the public shouting for more"—but it ends up vastly more complex and all-embracing in a pop world attended to by teenyboppers and students, business executives and revolutionary dropouts—a world split between singles and albums, TV shows and weekend festivals, stage concerts, dance-halls, discotheques and films, and under the constant if idle scrutiny of "quality" newspapers, tabloids, underground fortnightlies, weary Fleet Street musicpapers, and trendy paperbacks. You have to learn to dodge them all. Otherwise they burn you out before you're half-way there.

To a certain extent it's true that it's in the interests of the magazines to help you become a star—but they're not very subtle, they're slaves to precedent and just occasionally they decide to actively put the boot in. The British press, for example, killed off Terry Dene and P. J. Proby, and tried to do the same to Jerry Lee Lewis. The *Daily Sketch* even tried to pull down Dylan.

Monday, September 1st, 1969, WEATHER: Slight rain, some sun

DYLAN CUTS IT SHORT AFTER MIDNIGHT FLOP

Uproar broke out at the great pop festival at midnight when

Bob Dylan walked off the stage after singing for only an hour. The pop star, who was being paid £35,000 for a three-hour climax to the Isle of Wight Festival, staggered off helped by two friends ... The 150,000 pop fans ... had shown little enthusiasm for the American singer. He had kept them waiting three hours —until 11 pm—before strolling on to start his act ... Coke cans and beer bottles were thrown on the stage when he finally appeared ... And when the white-suited Dylan finally walked off the fans started shouting and jeering ... Earlier teenagers had romped semi-naked in a sea of foam pumped into one of the "side-show" arenas. And at the height of the freak-out a couple waded naked in the foam, openly making love. See centre pages.

That report came from Jane Gaskell and Christopher White, who were in the press arena immediately in front of the stage. I was in the press arena too, and was close enough to see that the only people who got beer bottles and coke cans thrown at them were appalling reporters like Jane Gaskell and Christopher White, and their even more appalling photographers, who kept jumping up and down, shooting off their flashbulbs and obscuring all view of the stage for the front rows of the audience.

But it isn't the facts, wrongly-reported, that show how much there is to avoid. The hopelessly deadening journalistic machine condemns itself with phrases like "Midnight flop", "staggered off helped by two friends", "before strolling on to start his act", "at the height of the freak-out", "openly making love" and that crude attempt at subtle condemnation, "the American singer".

The star not only has people like that to deal with, but he has to dodge, every day, a hundred other reductive approaches. In the early '60s in England, there was a programme on BBC Radio (the Light Programme) called "Saturday Club". This was a two-hour mixture of records and live appearances partly by pop artists and partly by played-out old dance bands/combos/foot-tappin' guitarists. Plainly, a programme to avoid. No true star would have touched it with the wrong end of his chromium-plated microphone. Yet plenty of famous pop names agreed to perform on it not just as newcomers but long after they'd become established. Bad strategy, bad management.

The man with the best manager was Presley. Once established,

Presley withdrew from all these lowly aspects of the pop scene, built up a reputation for declining huge appearance-fees, stopped talking to newsmen, avoided television like the plague—and consequently emerged as the best-selling, highest-paid, most god-like and untouchable dream since Greta Garbo.

Presley never came to Britain—turning down, among other things, an offer of £100,000 for one performance inside a magnifying bubble in the centre of a vast sports stadium. He couldn't, it was explained, afford to make the trip for "that sort of figure". It was "not quite what we had in mind".[5]

In contrast, Paul Anka performances were, in many parts of the world, two a penny. Result: Paul Anka became eminently touchable, the boy next door, one of myriad second-class stars. When you saw his name mentioned, momentary interest was engaged: you read the item. If he was coming to your home-town, well, maybe you'd go and see his show if the supporting acts weren't too awful and if the price was right. But when you read the name Elvis Presley, lights flashed—and you knew you'd go anywhere, pay any price, to see him.

He's lost a certain amount of this hold on people—he's made too many films (and very grim ones at that) and too many records which have been dully out of touch; but the image and the aura linger on to a remarkable extent. His TV Spectacular in 1968 (1969 in England: thanks again, BBC) was his first television appearance for over eight years. And that's the way to do it.

That's how Dylan does it too. You wouldn't catch Dylan on "Top Of The Pops", or in bed for peace *ad nauseam* on the front pages of the world's newspapers. His scarcity-value is enormous. Rumours about what he's doing are whispered around now and then; he limits himself, effectively, to albums, and never brings out more than one a year. When California was bursting with supposedly-incredible rock groups and was crowded out with every pace-setting Beautiful Person in the world, Dylan remained pointedly 3,000 miles away, in splendid isolation in New York State. "Involvement is death," he once wrote.

It sounds easy—refuse to appear for £5 and eventually someone will offer you £50. Do that once, throwing in a little controversy while you're at it—and then start refusing again. Easy or not, most people don't manage it: most people don't appear to even understand. They're delighted with any rush of publicity, they pose for fifty photographers and comply with every tasteless idea these men come up with, they commit themselves to films which, if they're lucky, will never get a general release—and a year or two later they're astonished to find themselves rated about as exciting as Ray Connif.

It's true that much of Dylan's uncooperativeness with the media is in response to their intrusions, their attempts to raise a man who is a great and a serious artist to their own level of vulgarity (on the journalistic Peter Principle); but it also comes from Dylan's shrewdness as an image-builder, a Garbo in rock music.

He plays with reporters brilliantly, showing up their bumbling, uncomprehending platitudes, keeping his distance, controlling them. A few examples. He allowed a film to be made, a semi-montage of parts of his 1965 tour of England. The reviews were a triumph for Dylan. The Cleveland *Plain Dealer* spluttered out this:

> Should be buried ... This is a cheap, in part, a dirty movie, if it is a movie at all ... It is certainly not for moviegoers who bathe and/or shave. It is "underground" and should be buried at once. Burn a rag, as was once said of filth. Phew!

It wouldn't have been very satisfactory if the Cleveland *Plain Dealer* had liked the film. Bad for the image. As for *Newsweek*, it really had to grovel—and in a way that must have amused Dylan greatly:

> "Don't Look Back" [said *Newsweek*] is really about fame and how it menaces art, about the press and how it categorizes, bowdlerizes, sterilizes, universalizes or conventionalizes an original like Dylan into something it can dimly understand.

Dimly understand was right. The *New Yorker* informed its readership that parts of the film "catch some moving essence of being young now".

Back in England four years later, for his one-hour appearance at the Isle of Wight, Dylan held a press conference. Not a convenient one, in London, on his arrival at the airport, but one instead on the Isle of Wight itself. They all flew out there to ask him their questions, of course, and the questions were what you'd expect:

REPORTER: A lot of the young people who admire you seem to

148

be mixed-up in a lot of drug-taking and so forth. Do you agree with this? What are your views on this problem?

DYLAN (assuming thick country accent): Oh I don't have any of them views; I sure wish I did—I sure would like to share them with y'all.

It isn't just funny answers, it's an ability to manipulate completely, to counteract instantaneously the amorality of the media—and that seems to me a gigantic achievement. In our mass society, it is revolutionary warfare. Norman Mailer must be proud of him; no one else in the western world has learnt to fight like this. The goat comes along, asks its questions, tries to have its customary shit—and Dylan, instead of evading like a politician, by mouthing other goat-like platitudes, cuts through it all and so manages to speak directly to the people who are still "out there" and who don't rely on the *Reader's Digest* to give them their world-view.

This triumph does more in the way of keeping Dylan a star than just maintaining his scarcity-value. It also allows him to feed secrets to his fans, which in pop is very important. There you are at home reading a rumour in *Melody Maker*, August '69. The rumour says that when Dylan comes to the Isle of Wight at the end of the month for his first appearance in Britain for over three years, he might finish his performance with a jam-session, with George Harrison, John Lennon, a couple of Rolling Stones, Eric Clapton and Ginger Baker, Humble Pie and the Bee Gees joining him on stage! And it's highly pleasurable to be in on a secret, to cut through this rubbish and know the mind of this incredible man—because you know all the while that he's let the rumour grow by simply not denying it, that he's watched in amusement as the snowball machine rolls it out: and you know perfectly well that it won't happen. He'll no more appear on stage with those people than he'll enter the Eurovision Song Contest.

There are lots more peripheral pleasures involved in the star-fan system in pop, and Dylan doesn't miss a trick. He's not just ten steps ahead of the media: he's three steps ahead of you too—which enhances the fun of sharing secrets. It's fun hanging on to the reins of his unfailing unpredictability.

You see him in concert in Liverpool in 1966. The board outside the theatre (which is really a huge, depressing cinema) says

2.45: THE SOUND OF MUSIC. 7 P.M. BOB DYLAN

—and that's a joke the newsmen (and the cinema management too) wouldn't even notice. Anyway, you go in, you wait, and Dylan comes on for the solo half of his performance. He tunes up carefully before every number, he hardly glances at the audience, he wears a shabby, crumpled grey suit—and he doesn't speak. No "Hi! It's wonderful to be here!", no "Thank you very much, thank you", no "I'd like to do a song now called. ..." The first time he speaks is in the second half, when the folk morons are booing and heckling. Somebody shouts out, uncomprehendingly, "Where's the poet gone?" and Dylan smiles, comes up to the microphone with a gentle corrective reproach: "Not where's the poet, where's the saint gone." And at the very end, no encore. Dylan almost runs off the stage at the end and is out of the theatre and away—with the audience still hoping against hope that he's still there really, that really he's just behind the curtain.

Great—the press don't understand it at all, but you do. You're in on the secrets and you've witnessed the agile rejection of all the showbiz charades.

And then you see him at the Isle of Wight and he twists it all around. "Thank you, thank you—great to be here," he says, in the little shy voice of a moderate man, as if he's ever so surprised to find all those thousands of people turning up just to hear him. And he's dressed immaculately in white, just for the flashbulbs and spotlights. Fifty-five minutes later, he says "We're gonna do one last song for ya now, It was a big hit for, I believe, Manfred Mann. Great group, great group." He sings *The Mighty Quinn* and walks off. The hoping against all hope begins—and back he comes, happy to please all the folks out there applauding. But the song he sings is yet another lampoon:

> Who's gonna throw that minstrel boy a coin?
> Who's gonna let it roll?

So where does that leave you, except still applauding twenty minutes after he has gone away? You stand there clapping not only the artist, but paying your tribute gladly to the idol as well.

4: EVERYTHING'S BIN RETURNED WHICH WAS OWED PART II:

Despite the influences of Holly, Presley, Berry and the rest, Dylan's work is far more original than derivative. In fact he has been the big influence: he has created a re-birth in rock.

Dylan goes beyond other people—with every new album there's a progression; and this has happened so fast that in one sense Dylan has always been an outsider in pop—has always been ahead of his time.

The first time a lot of pop fans noticed him was when *The Times They Are A-Changin'* came out as a single in 1964. To pop-trained ears, it was a laughable record. The singer had a voice that made Johnny Duncan and The Blue Grass Boys sound in the same league as Mario Lanza—and plainly, the man hadn't even the most elementary sense of timing. He brought in the second syllable of that titleword "Changing" far too soon—at a quite ridiculous point. What was the record-company playing at? Just because Bob Dylan was the writer of an interesting song called *Blowing In The Wind* didn't mean he could expect to start singing all his other songs himself.

With that behind him—and it was, in the end, what Radio Luxembourg calls a chart-bound sound—Dylan invented a new form, folk-rock. "Another Side Of Bob Dylan", his fourth album, is essentially rock music. The sound on the album is a rock sound, despite the fact that the backing is "really" just Dylan with solo guitar and harp—despite the fact that "really" it is his last solo album. The rock sound is evident everywhere on it, and Dylan doesn't achieve this by going mad on his guitar/harmonica/piano. He achieves it by implication.

Motorpsycho Nitemare is very much the same sort of song as *Bob Dylan's 115th Dream*, on the rock side of the 5th LP; but *Nitemare* doesn't differ from "Dream" in being solo-work rather than rock—it differs in having a better and a heavier implicit rock sound behind it. And the whole of the 4th album has exactly that same superiority to the 5th. The explicit backings on the latter are often thin and clickety but the music the 4th album puts into your head—perhaps especially on *Spanish Harlem Incident, I Don't Believe You* and *Chimes Of Freedom*—is dazzling: strong and rich. It has the sort of richness Dylan achieved in concert in 1966 (not just in the rock half of the concerts either, but on the solo *Mr. Tambourine Man* of that time too) and on tracks like *One Of Us Must Know* in the "Blonde On Blonde" collection.

But it's rushing ahead to mention "Blonde On Blonde" at this point. We were on a chronology of Dylan's entry into pop and we had reached folk-rock, just about. There, on the earlier rock albums, were sounds unlike anybody else's before him. With "Another Side Of Bob Dylan", and more so with "Bringing It All Back Home", many of the folk fans flinched away, and the pop world didn't really catch on either till it was spoon-fed with the singles of *Subterranean Homesick Blues* and *Like A Rolling Stone*. Even with these, Bob Dylan was still clearly an outsider not just because such records were different, but also because they were peculiar. They lasted longer than two-and-a-half minutes: very odd.

But they made an impact: and again Dylan's originality as a rock artist was very clear. The folk fans who carried on listening called his new music "folk rock" because, well, he was a folk-singer and yet there he was using electric guitars and things; and from the other side, the pop fans who began to listen also called it "folk rock" because, well, it was certainly rock and yet it was strange, it demanded intelligent attention.

Both groups of people were right. This was a new music, an original music. Dylan had made a profound connection between folk's articulacy and rock's virility. Here was rock music, part of the pop world, yet with it Bob Dylan was pumping out something of infinitely more dimensions than any one else had ever thought of in pop before. Pop had its isolationist policies torn away from it and was made to contemplate part of the real world too.

Perhaps it was just because Dylan was fully conscious of this achievement that he demanded such high standards from his rock musicians.

Even for his first appearance in rock music, at the Newport Folk Festival in 1965 (a slice of which is included in the film *Festival*), he only enlisted the best—they were, then, from the Paul Butterfield Blues Band. And as the words on Dylan's electric albums got more and more impressionistic, less and less specific, the music got ever more precisely "right". (And this is why by the time of "Nashville Skyline" the musicianship clinches Dylan's country stuff as both more commercial and more ethnic than other people's.)

If the oddness of Dylan as a pop figure, with all his perplexing innovations, suggested that intelligence was assaulting the pop scene, that didn't mean that no clever people besides Bob Dylan had ever made their mark in pop. It isn't true that success depends on stupidity, as outsiders tend to assume.

Being a bit dumb can help, of course: could Andy Williams vulgarize everything so gladly if he was sensitive enough to puke up after every show? How could a man like Tony Blackburn carry on if he could see himself as others see him? How could he even smile like that if he wasn't so contentedly stupid? And it's well known that in England pop as a business is kept going by cliques of sharp but brainless cockneys.

But you don't need to be thick. Phil Spector, Mick Jagger, John Lennon, even Ricky Nelson: they are not stupid at all. Yet they haven't used their intelligence to accomplish any fundamental changes, as Dylan has. They've come into pop accepting as permanent its conditions and restrictions as they found them: so all they've done is find themselves a corner each to sit in.[6]

In contrast, Dylan has used his intelligence to re-create the rock milieu. Far from accepting what he found and settling down in some lucrative little niche, he has burst the whole pop world wide open and built a new one (and with much more than the bricks of the old).

Before him, you could have said that pop was like football. Millions of people liked it—millions of people like fish and chips —but it didn't much matter. It was just a "mindless explosion of fantasy's dream". To make it important, you had to be an addict. Only very occasionally and by accident did it take on the function of art, by summing up, like a brilliant photograph, the nature of some reality in contemporary life. Flashes like Eddie Cochran's couplet:

> Six hot dogs oughta be just right
> After such a wonderful night

were entirely unconscious of their importance.

Dylan has made art possible in pop, quite unfortuitously. He has shown that a rock song can provide the appropriate form for universal statements, and that millions of people can respond to it. (Even the Ivy League universities have begun to accept rock as an art form. Princeton has given Dylan an honorary doctorate for his "services to music".)

So the pop world has split in two. Half, currently called teenybop or bubblegum, is the music that has rattled on regardless of change

153

—regardless of Dylan. (Much of this stuff has been affected instead by the glittery tunes and brave new chords of Lennon and McCartney.)

The other music, still labelled "progressive" or "underground", couldn't have happened without Dylan.

But you can't blame The Beatles for the "improvements" in bubblegum, and you can't blame Dylan for all the cheap and nasty developments which his work inspired before the serious musicianship of the underground found itself.

First, predictably, in Dylan's wake, came the Great Pop Protest Craze. The one worthwhile section of Richard Mabey's book deals with this insidious phenomenon.[7] It was, writes Mabey,

> not a very long-lived fad, nor in statistical terms a very successful one. But it aroused a spirited controversy and left a faint but seemingly permanent impression ... It had, in theory, every element that a truly popular form should have, and suffered, in practice, every injury that can befall such a form as it is shunted through our mass communications network ...
>
> ... When some of these songs began making seditious inroads into the Hit Parade, it was difficult not to feel delighted that they were reaching such a large public. But then ... things started to go wrong ... A new craze had been filed. Immediately ... singers who had not had a hit record for some time began producing songs which were as trite and generalized in their comments on war and freedom as most pop songs are on love. Because of the lack of discrimination in the pop scene, these camp followers put everybody's sincerity in question, and protest music, as a fashion, died a quick and rather embarrassing death ...
>
> Not many people inside the modern pop music business have ever been bothered about pop's lack of contact with our contemporary concerns. Most of the nagging about this has come from the outside, and has consequently been disregarded. ... Pressurized by sheer custom and the danger of disturbing a comfortable and receptive audience, the song-writers have stuck to safe, impersonal subjects. (This is a strangely anomalous convention, for the same young people who—however accidentally—have avoided overt sex, crime and war in their songs, will

flock to the cinemas and bookstalls for proxy excursions into these areas.) And strong is the allied belief that the appeal of lyrics is insignificant ...

... The first obvious landmark was raised when the Manfred Mann group played Dylan's *With God On Our Side* on "Ready, Steady, Go!" ... it was received tumultuously. But it was difficult not to be sceptical. What was the applause for? A good song? A sensitive performance? For famous Manfred Mann? Or just for fun, because "R.S.G." was a live-wire show, and if you didn't clap and cheer the temperature might drop? One could not get rid of a nagging doubt that, if the group had sung a number in favour of the saturation bombing of China, the reaction might have been exactly the same ... *With God On Our Side* set a pattern, in more ways than one ...

The two records which really established protest as a fashion were Donovan's *Universal Soldier* and Barry MacGuire's *Eve Of Destruction* ... [and] ... when *Universal Soldier* was played on Radio London, it was punctuated by shrieks and gun-noises from the disc-jockeys. During its spell in the Hit Parade, I saw servicemen listening to it on juke-boxes with what appeared to be pleasure. And when Donovan's name began featuring in advertisements for toothpaste, there was good reason to doubt if any of his songs were communicating in the way he intended:

Are you a Donofan? Folknik sweetie, profile blurred in
    cigarette-smoke,
how does your garden grow in the magic land of Folk?
For you, is one-name Donovan just the job or do you save
    up sighs for Dylan, Bob.
Whatever sort of folk you dig, of this be sure,
that dreaming face in cloudy shock of soft-brushed hair
    needs Gordon Moore's,
the modern cosmetic toothpaste that tints your gums a
    pink that sings,
shines teeth as bright as guitar strings.

... Barry MacGuire ... was delighted that the BBC had banned *Eve Of Destruction*: "I read somewhere that this sort of thing is the new way to get a hit in England." ... By October there were a dozen songs or more in the Top Fifty which were being filed under "protest" ... There was the Hollies' *Too Many People*, a song about over-population, which ended with the roar of an H-bomb explosion. One of the Hollies explained:

> It kind of says that God has ways of cutting down the popu-
> lation when there really are too many people in the world. War
> does away with a lot, and then there were things like the Plague
> of London. It kind of levels things up.

Their recording manager levelled things up a bit more by saying:

> I suppose it will be controversial, but that never did any
> harm. It's publicity, and with a record you're just selling a
> product.

Then there was Sonny's (of Sonny and Cher) *Laugh At Me*, a rather dismal piece of self-pity which he wrote after being ejected from a restaurant because of his appearance. ...
... "Parade" ... was typical of the reactions of the popular press:

> ... What with Joan Baez saying she regarded herself as a
> politician more than a singer, and Donovan sounding off here,
> there and everywhere, it seems to me that the young warblers
> are getting a shade too uppity.

If serious pop songs ever succeed in breaking through wide-spread attitudes like this it will be a miracle. In this comment are crystallized most of the values with which the operators shackle pop: the assumption that pop music's only function is to entertain, and that it is impossible for songs with a "message" to do this; that young people should not criticize society, par-ticularly if they are making money; above all, the total lack of discrimination ...
... By December 1965 the protest fashion had expired, de-flated by a surfeit of irrelevant and misleading publicity, an audience that was, as usual, getting bored, and the influx of a large number of spurious songs ... As Philip Oakes once re-marked, "You, too, can be a liberal: all you have to do is play the record."

The "seemingly permanent impression" the protest craze left was, nevertheless, that people in pop felt obliged or permitted to engage with the outside world: to be seen to have outside interests, to think, to produce material that was less mass-minded. Dylan had already said it—the protest free-for-all just tarnished the Dylan legacy.

Some of what happened afterwards *was* pretty tarnished too. In England, Maureen Cleave could legitimately include the following in a glance back over 1966:[8]

... pop singers in interviews said they were reading the works of Huxley, Sartre and Dr. Timothy Leary. One even claimed to be reading *Ulysses* ... But there were compensatory laughs ... Andrew Oldham said Scott Engel of the Walker Brothers was the Joan Crawford of pop music, and Scott Walker said no he wasn't—he was the Greta Garbo. The *Sunday Telegraph* described Andrew Oldham as the Rolling Stones' "creative manager" ...

Any pop singer, at a loss for something to say, said he was thinking of opening a boutique. (As Clement Freud so rightly pointed out, one feels such a fool without a boutique nowadays.) ... Mick Jagger took to producing: "Jagger", said an admirer, "who brought Nureyev to rock'n'roll is now the Zeffirelli of pop." We saw the story of Donovan's life on television: "My job," he said, "is writing beautiful things about beauty. You see, my life is beautiful." ...

Nervous exhaustion was all the rage. Scott Engel was exhausted nervously; so was a Kink, a Yardbird and a Cream. Mick Jagger was reported to be nervously exhausted after buying furniture for his new flat ... in the last few months even nervous exhaustion was on the decline.

It was replaced by the conviction that everything was beautiful, groovy and gentle. Pop singers floated around loving people in a patronizing manner that was even more infuriating than their protest songs. "When you are aware," Donovan said, "there are no such things as hate and envy: there is only love."

"This industry of human happiness," said Andrew Oldham crossly. Oh yes, there were laughs in plenty; but ... it was the end of an era ...

The pop singers themselves have grown old; their faces on television look old, world-weary; bored faces that have seen it all. The future is bleak ... but the present, while they sort

157

themselves out, is pretty sordid. Nineteen sixty-six is the year the whole thing turned sour. Many found they hadn't made the money they ought to have made. The shock reduced them to complete inactivity. . . . What, one wonders, will happen to them? They can't all be absorbed by boutiques. Will they . . . all go into pantomime? Or will they—which is what the richer ones do at the moment—stay in retirement, cut off from the world in their large houses, making home movies and having beautiful and groovy thoughts, far removed from the industry of human happiness? . . . And Andrew Oldham said: "This is the year of the crucifixion and only some of us have managed to pull the nails out of our fingers. Few will survive."

And yes, suddenly it was go to San Francisco with a flower in your hair, and after that Frank Zappa told the lefties at LSE that "revolution is this year's flower power".

You can't blame Dylan. He'd finished recording his "protests" in 1963, and on his last solo album (the one with the rock sound) had issued his dismissive evaluation, *My Back Pages*. By the time the Protest Craze was happening, it was one too many mornings and a thousand miles behind its founder.

Ironically, though, while it was student audiences for whom protest was more than a craze, it was also student audiences who first picked up on the music Dylan went on to create. The musical underground began under the patronage of the campuses.

With *Mr. Tambourine Man*, Dylan had started something else: the pop exploration of drugs. He carried it through—based, we all assume, on heavy personal tripping—and in the year that Maureen Cleave was characterizing as "sour", Dylan issued "Blonde On Blonde": acid-rock. It may not have been apparent at the time, but this was the great regenerative force. In terms of pop history, it was the single most important recording since Presley's *Heartbreak Hotel*.

It was less the drugs than what Dylan had done with druggy music that caused the "underground" explosion that followed "Blonde On Blonde"—an explosion of groups with (at first) strange names and genuine exploratory work. Dylan was father to all these groups—to Moby Grape, Big Brother & The Holding Company, The Doors, The Velvet Underground, Sopwith Camel, Country Joe & The Fish, Jefferson Airplane, The Byrds, Iron

158

Butterfly, Dr. John The Night-Tripper, Procul Harum, etc., etc., etc. They were all descendants of Dylan: and so was "Sgt. Pepper's Lonely Hearts' Club Band".

As his protest music had popularized and part-unified the anti-Establishment focus, so too his acid-rock/surrealist music made possible an alternative to that Establishment outside of tiny avant-garde minorities: he was catalyst in the mass adoption of the underground. If the Protest Craze had shown that serious expression in pop music would have to steer clear, in future, of the Hit Parade and the leeches down Tin Pan Alley, then Dylan had shown that a viable alternative really was possible, given a certain singleness of purpose and a thing pop had never recognized before —integrity. Dylan's protest songs survived the craze, on the whole; Dylan carried on exploring without regard for trends, never a slave to pop's unwritten rules.

So the underground groups were his offspring, for better or worse. The attempt to do one's own individual best—to compete against oneself instead of others—the willingness to stand alone, to face the changing times head-on if need be: Dylan showed everybody how, just as his songs were showing how possible it was for rock to handle real things instead of the conventional falsehoods.

Not only that. The attempt to learn from drugs, the attempt to recreate the acid experience, the rejection of commonsense logic and the acceptance of mystery—Dylan accelerated the awakening to all this. His has been the giant silhouette hovering above the crowds at the Rock Music Festivals. At Woodstock, the big secret hope was that to round it all off, to bless and perfect it, Dylan would appear, like a Moses come down from the Mount. That was certainly the feeling when he did appear, three weeks later, at the 2nd Isle of Wight Festival of Music. And if such festivals confirm that pop is not at all what it was and that "the new pop is concerned more with incantation than with communication" then Wilfred Mellers was clearly justified in introducing that phrase in the context of reviewing "Blonde On Blonde".

Dylan himself, characteristically, has always denied responsibility. No sooner had the Beautiful People scene, the-all-you-need-is-love-and-a-rock-band scene, reached breakneck speed in San Francisco than Dylan was, well, breaking his neck, or claiming so, and staying away.

After a two-year silence, he issued "John Wesley Harding",

159

which was a rejection of the new music, the love generation, drugs, revolution and almost every other underground solidarity set up and encouraged by his earlier work. As Jon Landau wrote in *Crawdaddy*, May '68:

"John Wesley Harding" is a profoundly egotistical album. For an album of this kind to be released amidst Sgt. Pepper, Their Satanic Majesties Request, Strange Days and After Bathing at Baxter's, somebody must have had a lot of confidence in what he was doing . . . Dylan seems to feel no need to respond to the predominate trends in pop music at all. And he is the only major pop artist about whom this can be said. The Dylan of "John Wesley Harding" is a truly independent artist who doesn't feel responsible to anyone else, whether they be fans or his contemporaries.

It wasn't really a pop album at all; it certainly hadn't got a rock sound, except for the country-rock of the last two tracks—and they were less integral parts of the whole than signposts to yet another future. *Down Along The Cove* and *I'll Be Your Baby Tonight* equalled some in "Nashville Skyline".

"John Wesley Harding" was out of even the new pop world (which was by then different enough from the old for the word "pop" to seem embarrassing and inappropriate and the word "rock" just had to replace it). But the new world rolled on, from the opportunity-blueprints of "Blonde On Blonde", using the medium as an art form and producing, at its best, an abundance of creative, self-made music.[9]

Even where the sources were musically/lyrically very different, it was still Dylan who had opened the door. Frank Zappa and the Mothers of Invention, for instance, didn't need "Blonde On Blonde" (or "Highway 61 Revisited") musically but they needed Dylan to establish that "pop" artists could claim and merit serious attention. And they, like all the rest, needed the example of his successfully ruthless focus on established values. Without him, the Mothers really would have been a freak show, largely unheeded and soon forgotten.

Bob Dylan, single-handed, had created the sheer possibility of the situation Paul Williams was able to describe in the issue of *Crawdaddy* that was quoted above:

Rock groups who take themselves seriously [wrote Williams]

160

are not always eager to cater to what they believe is the public taste—and of course their direct contact is not with the public but with the record companies and the radio stations, who have their own ideas as to what the public taste might be. So even if you agree to appeal to the great unwashed, it is nigh-impossible to agree about what they really want. Problems: disparate goals (making music versus making money); disparate perception of the situation ("What does he know about what the public wants?"); and strained relations beyond the level of surface courtesy ("It's impossible to talk to those freaks/money-mongers").

The performer, then, is in a difficult position. Should he try to please the public, the record company or himself?

Before Dylan, that question would never have got asked. Before Dylan, everyone put the public first. They all bowed to what they imagined were the common denominators of public taste. Dylan not only showed them all, or their successors, that you didn't have to go along with this: he also showed that when you didn't go along with it but offered honestly some personally satisfying alternative, you could release an undiscovered openness in the public.[10] Bob Dylan unchained public taste. He has done more than anybody else—and far, far more than formal mass-education systems—to develop in a mass audience the kind of receptiveness to things imaginative and non-trivial that was, before, the sole prerogative of elite minorities. Dylan has done more than Spock and Montessori to enhance the inside lives of America's youth, and more than Nuffield projects can ever do for its English equivalent.

That's a sizeable claim, but it's well worth standing by. Dylan himself, of course, wouldn't dream of standing by it. The interview he granted *Rolling Stone* (December 13th, 1969 issue) served to emphasize this:

RS: Many people ... all felt tremendously affected by your music and what you're saying in the lyrics.
BD: Did they?
RS: Sure. They felt it had a particular relevance to their lives ... I mean, you must be aware of the way that people come on to you.
BD: Not entirely. Why don't you explain it to me.
RS: I guess if you reduce it to its simplest terms, the expectation

161

of your audience—the portion of your audience that I'm
familiar with—feels that you have the answer.

BD: What answer?

RS: Like from the film *Don't Look Back*—people asking you
"Why? What is it? Where is it?" ... Do you feel responsible to those people?

BD: I don't want to make anybody worry about it ... if I
could ease somebody's mind, I'd be the first to do it.
I want to lighten every load. Straighten out every burden.
I don't want anybody to be hung-up ... (laughs) especially
over me, or anything I do. That's not the point at all.

RS: Let me put it another way—what I'm getting at is that
you're an extremely important figure in music and an
extremely important figure in the experience of growing
up today. Whether you put yourself in that position or
not, you're in that position. And you must have thought
about it—and I'm curious to know what you think about
that.

BD: What would I think about it? What can I do?

RS: You wonder if you're really that person.

BD: What person?

RS: A great "youth leader" ...

BD: ... there must be people trained to do this type of work.
And I'm just one person doing what I do. Trying to get
along—staying out of people's hair, that's all.

RS: You've been also a tremendous influence on a lot of musicians and writers.[11] They're very obviously affected by
your style, the way you do things—

BD: Who?

And later in the same interview—with the interviewer, Jann
Wenner, *Rolling Stone*'s editor, still trying for an answer of
acceptance somewhere in the same context—there is this final
refusal to accept:

RS: Do you think that you've played any role in the change
of popular music in the last few years?

BD: I hope not (laughs).

Anyone who handles an interview like that has to deserve
applause—but no one else besides Dylan should concur with his

162

denials of responsibility. It certainly hasn't been the aim of this chapter to go along with such denials.

NOTES

[1]Not that it didn't stay complacent. Complacency is in its nature, so that Bing Crosby could remark that you "can't go on singing *Hound Dog* forever", and could go on singing *White Christmas* indefinitely himself.

[2]Since writing this, the BBC has done it again, and this time to Dylan himself. Mr. Bill Cotton, Head of Light Entertainment (how typical that a man in that capacity should be involved at all) has decided not to put on TV in Britain the 1969 Johnny Cash Television Show which featured Dylan, and has so decided because he thinks Dylan gave "an inferior performance". Mr. Cotton explained, in a statement to *Melody Maker* (published October 24th, 1970), that naturally if Dylan wanted to do a "good show", like the two concerts done for the BBC in 1965, then he, Mr. Cotton, would be glad to "employ" Dylan.

[3]The debts of *particular* Dylan songs to *particular* earlier records are not, of course, always this direct or significant. It is of interest but not of great import, for instance, that Dylan's basement-tape song *Yea Heavy & A Bottle Of Bread* trades on the amazing and largely-forgotten *Stranded In The Jungle* by The Cadets.

[4]There is, all the same, one country album that seems to justify the "influences" approach to Dylan's country output. The smooth and gentle "Nashville Airplane" (!) by the re-united Flatt & Scruggs can claim a special relevance. The back-up musicians are the same on "Airplane" and "Skyline"; several of the tracks of the former are Dylan songs—but not, in the main, his country songs: songs instead like *Rainy Day Women Nos. 12 & 35* sung country; and one track, by Flatt & Scruggs, *Freida Florentine,* is very much a dress rehearsal for Dylan's *Nashville Skyline Rag.* But then again, Dylan's own *Cough Song*, recorded years earlier, is also very like *Nashville Skyline Rag.*

[5]The use of the royal "we" is an interesting detail. Dylan uses it, as Elvis did. "We're going to do one last song for you now," he said at the Isle of Wight, and it didn't sound as if he just meant him, singular, plus The Band, plural. And certainly, Albert Grossman uses it like Colonel Tom Parker, Elvis' manager.

[6]The extreme example of this is perhaps the case of Jonathan

163

King. To accept rather naïvely, the myth that King's IQ is among the Western World's top 4% is to find it depressingly clear how such a potential advantage can be so lightly frittered away.

[7] *The Pop Process* by Richard Mabey, Hutchinson Educational Ltd., 1969.

[8] I take this from the Maureen Cleave article as quoted in full in the Mabey book.

[9] It would seem to be in direct contradiction of such an assessment of "Blonde On Blonde's" importance to note, as Jon Landau noted (*Crawdaddy* Magazine, May 1968), that it has been said of the album that the total musical effect is muzak—thus contrasting a soft backing with a hard voice. One can see what people meant—and indeed the "muzak" backing crops up earlier than "Blonde On Blonde": it is there on *Positively 4th Street* (1965), and *Queen Jane Approximately*, from the same year, has an almost Johnny Mathis piano intro. But the point is that all of this is oversimplification. On "Blonde On Blonde", actually, it is often the *voice* that is soft—and blurred acoustically as opposed to pronunciation-wise—and it is often the backing that is "hard". Consider *Absolutely Sweet Marie* with its harsh "headache" harmonica, its tough drum-rhythms, and its smoke-soft voice—a voice never more softly eloquent than at the end, with that great line "In the ruins, of your, balcony".

[10] Without Dylan, The Band would still be The Hawks; one of Crosby, Stills, Nash & Young would still be a leading Holly; the Stones would not have gone back to being true to themselves; The Beatles would still be doing "Eight Days A Week".

[11] Not least, one might add, on writers like those who put *Rolling Stone* together. And a small but eloquent testimony to this effect is provided merely by the headlines in "the alternative press". Dylan phrases, as if they were the Western World's Mao's Thoughts, are littered continuously throughout the underground's literature. It is one of Dylan's most minor achievements (though it hints of greater ones) that his songs have answered a thousand sub-editors' prayers.

5

The Images To "Blonde On Blonde": Aspects Of Language

There really seems no need to try to surmount the difficulties involved in defining "imagery" and so on. In what follows, the meanings I intend for such words should be obvious enough from the contexts. As if to underline a disregard for such definitions, I begin the present chapter by quoting part of a David Horowitz article which refers happily to Dylan's "symbolic language" without saying what that means. Maybe it's worth my noting that Horowitz' term covers what, in dealings with the same song, I would mean by "imagery". The song is the early one *A Hard Rain's A-Gonna Fall*, and Horowitz writes:

> The artistic problems involved in treating such a subject (the threat of nuclear wipe-out—raised at the time of the song's composition by the 1962 Cuba Crisis) seriously (Dylan has given it a splendid satiric treatment in *Talking World War III Blues*) are seemingly insurmountable; but Dylan has taken long strides in the direction of their solution. He has done so in the only way possible: by employing an approach that is symbolic. Only a symbolic language could bear the strain of an event as absolute and apocalyptic as the total destruction of life on earth. Dylan's instinctive awareness of the capacities of symbolism is, in this song, turned to brilliant use. In *Hard Rain*, Dylan has adapted the melody and refrain of the traditional English song, *Lord Randall*, and by this very fact has set his own "story" in a frame of concreteness:

> > O where have you been, my blue-eyed son,
> > And where have you been, my darlin' young one?

But the actual tale which is told in answer to the traditional question takes place on an altogether different plane of reality from that of its source:

> I've stumbled on the side of twelve misty mountains
> I've walked an' I've crawled on six crooked highways
> I've stepped in the middle of seven sad forests
> I've bin out in front of a dozen dead oceans
> I've bin ten thousand miles in the mouth of a graveyard
> An' it's a hard, it's a hard, it's a hard, an' it's a hard,
> It's a hard rain's a-gonna fall.

The cumulative effect of these images [ah ha!], an effect which is reinforced by the repeated rhythmic figure of the guitar accompaniment, is little short of overwhelming. We are besieged with images of dead and dying life, a kind of dynamic stasis, a perfect figurative medium for the vision at the brink:

> I met a young child beside a dead pony
> I met a white man who walked a black dog
> I met a young woman whose body was burning
> I met a young girl, she gave me a rainbow ...

We have the start of many stories here, never to be finished, and in the very fact of this arrested promise an accurate rendering of the meaning of that awful apocalypse that may await us. Aptly, this style, which is so tuned to the reality, was actually dictated by it. For, as Dylan explains, "Every line in it ... is actually the start of a whole song. But when I wrote it, I thought I wouldn't have enough time alive to write all those songs, so I put all I could into this one." Because of the precision of the tone and the adequacy of the vision, when it is over, and the respite won, the poet's resolve carries absolute conviction:

> And I'll tell it and speak it and think it and breathe it
> And reflect from the mountains so all souls can see it
> And I'll stand on the ocean until I start sinkin'
> And I'll know my song well before I start singin'
> And it's a hard, it's a hard, it's a hard, and it's a hard,
> It's a hard rain's a-gonna fall.

There is little to quarrel with in this account; it only seems misleading in one significant sense. It accepts too readily that Dylan's articulacy is not so much individual as traditionally "skilful"; it rests on the assumption that Dylan's early work compliantly fits in his non-literal language according to the long-established literary rules.

This doesn't seem to me to be the case. If you look from the rules to the work Dylan has produced—if that is your method of measuring Dylan's achievements (and it appears to be David Horowitz' method)—you will soon get entangled in listing Dylan's "failures", or, to put it another way, in emphasizing Dylan's "lack of sophistication" in handling language, or defensively referring to his "instinctive" talents.

Such entanglement will reveal, in fact, not *Dylan*'s faults so much as a wrong perspective on the listener's or critic's part. Full as Dylan's work is of "unsophisticated" imagery, the success—the eloquence and impact—of such language *in Dylan's hands* makes it necessary to review one's weighting of "sophistication" as an evaluative term.

All the same, it is a feature of Dylan's early work that the good the bad and the ugly often go hand in hand. In *I'd Hate To Be You On That Dreadful Day*, for instance, bad things abound (Dylan never released a record of the song), like this:

> Well your clock is gonna stop at Saint Peter's gate,
> You're gonna ask him what time it is, he's gonna say
>   It's Too Late
> Hey, hey, I'd sure hate to be you on that dreadful day.

I would imagine even Barry MacGuire would have rejected that; and yet the same song included this why-didn't-anyone-express-that-before idea:

> You're gonna have a nightmare and never wake up!
> Hey hey, *etc.*

As for the comparably gloom-ridden *A Hard Rain's Gonna Fall*, it is true that to a very large extent, Dylan's use of images is, as it happens, dictated by tradition. On the other hand, such dictation must be recognized as uncharacteristic of Dylan's early work; and in some ways even this particular song offers a rather special use of imagery.

Line upon line the pictures are piled up, some containing their own "moral" via paradox:

> I saw a new-born babe with wild wolves all around it ...
> I saw guns and sharp swords in the hands of young children ...
> Heard one person starve, I heard many people laughin' ... ;

others with the same purpose but taking longer to say it:

> I met one man who was wounded in love,
> I met another man who was wounded with hatred ...;

and others which, citing two pictures, offer an analogy or parallel:

> Heard the song of a poet who died in the gutter,
> Heard the sound of a clown who cried in the alley ...

Then again, there are images which stand alone, entirely detached, and which do not apparently operate as direct moral diagrams:

> I bin ten thousand miles in the mouth of a graveyard ...
> I saw a highway of diamonds with nobody on it ...
> I saw a white ladder all covered with water
> I met a young girl, she gave me a rainbow ...

The most interesting thing, perhaps, in terms of Dylan's achievement, is that although the fifth verse draws the morals almost specifically, and although the deliberate fragmentedness of the other verses does fit into a cohesive moral *theme*, the effectiveness of this theme still depends on the pictures rolling past, as if on and then off a screen, without opportunity of recall. In other words, there is a simple but none the less strange sense in which for the song as a whole to succeed, each image within it must have a segregated life of its own. Even the common factor that makes most of them fit Horowitz' description of them as "images of dead and dying life" must remain a very, very loose-fitting cover.

Clearly, then, even as we note that Dylan's use of imagery in *A Hard Rain* is uncharacteristic in some ways, we must still make our assessment largely on Dylan's own terms—and we would fall down were we to attempt assessment by a process of moving from an idea of the traditional rules towards an idea of Dylan's talents. Even where Dylan can be said to use traditional images (and indeed there are a preponderance of them in his early work) he cannot be said to utilize them along traditional lines.

I think, to take a small but telling example, of the traditional rendering of someone's personality or spirit in terms of a "light". Someone thus referred to as giving out light is conventional and unsurprising enough; but the reference is normally indirect—like this perhaps:

168

1. Bob Dylan in 1963

2. In Paris, 1966

In Sidney, Australia in 1966

4. At the Isle of Wight Festival, 1969

At the Bangla Desh Benefit Concert, held
Madison Square Gardens, New York, in 1971

6. At the Mariposa Festival in 1972

At The Band's New Year's Eve Concert, 1971-2, held at the Academy
of Music, New York City

As Hartley's eyes swept the ballroom, his attention was called back, again and again, to the same animated face. Miss Satterthwaite (for indeed the face was hers) seemed to radiate an ethereal yet energetic light—and it was not long till Mr. Hartley stood breathless in the glow of it.

That, or at least the kind of thing which that tries to emulate, is very elegant and so on, but the image of light is almost asleep: it is a traditional image traditionally used. Dylan, employing it more casually, rejuvenates it by his non-traditional usage. He takes it from the context of third person narration and plunges it into a direct conversation: and so it emerges with a refreshing kind of bluntness:

> It aint no use in turnin' on your light, babe—
> That light I never knowed

and is given an effective extension:

> An' it aint no use in turnin' on your light, babe—
> I'm on the dark side of the road ...

There is, finally, one further general point that needs to be made in the context of Dylan's "unsophisticated" imagery: and that is simply that where it can legitimately be called unsophisticated, it usually carries corresponding strengths.

Often, for instance, with Dylan's least subtle imagery, he relies quite rightly on a combination of simplicity itself with a mood of anger, to yield a considerable effectiveness. It seems to me that this method works well enough here, for example, in *Masters Of War*:

> But I see through your eyes and I see through your brain
> Like I see through the water that runs down my drain.[1]

We can equally consider the *simple* effectiveness of the imagery in *The Ballad Of Hollis Brown*. There, the words are so riveting and so didactically visual that Dylan can even afford to echo the nursery-rhyme about the crooked man without posing any danger of distraction:

> You looked for work and money
> And you walked a rugged mile
> You looked for work and money
> And you walked a rugged mile ...

Neither are we distracted when we come to an apparently histrionic analogy like this:

> Your wife's screams are stabbin'
> Like the dirty drivin' rain.

The very lack of balance in the construction of that analogy enforces its realism. It is a way of the narrator saying "I understand your desperation—*your* imbalance".

And this relationship between narrator and subject gives the song a strength that is more widely distributed than the isolated quotation above can indicate. We can turn back to David Horowitz' article for a fuller explanation of this point. Horowitz writes:

> Technically speaking, *Hollis Brown* is a tour de force. For a ballad is normally a form which puts one at a distance from its tale. This ballad, however, is told in the second person, present tense, so that not only is a bond forged immediately between the listener and the figure of the tale, but there is the ironic fact that the only ones who know of Hollis Brown's plight, the only ones who care, are the hearers who are helpless to help, cut off from him, even as we in a mass society are cut off from each other.

When we can recognize that even such an early song as *The Ballad Of Hollis Brown* has such strengths, it becomes more than useless to talk of his "unsophisticated" approach—unless we are to merely use that adjective to be synonymous with a word like "honest".

Following on from this, Horowitz points to the power of the blues in Dylan's hands; and in this connection equally, it is fruitless to measure such tools by traditional literary criteria. Why describe Dylan's imagery in traditional terms since it works in a different way? Purely for interest's sake, I should add here, it is worth a final glance at Horowitz' article. With reference to Dylan's use of his blues background, Horowitz argues:

> Indeed, the blues perspective itself, uncompromising, isolated and sardonic, is superbly suited to [Dylan's purpose, which in *The Ballad Of Hollis Brown* at least, is to] express the squalid reality of contemporary America. And what a powerful expres-

sion it can be, once it has been liberated (as it has in Dylan's hands) from its egocentric bondage!

A striking example of the tough, ironic insight one associates with the blues (and also of the power of understatement which Dylan has learnt from Guthrie) is to be found in the final lines of *Hollis Brown*:

> There's seven people dead on a South Dakota farm,
> There's seven people dead on a South Dakota farm,
> Somewhere in the distance there's seven new people born.

How much of the soul of contemporary American society and its statistical conscience is expressed in this sardonic image!

Let us take advantage of the fact that Horowitz takes us, in the above, both to the end of *The Ballad Of Hollis Brown*—which we can therefore reasonably leave—and back to the question of imagery.

We were considering examples of Dylan's using conventional figurative language, especially in the earlier work; and in fact from one of the very earliest of his published compositions, we have a thoroughly conventional, yet quietly effective example. In *Song To Woody*, Dylan takes the obvious but worthwhile step of personifying the "funny ol' world" which

> Seems sick an' it's hungry it's tired an' it's torn
> It looks like it's a-dyin' an' it's hardly bin born.

Of another "travelling" song from Dylan's early output, *Down The Highway*, it could be said that the figurative language is so conventional as to be automatic and consequently careless; that, for instance, it is an arbitrary drift which takes us from the visual image that is to be taken quite literally in the first two lines—

> Well I'm walkin' down the highway
> With my suitcase in my hand

to the almost accidental visual picture offered, dimly and at a distance, by a colloquial figure of speech at the end of verse three:

> Please don't take away my highway shoes.

There is an equal, but more successful, reliance on conventions of the figurative in the unreleased *Train A-Travellin'*, where we

171

have an extended metaphor which uses a reality of pleasant associations to stand for an unpleasant ethos:

> There's an iron train a-travellin' that's bin a-rollin' thru
>   the years
> With a firebox of hatred and a furnace full of fears ...
> Did you ever see its passengers, its crazy mixed-up souls?

The eloquence achieved by simple alliteration (in the second line above) is utterly typical of Dylan's "unsophisticated" work. The use of the train metaphor is, as I have hinted, a little more complex: "iron" is usually associated with an animate machine such as a train in an approving way—as a coloured term indicating strength; in the above, though, it is associated with blindness, or stubbornness; it condemns a dogmatic quality (the direction of which is, of course, shown by that "firebox of hatred").

If the early simplicity of language I've been noting derives some strengths of its own from its very simplicity, it often works in a rather different general direction. That is, rather than just ignoring traditional literary rules, Dylan often actually breaks them—and the effects are not then so simple.

Consider, for instance, these two tiny lines from *Eternal Circle*:

> Thro a bullet of light
> Her face was reflectin'

They provide not the visual image one might expect—because visualization is just about impossible. The picture that we might construct easily enough from "bullet of light" is quite contradicted, and so cancelled out, by the reflectin' *face*—for face is an unanswerable challenge, by its very roundness of shape, to any idea of light like a bullet, which is to say, like a fast straight line. Yet if there is no visualization, there is still a response to that "image", and still a purpose in its being there. We could usefully call it a word-sound image; it is there because its *sounds* are attractive—and they give the voice a kind of equivalent articulacy to the wiry strength of the accompanying guitar-sounds.[2]

I noted much earlier that, often, the simplicity of Dylan's use of language is made effective in conjunction with an overriding anger in the tone and delivery; but naturally enough, this isn't always the case. As we begin to look towards slightly more recent work, we find that even an ultra-simplicity of imagery is partnered frequently by an opposite sort of quality to one of "overriding anger"—partnered, that is, by an understatement (which, incidentally, was in evidence in the very, very early *Song To Woody*). There is no anger here—although there might have been, if, for example, Dylan had rocked up the song in his 1966 concerts— and there is nothing complex either; but the effectiveness is un- deniable:

> Oh a false clock tries to tick out my time
> To disgrace, distract and bother me
> And the dirt of gossip blows in my face
> And the dust of rumors covers me
> But if the arrow is straight
> And the point is slick
> It can pierce through dust no matter how thick:
> So I'll make my stand
> And remain as I am
> And bid farewell and not give a damn.
>
> (*Restless Farewell*)

None of those would be called complex images—or great ones— but in that an image's function is not to sit glistening for the critic's entertainment but rather to make more vivid the artist's idea, then they work perfectly. And they don't need the energy of a *Masters of War* anger-blanket to help them.

They are far from clichéd; and yet they *are* standard images— they involve no surprise. They assist the song but they don't strike hard. And indeed, really striking imagery is uncharacteristic of early Dylan.

By the time of the fourth album, "Another Side Of Bob Dylan", one very characteristic type of image has certainly emerged: images invoking the elements. Dylan notices winds, rains, and so on very keenly, and represents them as forces which impinge strongly, if not theatrically, in the action of his songs. His presentation of them is distinctive—so much so that anyone familiar with even a few Dylan songs would recognize all the following lines as being from his work:

> The night comes in a-fallin' ...
> The wind howls like a hammer ...

And the firing air it felt frozen ...
An' the silent night will shatter ...
Through the mad mystic hammering of the wild ripping
    hail ...
The stars one by one they're a folding ...
The sky is folding. ...

plus, to choose four lines together (from the unreleased *Walls of Red Wing*):

As the night laid shadows
Through the crossbar windows
And the wind punched hard
To make the wall siding sing

or, to add a phrase that only strays slightly from an imagery of the elements:

... electric light still struck like arrows.

That line is from the 4th-album song *Chimes Of Freedom* which is in one way the central song of the album. Ostensibly, the opposite is true: it is the last explicit protest-song: the words have a message. Yet the message is not the important point—and it is almost as if Dylan uses this apparent "message song" to show his listeners that significance lies elsewhere. In doing that, the song offers the motto for the whole album. And indeed it has the album's "sound" to note which brings us to what *is* the importance of *Chimes of Freedom*: namely, that with this "sound"—the echo, the voice, the chiselled word-*shapes*; the sculptured, hard-grained phrasing—Dylan creates a world. It is in notable contrast that in the later, more "out-of-this-world" Dylan work, its force is, paradoxically, an interpretative one, not a sculptural.

So far, I have focused on simplicity in Dylan's language, with only the occasional qualification. But Dylan is far more famous (albeit due to misconceptions, on the whole) for the very antithesis of this—a complexity of language that runs over so the charge goes—into the positively obscure. As we turn our attention towards the album mentioned just above, "Another Side Of Bob Dylan", we can begin to see the development of the new complexity. The first hints of it came even earlier.

The previous album, "The Times They Are A-Changing", offers

an interesting example of poetic transference (if I can use that phrase) on the beautiful *One Too Many Mornings*. The attributes of one thing are transferred onto another in the following:

> And the silent night will shatter
> From the sounds inside my mind ...

The prose equivalent, stripped of this transference, would be that the silence (of the night) will be shattered; as Dylan has it, the night will shatter.

This transference succeeds, of course—which is to say, it comes across as a natural and unobtrusive mode of expression. It is in any case conceptually quite plausible, since it urges the inseparability of the night and the silence. It involves the implied idea that if the night were no longer silent, it would not be the same night.

There is a line in the unreleased *Long Ago, Far Away* (1962) which offers, in a sense, another instance of transference—one involving slighter implications but an arresting visual picture: the line runs

> People cheered with bloodshot grins.

From the fourth album, perhaps the most historically interesting song is *Spanish Harlem Incident*; which begins with this:

> Gypsy Gal, the hands of Harlem
> Cannot hold you to its heat

which, as far as his figurative language is concerned, is like a stylish and immediately impressive declaration of independence on Dylan's part. It's a prety good image, and very individual.

Thus with *Spanish Harlem Incident* we find the really substantial beginnings of Dylan's famous complexity—the beginnings of what 1965 brought out with an explosion, and what 1966 sustained in the "Blonde On Blonde" double-album. (By the 1965 explosion, I mean that that year saw a huge list of great Dylan songs, great Dylan recordings: *Ballad Of A Thin Man*; *Can You Please Crawl Out Your Window?*; *Desolation Row*; *Farewell Angelina*; *From A Buick Six*; *The Gates Of Eden*; *It's All Right Ma (I'm Only Bleeding)*; *It Takes A Lot To Laugh, It Takes A Train To Cry*; *Just Like Tom Thumb's Blues*; *Like A Rolling Stone*; *Love Minus Zero/No Limits*; *On the Road Again*; *Outlaw Blues*;

175

Positively 4th Street; *She Belongs To Me*; *Subterranean Homesick Blues*; and more besides—all from 1965. An amazing, breathtaking burst of prolific creativity.) *Spanish Harlem Incident* is therefore especially interesting—*historically* interesting, as I noted above, precisely because it is creatively pioneering in the context of Dylan's output.

> I am homeless, come and take me
> Into reach of your rattling drums.
> Let me know, babe, about my fortune
> Down along my restless palms.

In the first two of those lines, we find the individual style of impressionism which Dylan cultivated (and which attracted so many unfortunate imitations—including much from The Beatles, with their "plasticine porters" and "marmalade skies"). Dylan's own impressionism works because his imagery is knowingly, not fortuitously, used. Above, the poetic statement begins simply enough, with that non-literal, non-physical, "homeless"; and while it moves into that apparently vaguer "rattlin' drums" yet the adjective there has a precision of its own: one is shown how appropriate the phrase is to the spirit of the girl as Dylan sees her. Again, there is a precision of function in the uniting of the two ideas focused by "my restless palms"—the validity of the fortune-telling allusion being sympathetically strengthened by its connection to the singer's admitted desire for hand-in-hand contact. And the wish implicit there harks back to that "come and take me" in the earlier line:

> Gypsy Gal, you got me swallowed,
> I have fallen far beneath
> Your pearly eyes so fast an' slashin'
> And your flashin' diamond teeth.

There is nothing contrived here, as the context and the recording yield up those lines. "Swallowed" works undisturbingly, and the unobtrusive reversal of the usual teeth and eyes metaphors strikes the listener as entirely unforced and appropriate to his idea of the girl and song addresses.

It is in terms of the girl that this near-Gothic effect works also:

> The night is pitch black, come an' make my
> Pale face fit into place, ah! please!

For such a girl, the night *would* make itself dramatic. And similarly, we can feel that it is the girl's personality which draws out this, in the final verse:

> On the cliff of your wildcat charms I'm riding,
> I know I'm round you but I don't know where.

In fact the first of those two lines gives a perfect summary of how the writer stands for the creation of the song. His language, throughout, is dedicated to eliciting a captivating vision of those "wildcat charms"; and the singleness of purpose places Dylan's impressionistic imagery a long way away from the random hit-and-miss impressionism of the hosts of Dylan's imitators. Theirs is exhibited for its own sake and is its own reason for being; Dylan's is there to assist the communication of specific and personally realized themes.

Correspondingly, it is when he has no such theme—when he is expressing nothing more personally valid than a recognizable public feeling—that he is led into a vagueness of language, a sloppiness of language which resembles that of his imitators.

It seems to me that this sort of thing happens in Dylan's very famous archetypal protest song, *The Times They Are A-Changin'*. With that song, his aim was to ride on the unvoiced sentiment of a mass public—to ride, that is, as the spokesman for people who wanted to hear just such "a fuck you of enraged self-assertion". (That phrase is Elia Katz'.)

As a result, the language of the song is weak—imprecisely directed and conceived too generally. It offers four extended metaphors, and makes no more than an easy politician's use of any of them. The four are: change as a risin' tide; change dependent on the wheel of fate; the Establishment as an edifice; and yesterday and tomorrow as roads to be opted for.

People enjoy the song in the sense that they approve of its theory; it is a less satisfying alternative to Country Joe & The Fish's *Fish Cheer*, Woodstock Version—which is, of course, the ultimate fuck you of self-assertion, and which offers the logical conclusion of public spokesmanship in that it gets its mass public actually in on the speaking.

When *The Times They Are A-Changin'* was released, of course, the *Fish Cheer* had not yet replaced it, so that the Dylan song, was, to those it tried to speak for, uniquely pertinent. It was certainly prophetic—but it has been outdated: and the important outdating has been done by the changes that the song itself threatened. Its message is *politically* out of date. On the one hand "mothers and fathers throughout the land" are as ready as ever to criticize what they don't understand, and on the other hand the people who have pioneered neo-social change have gone beyond the optimism of expecting senators and congressmen to heed their political calls.

When The Ship Comes In prophesies a socio-political ideal future too—and offers us Dylan singing of the coming change in terms of an arriving ship—which seems as unsurprising as the use of roads, tides and so in *The Times They Are A-Changin'*. Yet *When The Ship Comes In* has *not* been outdated by events. It survives because it is wisely unspecific and because this lack of specificity is not the result of vagueness. It doesn't stem from an attempt to provide a common-to-everyone account; it stems from a personal realization of the song's subject-matter. Necessarily and rightly, its references to the coming changes are general and figurative (to the point of allegory—"Like Goliaths they'll be conquered!") because the important thing is (by contrast) the *personal* responses of the writer towards the anticipated arrival. The details, figurative, metaphorical, allegorical and symbolic as they are, serve delicately to define and illustrate these responses.

Whereas, therefore, *The Times They Are A-Changin'* fails to offer anything much with which to identify—it gives us no sense of proximity to any individual's sensibility—*When The Ship Comes In* offers a vision that is sincere. It *does* put us in contact with a real and a very *fine* sensibility. It doesn't lean on mass sentiment at any point; mass sentiment can, if it likes, lean on it.

It is in a partially connected sense that *When The Ship Comes In* thereby reminds me of the truly charming Richard Lovelace poem, "To Lucasta, Going To The Wars":

> Tell me not, Sweet, I am unkind
> That from the nunnery
> Of thy chaste breast and quiet mind
> To war and arms I fly.

> True, a new mistress now I chase
> The first foe in the field;
> And with a stronger faith embrace
> A sword, a horse, a shield.

178

Yet this inconsistency is such
As thou too shalt adore;
I could not love thee, Dear, so much,
Loved I not Honour more.

Lovelace died in 1658, and must therefore have written that poem in an age when the simplistic gallantry, chivalry and patriotism it evinces were just what the public approved of; yet Lovelace has so steadily offered not the *public* view but a highly *personalized* glimpse that the poem retains its charm and its impetus even today. It achieves this despite the demonstrable fact that the poem's attitude to war could hardly be more estranged from our own. Because Lovelace didn't lean on a *public* attitude, his poem has not been castrated by that public attitude's collapse. Something about it, through which its delicate self-reliance shines—still appeals considerably.

Similarly, it seems to me, while *The Times They Are A-Changin'* has been castrated, and will be altogether buried by changing times, *When The Ship Comes In* is bound to last. (For a more detailed commentary on it, see Chapter Two.[3])

Since *Spanish Harlem Incident*—4th album—has been praised and *The Times They Are A-Changin'*—3rd album—disparaged, perhaps I have given the impression that by the time of that 4th album, Dylan had really left the bad things behind. It is only right, then, to look at a song very different indeed in quality from *Spanish Harlem Incident*—*Ballad In Plain D*.

Ballad In Plain D is a very bad song—partly because the words seem forced to fit the tune (and forced into rhymes also: "Beneath a bare lightbulb/The plaster did pound/Her sister and I/In a screaming battleground/And she in between/The victim of sound". What else but the obligation to rhyme could account for the absurd inaccuracy of statement in that last part quoted?) and partly because words and tune so obviously *don't* fit. The lyric is full of Sensitive Teenage hysteria; the tune is Reflective and rather morose.

The hysteria shows up an even more fundamental fault—that the telling of what is a tale of adolescent-love-frustrated is done not from outside, not with a detachment capable of reassessing the significance of the things experienced; the narrator is the artist, and the artist is still inside, so that the assessment is as teeny and

179

entangled as the experience. Dylan could only have made the song worth having if he had handled his theme "afterwards": if he could have judged from a non-adolescent perspective (which is not, of course, to say he should have judged without sympathy). The song deals with a stage of immature development and yet Dylan refuses to see it as such. His allegiance is to the state of mind which experienced the story; his attitude towards his own immaturity is a long way from mature.

There is, throughout the song, a pretence at the quality of assessment that is so patently missing.

> Myself for what I did
> I cannot be excused
> The changes I was going through
> Can't even be used.
> For the lies that I told her
> And hope not to lose
> The could-be dream-lover
> Of my lifetime.

It doesn't convince. Somehow by the time we've got past "The changes I was going through" we are aware of a sort of self-idealization on the narrator's part, enforced by that "Myself ..." as it is cushioned and coddled by the tune, and emphasized also by the hint of deliberate mysteriousness. We don't get told about the changes, nor about the "lies", but their existence (and apparent importance) is thrust at us with an exaggerated solemnity we are supposed to take at face-value—to take with an equal, corresponding solemnity.

The reliance on face-values leads Dylan to some embarrassingly bad lines:

> Of the two sisters
> I loved the young.
> With sensitive instincts
> She was the creative one.

Nothing in the song (and it has thirteen verses) shows us any of this. We are rebuked into swallowing it—which does the opposite of encouraging our credence.

There is, of course, another factor—Dylan's performance—which predictably goes a long way to minimizing the song's faults.

With some lines, his voice can enhance sufficiently to give positive pleasure, as for instance at the very beginning:

> I once loved a girl,
> Her skin it was bronze ...

and it is also true that there is one instance where the vagueness of imagery (which comes across, generally, as a kind of sulkiness) rolls back to give us an impressive glimpse of the boy-girl relationship gone wrong:

> Till the tombstones of damage
> Read no questions but Please,
> What's Wrong?
> And what's Exactly The Matter?

Throughout the rest of the song, we have to struggle hard against a dominant impression that despite that "once" in the opening line, it all happened about two days before the song was set down, and that the motivation for the writing was entirely bound up in the unsorted, ill-articulated aftermath of the experience.

It is not easy to understand how such a bad song could have come from Dylan at any time, let alone at a time when so many distinctively good ones were emerging. Perhaps any transition period (as 1964 certainly was in Dylan's development) makes for vulnerability.

At any rate, 1965 was far more hectic and found Dylan's use of language in a far greater state of flux.

At one end we have *It's All Right Ma* (*I'm Only Bleeding*), which is merely a more circumspect re-working, in tone and area of theme, of, say, *Only A Pawn In Their Game*, yet merges this old approach to new language. Part of the song's impact is thereby its very patchiness—the way it keeps wowing from one sort of articulation to another. Thus Dylan makes even transitional experiment work for him not just as a way forward but as a procedure in its own right and for its own sake.

One minute the listener hears of

> Advertising signs that con you
> Into thinking you're the one
> that can do what's never been done

181

> that can win what's never been won
> Meantime life, outside, goes on
> all around you.

—all absolutely straightforward. Not so this:

> Temptation's page flies out the door
> You follow, find yourself at war,
> watch waterfalls of pity roar ...

The struggle towards a figurative language keeps bursting through in such flashes as this, though varying, naturally, in its effectiveness in local contexts. The image that takes us to the edge of the waterfall, to the juxtaposition of "pity" and "roar" is only one of many "deepening-points" in the song: it is felicitous and abrasive in a way more inward than we would have expected from the earlier social-commentary songs. It is more real than the mirror of his older "realist" songs.

This veering away from mere external (political) generalization goes hand in hand with a paradoxical change in external attitude. It appears (though not for the first time: *North Country Blues, The Lonesome Death of Hattie Carroll* and others all have their personalized moments) along with a more resigned, accepting posture:

> It's all right, Ma, I can make it ...
> It's all right, Ma, It's life and life only

and along with a more savage and jaundiced vision of what he bitterly calls "people's games":

> Disillusioned words like bullet bark
> as human gods aim for their mark,
> Made everything from toy guns that spark
> to flesh-coloured Christs that glow in the dark
> It's easy to see without lookin' too far
> that not much
> is really sacred

All these changes seem to me to stem from Dylan's discarding of an anger that was the child of *optimism*—an indignation (as, for instance, we meet it in *Masters of War*) which could only be sustained so long as the belief in enlightened-congressmen-about-to-heed-the-call could itself be sustained. Dylan's graduation from the *Masters of War* approach towards real poetry—the poetry of real experience—can in this way be seen as prompted not by a change in political *belief*, nor by a *rejection* of politics (which is the same thing) but a change in *assessment* of his political vision. To put it over-simply, Dylan became a serious artist when profound political pessimism set in. The spectre of pessimism showed up pamphleteering songs as pitifully inadequate and rather silly:

> While one who sings with his tongue on fire
> gargles in the rat-race choir—
> bent out of shape by society's pliers ...

It's All Right Ma is not the last of Dylan's protest songs, but it is the last in which the vestiges of the old attitude remain—the last of the type wherein anger (and anger of the kind that pleads for help from Senator Fulbright) replaces analysis with accusation: and, like *My Back Pages*, it specifically abdicates the protest function. The contemporaneous *Gates Of Eden* (see Chapter Three) is very different in vision and organization and utterly different as an indicator of what Dylan had come to expect of himself as an artist.

Thus too the change by the time of *Desolation Row*—which gives classic illustration of the distinction between accusation and analysis. *Desolation Row* is a brilliant *political analysis* of American society. And from the most cursory glance at it, the connection between the pessimism and the seriousness of intention is apparent.

Dylan chooses to offer his narration from inside Desolation Row itself, and so he can communicate one part of his gloom in a personalized way:

> When you asked me how I was doing
> Was that some kind of joke?

The intention of the whole, however, is not to repeat the theme of, say, *North Country Blues*, which was basically the chronicle of a community's suffering in the face of encroaching penury. In *Desolation Row* Dylan is dealing with contemporary America in terms of its infection of human values. He is no longer treating a particular side-effect of capitalism as a sort of overlying weight which affronts the pockets of golden-hearted miners and the conscience of liberals. Dylan is recognizing a pervasive Amerika, one that trades in human vanity and offers insinuatory as well as polarizing challenges: challenges against which the old liberal blueprints are worse than useless. Dylan no longer expects solutions to arise out of reforms or legislation or any equally bland leftie alternative. And there is no point rallying around the new home-comforts of *We Shall Overcome*. There *is* no broad solution. The most Dylan expects is some major effort towards developing, *individually*, an unwarped perspective:

> Right now I can't read too good
> Don't send me no more letters, no:
> Not unless you mail them from Desolation Row.

Excepting its final verse, the song is Dylan's necessarily tentative expression of such a perspective for himself.

He emphasizes the complexity of the subject-matter, in the first place, by a sustained reversal of norms within the song: the beauty-parlour is filled with big hairy U.S. Marines and it is the riot squad that needs putting down. Casanova, the sophisticate, is being spoon-fed; Romeo is moaning.

If nothing else on first hearings, the song is a striking and a sinister parade—and we come to see the chaos with clarity, come to see in the parade a barrage of folk-heroes in careful disarray: participants, victims and agents of a disordered, sick society.

The other general characteristic of the song is associated with the "sinister" element: the song confronts us with recurring hints of imminent disaster.

For analysts of America committed to Big Bang Revolution, such hints are taken, of course, as signs of promise; but Dylan declines to go along with this approach (which, in order to simplify the "solution", must warp the truth about the problems to be solved—must posit them as equally simple). In *Desolation Row* the imminent disasters are past and present as well as future. The verses pile up and pile up, the sinister intimations pile up with them, and there is no suggestion (no "hope", in other words) that the crescendo will ever be curtailed.

If it wasn't for the last verse, with its different function, the song could be circular: which is to re-assert that the parade could pass not once, or even several times, but endlessly: timelessly. The very lengthiness of the song enforces this impression, as it is meant to, and so does the long and rather formless instrumental section which comes between the penultimate verse and the last. A variant effect, though a closely connected one, of this instrumental section is to take the last verse away from the circular plane of the rest and set it aside. Only on the page does it "follow on" from the other verses; in reality it is off to one side, a satellite, alone but with a special focus which can be brought to bear on the rest at any point. When people consequently say that *Desolation Row* has two endings, they could more usefully say instead that it doesn't have an ending at all.[4]

But though the climactic holocaust never quite comes, Dylan's intimations of disaster build up towards one. They come with ever-increasing intensity and there is, of course, in any case, a cumulative effect. At the beginning, the commissioner—who is blind —is tied by one hand to the tightrope walker; the riot squad is bound to burst out somewhere; furtively, the ambulances move in and depart. Then we get these lines:

> Now the moon is almost hidden
> The stars are beginning to hide
> The fortune-telling lady
> Has taken all her things inside ...

With these lines, Dylan carries us further into the darkness, as he correlates the blanching of the moon and stars with the ominousness of the astrologer packing up and gravely going home after glimpsing the future. The correlation has a neatness and power which, as much as anything else in the song, shows Dylan's success with a new economy of language.

The lines that follow on from those just quoted have a neatness of not quite the same kind:

> All except for Cain and Abel
> An' the hunchback of Notre Dame
> Everybody is makin' love
> Or else expecting rain

and by this point in the song, we've had enough opportunity to note what a curious amalgam it is—part surrealism, part impressionistic metaphor, part allegory and part riddle: an anti-logic nightmare.

185

The most striking evocation of impending catastrophe is, however, achieved very simply—in the one arresting line

> The Titanic sails at dawn.

That summarizes, with all the conciseness a well-played allusion can offer, the tone and colouring of the whole song. For all its simplicity—perhaps because of it—the analogy as it is urged does not take away from the complexity of the overall vision. Dylan merely provides a good guide-line by taking the *Titanic* to represent contemporary America: for the Titanic was the ship of the future, the "proof" of man's civilization and progress, the unsinkable ship which, on her maiden voyage, sank. And, according to the best stories (and Dylan relies on their currency—a fine case of poetic licence) when the ship began to sink the passengers refused to believe that it was happening. The palm-court orchestra kept playing and the people in the ballroom danced obliviously on.[5]

The different kinds of oblivion and denial in America—the various ways in which the dancing continues—are presented with an incisiveness maintained throughout the song. The focus on all this escalating malaise is kept very strictly under control.

The cumulative effect mentioned earlier is, in this sense, fully allowed for. The swelling up of evil as we are given it never becomes histrionic: yet it operates powerfully as it grows through from the postcards of hangings, via the cyanide holes, and on past the factory

> Where the heart-attack machine
> Is strapped across their shoulders
> And then the kerosene . . .

The first two verses of the song are actually very general: introductory in a conventional way: "Here is the parade." It is when he gets to the third verse that Dylan begins to focus on specific components of the overall chaos and disease.

Appropriately enough, he fixes first on the modern liberal conscience:

> The Good Samaritan he's dressing,
> He's getting ready for the show
> He's going to the carnival tonight on
> Desolation Row.

186

By the time we meet this Good Samaritan preparing for his visit to the carnival, the moon has already hidden and the stars are retreating. The darkness is closing in, and it is not the kind of darkness that should encourage dressing for dinner. Like everybody's making love, it is an inappropriate response. The wrong gesture at the wrong time. It is part of the lethal unawareness against which Dylan is concerned to speak out.

In their own ways, the other verses all argue the same case—and the shift of perspective in the final verse just emphasizes and reiterates the same point. It's a world of commissioners; we're all blind.

In the verse quoted above, the argument applies—in so far as poetic language can be paraphrased down into particulars, which it mostly can't—in that the liberal conscience marries an indiscriminate humanitarianism to an equally effete set of fashionable reforming aims, never achieves sufficient vision to begin to transform society and thus gets nowhere. The Good Samaritan is blown from aim to aim and from idea to idea by the prevailing outrages and ailments of a society in flux. Dylan is urging instead the primary need to recognize and assert essential human values which must ultimately be re-established. The one place where the possession, or rediscovery, of the necessary detachment and honesty of response is possible is, of course, on Desolation Row. It is worse than useless to go there in carnival mood.

Such blindness, manifest in other ways, comes under attack most urgently towards the end of the song, and in the eighth and ninth verses is given a kind of cause-and-effect examination.

If the seventh verse can be said to berate the bourgeoisie ("Across the street they've nailed the curtains"; "They are spoon-feeding Casanova ... poisoning him with words") the eighth verse indicts the American education system which that bourgeoisie has established. A system organized to enforce and perpetuate ignorance, Dylan portrays it as an essentially nightmarish machinery for bringing into line the potential enemies of the state—which is to say, of the *status quo*—the independent thinkers:

> Now at midnight all the agents
> And the superhuman crew
> Come out an' round up everyone
> That knows more than they do.

How eloquent that is. That "crew", in the context, asserts, in association with the opening phrase "At midnight ...", the telling connotative suggestion of collective vandalism, political purges and press-gangs.

Those lines insist, equally acutely, on an overriding presence of violence; it is evoked in the first two lines of that verse, and so we are forewarned of the "heart-attack machine" and the kerosene; and we find impressed upon us too the near-impossibility of escape.

To register *that*, of course, is to note that Dylan has slid us away from particulars again, and back towards the general features of society's ills. It isn't, after all, a song for Huey; it's a song for all of us.

The remainder of that eighth verse takes advantage of this return to generality at the same time as planting in us a strong consciousness of violence; and so Dylan urges upon us anew a sense of the powerlessness of the individual ...

> ... brought down from the castles
> By insurance men who go
> Check to see that nobody is escaping
> To Desolation Row.

The allusion, clinched by that "castles", to Kafka's visions, makes this pessimism unequivocally clear. Dylan has not merely argued, but has created for us, the powerlessness just mentioned. It is not a polemic but a vision that he leaves us with, and which insists that all *any* individual can do is hold to some integrity of personal perspective. And such a perspective is, in the end, exactly what "Desolation Row" offers.

I noted earlier that *Desolation Row* showed a strange mixture of language. It might be added here that this mixture, which has every appearance of carelessness, actually works better than one could easily imagine of a more scrupulous technique. Towards the end of Chapter Three I argued that, like T. S. Eliot, Dylan has challenged the validity of traditional distinctions between poetic "seriousness" and levity; it strikes me as equally true that Dylan has challenged with equal authority the traditional conceptions of "serious" (which is to say scrupulous) technique.

Not only *Desolation Row* offers this challenge: it is also thrown up by many another of the songs that date from 1965, and which all dispay a similar chaos of language—an amalgam to some degree of blues vernacular, impressionism, allegory and more.

Like A Rolling Stone is one such song. Its opening verse is straightforward, almost monosyllabic slang:

> Once upon a time you dressed so fine
> Y'threw the bums a dime
> in your prime, didn' you?
> People'd call, say Beware Doll,
> You're Bound T' Fall—
> you thought they were all
> kiddin' you;
> you used to laugh about
> ev'ybody that was hangin' out
> Now you don't talk so loud
> Now you don't seem so proud
> about havin' t' be scroungin' your next meal—
>
> How does it feel?! Ah! How does it feel?! ...

The brevity and crispness of the language—city language, straight from the streets—combines with the pile-up effect of all those internal rhymes, fired past the listener as from a repeater-rifle, and so establishes at once the tone of bitter recrimination. The tone is modified as the language changes, in so far as it accommodates a broader theme, a heightened appreciation on the narrator's part of the girl's fall to "homelessness":

> You said you'd never compromise
> with the mystery tramp, but now you realize
> he's not selling any alibis
> as you stare into the vacuum of his eyes and say
> do you want to
> make a deal?—
>
> How does it feel?! Ah! How does it feel?!

Here the words are longer, those "ize" sounds slow-fading, the phrasing much less colloquial, the "meaning"—measured in prose terms—vaguer. This change of language keeps its momentum, and paradoxically, as the language gets "vaguer" so the meeting of eyes between the narrator and Miss Lonely is seen to have intensified: they reach the point where understanding is searching and personal, and where communication can therefore be achieved at this pitch:

> You never turned around to see the frowns on the
> jugglers an' the clowns when they all did
> tricks for you . . .

> You used to ride on your chrome horse with your
> Diplomat . . .

> You used to be so amused
> At Napoleon in rags and the language that he used—
> Go to him now, he calls you, you can't refuse . . .

This calculated lack of specificity becomes, in Dylan's hands, a positive entity grown out of and beyond the specific; and it opens up the way for the re-creation of many different universal relationships. As this use of language becomes a dominant characteristic of Dylan's writing (as it does in 1965) so he provides a whole series of songs which are indeed studies of human relationships. The listener is no longer just witness to incidents from Dylan's own life (as he was, say, with *I Don't Believe You, Girl From The North Country* and *Boots Of Spanish Leather*) nor just a witness to incidents from other people's lives (as with *North Country Blues, Hattie Carroll* and *Hollis Brown*). Just as Lawrence moved from making art out of direct autobiographical experience to making much greater art out of universal experience, so the Dylan of the mid-sixties has moved in a similar direction.

Perhaps the very easiest song to cite so as to clarify these remarks is actually a later one, *Dear Landlord*: for the point of that song is that it doesn't matter "who the landlord is"—it is simply "Dear Someone"; the song captures the essence of a relationship we can recognize as possible between any two people. It no longer needs Dylan the man to take one of the parts.

But if this use of language (which is still in transition in *Like A Rolling Stone*) no longer offers us autobiography, its universal glimpses are of course rendered as through Dylan's eyes. And so, like any great artist, Dylan bequeaths us a part of reality we could not otherwise have received. To render things that are real in a

190

genuinely new way (which takes more than an "original style") is actually to have *created* something new and at the same time true.

Like A Rolling Stone is, naturally, not the only song from 1965 which is, in the sense discussed, transitional. *It's All Over Now, Baby Blue*; *Positively 4th Street*; *On The Road Again*—all these are half-way houses in the same sense. And it is also true that many other Dylan songs from 1965 make no demands on the "Napoleon in rags" type of language; and there are yet others in which that language is subjugated to themes which are still clustered around autobiography. Into these categories come, at a minimum, *Bob Dylan's 115th Dream*; *Highway 61 Revisited*; *If You Gotta Go, Go Now*; and *Subterranean Homesick Blues*.

There are also songs full of the calculatedly unspecific which operate differently again—as, for instance, *Ballad Of A Thin Man* (see Chapter Three) and those two great songs *Love Minus Zero/No Limit* and *She Belongs To Me*, along with others in which words function mainly by helping Dylan's voice to be the masterpiece of rock-*musicianship* which it had become by 1965. (I am thinking here, in particular, of *From A Buick Six*.)

Nevertheless, there is a general direction to which, as I have been trying to suggest, songs like *Like A Rolling Stone* are signposts.

The first song that truly marks the arrival of the new type is one which, perhaps appropriately, was issued as a single (though with little commercial success, as it happened): *Can You Please Crawl Out Your Window*. In this song, the language flashes and sculptures, takes a hundred different photographs, captures a human possibility which comes across as always having been there, recurring and recurring, but never detected or seen in focus before. It needn't be a relationship that has happened to us for it to impress us as true—as accurately stated and real; and only the most insensitive listener would feel a need to ask what the song "means".

It almost stands up just as words on the page; and yet the recording is perhaps the very finest thing that has ever come out of rock music (and actually there are *two* recordings—the unreleased one forming part of the "Stealin'" bootleg album).

The language of the song, though, is at least as interesting as its music. It strikes me that there are three stages in Dylan's

191

acquisition of surrealistic writing. He begins with simple, rational telescoping—for instance with that phrase "the night blows raining" in *Love Minus Zero/No Limit*. The second stage involves a more complex telescoping—as, for example, in that expression "his genocide fools". The third stage Dylan reaches is that of *ir*rational juxtaposition, and stems partly from the very *habit* of juxtaposing which the earlier stages imposed.

A couple of special effects in *Can You Please Crawl Out Your Window* are worth special note. First, "fist full of tacks". Dylan seems to me to use that in at least three main ways. First, it gives us a visual image of sorts—it directs our awareness towards the man's hands: and these are implicitly kept before us when we come, later in the same verse, to his "inventions" and again later when we come to "hand him his chalk". Second, "fist full of tacks" gives us a vivid metaphor *at the same time* as yielding a neat juxtaposition.[6] The juxtaposition is of course that in the first half of the relevant line we get the man and the sweep of the room and are then zoomed down to the (much more precise) tiny contents of his closed hand. The metaphor is characteristic of Dylan— and takes us all the way back to *Talkin' New York*, on his very first album, where he says:

> A lot of people don't have much food on their table
> But they got a lot of forks,
> an' knives,
> an'—they gotta cut somethin'.

Those lines are explaining why his initial New York audiences were hostile: it is a figurative explanation. "Fist full of tacks" operates similarly. It could be swapped, in a prose précis, with the word "aggressively".

Yet it does a lot more than the word "aggressively" could do: and the third way it works is simply in establishing a tone of verbal precision—it is an incisive, sharp phrase—which is important throughout the song. It influences the sound, later on in the song, of words like "test" and "inventions", "peel", "righteous" and "box", and links up, in effect, with that phrase "little tin women" in the final verse. "Little tin women" is of exactly corresponding brittleness and precision. This impression is enforced in the music, too, by the guitar-work in particular and by various xylophonic effects in general. Finally, one notes that Dylan provides a contrast to all this "tin tack" atmosphere—it is beautifully contradicted by that gangling chorus line

> Use your arms and legs, it wont ruin you.

where the words enact the motion, where the listener is actually a part of the flailing limbs swimming out of the window—where, in other words, the sounds and impressions are rounded instead of thin and soft rather than sharp. More generally, the whole of the chorus takes part in this exercise of contrast: the qualities of "crawl", "use", "ruin", "haunt", and Dylan's long-drawn-out "want" are all antithetical to the qualities of that initial "fist full of tacks".

Another interesting ingredient in the same song is connected with that tremendous line

> With his businesslike anger and his bloodhounds that
> kneel . . .

because in fact until we isolate that line, it doesn't occur to our visual response to have our murky, semi-existing bloodhounds actually *kneeling*. Dogs cannot easily kneel at all; yet in the sense that they are humble/faithful/servile etc., they are kneeling, figuratively, while they are standing. And so we meet the Dylan phrase accordingly: we visualize the *atmosphere* that corresponds to silent, standing bloodhounds ranged around the man—and ranged, in fact, around his knee. It is thereby the man's that comes into our picture, and not the dogs' knees at all.

What needs to be stressed in the end, however, is that none of this kind of investigation into the lyric's effects is at all necessary to the working of such effects, and indeed by drawing them out of the song's own succinct phrases and stretching them into long prose explanations, one can't avoid warping what one is trying to clarify.

No other song could illustrate this point better than the one which seems to me to stand altogether alone in Dylan's 1965 output—one which is quite outside any pattern that can be devised for tracing the development of his art. That song is *Farewell Angelina*. There is no available recording of this by Dylan himself, and the best-known version of it is by Joan Baez. One tends, therefore, to think of the song as really a poem—as words-on-the-page.

Doing so, it appears that the song *does* fit a pattern: it seems half-way from *Can You Please Crawl Out Your Window* to "Blonde On Blonde". Yet it isn't actually like that at all. *Farewell Angelina* seems to introduce surrealistic language with a bang: that is to say, in a new way for Dylan; and by the time of "Blonde On Blonde" he has adjusted that language almost out of recognition. It is in this sense that "Angelina" stands alone. Where "Blonde On Blonde" works as a sort of contemporary Technicolor surrealist movie, *Farewell Angelina* seems like a black-and-white 1940 surrealist short (and *Can You Please Crawl Out Your Window* is not like a film at all):

> Just a table standing empty by the edge of the sea ...

—that is the line that encapsulates the song—its essential tone and its distinctive kind of image: and it is nearer to one of those old shorts in which someone like Dali had a hand than it is to any of Dylan's other work. A strange song: and the fact that there are still things in it that do seem characteristic of Dylan's other work does not make it, in overall effect, any the less strange—quite the opposite.

The melody *is* typical Dylan, if only minority-Dylan: it has a similar expansive lightness and brightness to the near-contemporaneous *Mr. Tambourine Man*.

Some of the lines in the lyric add to this similarity:

> The triangle tingles and the trumpets play slow
> The sky is on fire, and I must go ...

and

> ... In the space where the deuce and the ace once ran wild
> Farewell Angelina, the sky is folding ...

Perhaps the attempt to explain "Angelina's" relation to other Dylan songs by means of a movies analogy is a clue to its very singularity—namely that unlike most of Dylan's imagery, that in *Farewell Angelina* is emphatically and fundamentally visual. It is, almost uniquely, simply a series of *pictures*, sometimes switching suddenly on and off, sometimes sliding into each other:

> King Kong little elves on the rooftops they dance
> Valentino-type tangos while the make-up man's hands
> Shut the eyes of the dead, not to embarrass anyone:

194

Farewell Angelina, the sky is embarrassed, and I must be
   gone.

Even that remarkable "the sky is embarrassed" is an assertion
we visualize; we picture the sky, and picture it in relation to the
song's other protagonists, throughout the song. And this is all
that is offered or required; if we receive all the visual glimpses,
if we really can, instantly,

> See the crosseyed pirates sitting perched in the sun
> Shooting tin cans with a sawn-off shot-gun

then the song has worked.

When we come to "Blonde On Blonde", things are not so simple.
We come to material where visual imagery is only one factor, and
one that fluctuates enormously in importance even within a single
song, and we come to a surrealist language distinctly *unlike* the
surrealism of Dali or Magritte. In one important sense, Dylan's
vision throughout "Blonde On Blonde" much more closely resembles that of Bosch. There is no suggestion that the narrators
in these 1966 songs stand, like Magritte, on the threshold of mad-
ness. On the contrary, they are sane men surrounded by the mad-
ness and chaos of other people and other things. The surrealistic
pile-ups of imagery do not reflect the state of a narrator's (or
Dylan's) psyche: they reflect the confusion which a calm and
ordered mind observes around it.

In this sense, the album is a whole and the individual songs are
only parts; and it doesn't matter that sometimes the chaos seems
to be America and sometimes seems to be the city life of particular sorts of people. It doesn't even contradict the spirit of the
whole that a couple of the songs evoke a chaos that is inside the
emotions of the narrator—the chaos of happy infatuation in *I
Want You*, or of non-comprehension in *Temporary Like Achilles*.
I Want You propounds a relationship between the lovers and the
outside world which does fit the general pattern of the album in
that it lends itself, as a dichotomy, to a relation between internals
and externals—between chaos and order:

> The cracked bells and washed out horns
> Blow into my face with scorn
> But it's not that way, I wasn't born
> To lose you ...

> ... She is good to me
> And there's nothing she doesn't see
> She knows where I'd like to be
> But it doesn't matter—

The chaos is there all right. And *Temporary Like Achilles* bears some resemblance to this:

> Well I lean into your hallway
> Lean against your velvet door
> I watch upon your scorpion
> Who crawls across your circus floor

That "your hallway" suggests a place of refuge, and so raises again the fact of there being a gulf between narrator and outside world. The *strength* of the sense of refuge-seeking urged on us ("your hallway" is followed up by the repetition of the possessive adjective—"your velvet door", "your scorpion", "your ... floor") has been established earlier in the song by the eloquence of this:

> Kneeling 'neath your ceiling
> Yes I guess I'll be here for a while
> I'm trying to read your portrait
> But I'm helpless, like a rich man's child.

And when we say that those lines *are* so very eloquent, we come to recognize them as having many of the characteristic strengths of Dylan's mid-sixties' work, and having emphatically the strengths of the "Blonde On Blonde" collection.

In the first place, there is the refusal to incubate a "serious" poetic language. How else could the slightly lugubrious voice relish its delivery of "Kneeling 'neath your ceiling/Yes I guess I ..."?

Thrown in for good measure, in the second place, is the sort of abrasive little generalization that epitomizes part of Dylan's intelligence: "... helpless like a rich man's child". And this kind of side-remark is always an odd mixture of humour and high seriousness. It is there to bring a smile but it has an open moral insistence behind it. However lightly introduced, the contrast Dylan makes in this instance between her "poetry" and his equivalent of a debilitating richness is made with real severity.

It is equally characteristic as a sample of "Blonde on Blonde" in the way figurative language is the norm (as with "your poetry") yet mixes easily with the literal.

It has also the vision of chaos which dominates all of "Blonde On Blonde"—"Kneeling ... I'm trying ... But I'm helpless"—and the corresponding richness or organization (all that internal rhyming and odd southern emphasis) and richness of sound. The words purr across the airwaves to the listener: kneeling, 'neath, ceiling, while, poetry, child.

But even though it is so typical of the album, *Temporary Like Achilles* is not by a long way the album's best song. A far better one—a truly superb song, in fact—is *Absolutely Sweet Marie*, in which the words are borne along on a sea of rich red music, bobbing with a stylish and highly distinctive rhythm. Dylan's voice is at its very best, handling the repeated line which caps each verse with as much variety in delivery as would be humanly and still felicitously possible. Each time it arrives, the line is different —more insistent yet always spontaneously mooded.

Dylan's harmonica also excels itself with an invincible, searing solo that bequeaths new boundaries and new life to any concept of the blues.

The lyric overflows with all the qualities we specially associate with the "Blonde On Blonde" collection.

> Well your railroad gate know I just can't jump it
> Sometimes it gets so hard you see
> I'm just sitting here beating on my trumpet
> With all these promises you left for me
> But where are you tonight, Sweet Marie?
>
> Well I waited for you when I was halfsick
> Yes I waited for you when you hated me
> Well I waited for you inside of the frozen traffic
> When you knew I had some other place to be
> Now where are you tonight, Sweet Marie?

The challenge to distinctions between "serious" and "light" poetic language is clear enough there, and so are the abrasive little philosophical points, flashed out with smiles:

> Well anybody can be just like me, obviously

is about as ambiguous as anything ever could be, and just as a

197

joke pay-off line is clipped on to it, so later on in the song we come to this delightful alliance between sincere observation and jest:

> But to live outside the law you must be honest
> I know you always say that you agree . . .

Of course, to get the tone of that last-quoted line you need to go to the recording; and so do you to get the full and incredible richness of sound that comes not only from the swirling, oceanic music but also from Dylan's bending of the the words, as he breathes indelible cascades of life into lines and phrases like these: "your railroad gate you know I just can't jump it"; "with all these promises"; "And now I stand here, looking at your yellow railroad/In the ruins of your balcony/Wondering where you are tonight Sweet Marie". Actually, Dylan's handling of the single word "balcony" is sufficient indication of how much and how appropriately he can reawaken our tired old vocabulary and language.

Absolutely Sweet Marie has also, of course, its share of the glimpses of chaos, the effective communication of which depends on largely figurative expressions. It is easy to see how the metaphoric technique lights up the chaotic vision:

> . . . I just can't jump it
> Sometimes it gets so hard to see
> I'm just sitting here beating on my trumpet . . .
> But where are you . . . ? . . .

> Well I don't know how it happened but the riverboat
>   captain
> he knows my fate
> But ev'ybody else . . .

> . . . you see you forgot to leave me with the key.

The song also holds a characteristic richness of organization: a well-integrated, almost self-perpetuating system of internal rhymes and subterranean rhythms. These features work together perhaps most obviously in the second verse. And that verse also yields Dylan's humour, in his self-conscious—almost self-parodying—rhyming of "halfsick" with "traffic". The humour is there later

198

in the song as well, in his mischievous matching of the ambiguous, ostensibly humble "obviously" with that acidic fullstop on "fortunately".

The humour, however, is not achieved at the expense of seriousness. Throughout the song, we are conscious and appreciative that the narrator stands for self-honesty. His message is be true to yourself, and as it is given in that epigrammatic "to live outside the law you must be honest" its earnestness comes across.

It is also true that with each (freshly-delivered) return to the "But where are you ..." line, we are returned to a mood appropriate to what is fundamentally a very eloquent and outgoing love-song. All of the imagery works appropriately at maintaining this. The frustration of "I'm just sitting here" is ennobled, on the quiet, by that "trumpet"; the "promises" tumble from the tune with a kind of reverential flutter and poignancy; and the reproaches all work, essentially, at widening our impression of the scope of the narrator's love—look, that is to say, at what he has been through. Even the use of what is probably, in intention, just drugs jargon gives us, as it fits into the song as a whole, visual images of romance: "... the riverboat captain/he knows my fate" evokes, however illogically, snapshot glimpses of real riverboat journeys on waters bedecked with weeping willow trees. And the final verse perpetuates this romantic insistence, and gives it a conclusive emphasis: "In the ruins, of your, bal-cony ...".

To turn from the romantic associations of "balcony" in *Absolutely Sweet Marie* to the song that immediately follows it on the "Blonde On Blonde" collection is to be given quite a contrast.

4th Time Around is, on one level, just a parody of the Beatles' *Norwegian Wood*. It isn't uncommon for a parody to *outweigh* as well as outshine its victim and Dylan's song certainly does it. It has more subtlety and greater range than *Norwegian Wood*: and it uses a truly creative language, a language that lives and operates concretely (as opposed, one might conclude the comparison by adding, to a language characteristic of the Beatles, a language that merely fondles everything sentimental that lurks within the listener's mind).

4th Time Around begins as a cold, mocking put-down of a girl and a relationship untouched by love. For extra sarcasm's sake, it is set against a backing of fawning, schmaltzy guitar-work. But the drumming hints from the start at something more urgent and compelling than cold mockery, so that by the time the lyric switches attention to a second and love-tinged relationship, the tone of the whole song has been miraculously switched over too.

The contrast between the two women is plain enough:

> She threw me outside ...
> You took me in

but the song and its perspective is not that simple. The vast majority of it focuses on the "she" part, not on the "you" (and the fact of these proportions suggests the narrator's personal weakness and perhaps vulnerability); and in consequence this majority consists of language soaked in coarse sexual innuendo—language that brings out brilliantly Dylan's skill in pursuing the suggestive. (The songs on what's generally known as the basement tapes, recorded the year after "Blonde On Blonde", indulge in the suggestive to an unprecedented extent for Dylan, with lines like "I bin hittin' it too hard/My stones won't take", "that big dumb blonde with her wheel gorged", and "slap that drummer with a pipe that smells", plus the whole of *Please Mrs. Henry* [see Chapter 7].)

Dylan's technique for delivering all this is very interesting, in *4th Time Around* at least. It is almost like a parody of a schoolboy reading Shakespeare aloud in class: instead of the frequently-required line overflow, there is a pause—encouraged, but not exaggeratedly, by the tune—at the end of odd lines in the lyric. Into each pause comes all the innuendo and ambiguity that Dylan can muster:

> I
> Stood there and hummed
> I tapped on her drum
> I asked her how come
>
> And she
> Buttoned her boot
> And straightened her suit
> Then she said Don't Get Cute.
> So I forced
> My hands in my pockets and felt with my thumbs ...
>
> And after finding out I'd
> Forgotten my shirt

200

I went back and knocked.
I waited in the hallway, as she went to get it
And I tried to make sense
Out of that picture of you in your wheelchair that leaned
   up against

Her
Jamaica rum
And when she did come
I asked here for some.

The pause Dylan creates at the end of "And I tried to make sense" has, of course, a different purpose. (And after it, the lapse back for that pointed "come" has an added force—it seems in every sense uncontrollable on the narrator's part.) With that "tried to make sense" the pause is to allow a change of mood to begin impinging. The tone is no longer jaundiced but rather it is from here on open and alert and more sensitive; for from the midst of the imagery appropriate to the narrator's sexual, loveless encounter, Dylan—and here is the touch of genius—produces a clear and striking counter-image:

   ... that picture of you in your wheelchair

With that, the song has established the hint that here, in the offing, is something with a warmer potential—something for which it is worth the narrator's while to salvage his own sensibility.

   Yet having produced the counter-image (and it hardly needs stressing that by the time we've got this far the song has long since ceased to concern itself about parodying *Norwegian Wood*) Dylan allows it to recede and settle at the back of the listener's mind. Only at the very end is it reintroduced, to fuse into one clear perspective all the different threads in both the pattern of feeling and the pattern of imagery which run through the song: It ends:

And
When I was through
I filled up my shoe
And brought it to you;
And you,
You took me in

You loved me then
You didn't waste time
And I,
I never took much
I never asked for your crutch
Now don't ask for mine.

That "crutch" has all the complex functioning a pun can ever have. As we are presented, triumphantly, with the mental cadence from "wheelchair" down to that "crutch" at the close—in the sweep of which the "picture" is brought sharply to life—we have one of those fine, rare moments in poetry where although the technical device is *seen* functioning it does so with such supreme calculation and panache that its "intrusion" has to be recognized as an enriching factor in the finished work.

However good *4th Time Around* is, and however clever, there is still an important sense in which it is one of the minor works on "Blonde On Blonde". It is useful to look at others before coming to what are the generally-acknowledged major works on the album.

Just Like A Woman is one of Dylan's bad songs. The chorus is trite and coy and the verses aren't strong enough to compensate.

... she aches just like a woman
But she breaks just like a little girl.

That is a non-statement. It doesn't describe an individual characteristic, it doesn't say anything fresh about a universal one, and yet it pretends to do both. What parades as reflective wisdom ("... woman but ... girl") is really maudlin platitude. It hasn't even engaged Dylan's skill in minimizing the badness. It would, for example, be less bad if the "But" of the pay-off line was an "And"—for at least we would then be spared that lame and predictable "paradox".

On the other hand the part that we might as well call the "middle-eight" is beautifully done:

It was rainin' from the first an' I was
Dying there of thirst an' so I
Came in here
An' your long time curse hurts but what's worse is this
Pain in here, I can't

Stay in here,
Aint it clear that

I just can't fit . . .

Exactly *what*, in that, is "beautifully done" can be understood only from the recording, even though I've tried to set it down indicatively just above. It is inevitably a question of delivery, and that can be described only in the vaguest of ways—as a kind of three-dimensional achievement. Singing those words, those unit-construct lines, Dylan somehow moulds and holds out to us a hand-made object, a sort of clever toy with a lot of tactile appeal. In particular, you need the recording for the indescribably plaintive resonance the voice yields up on those simple little words like "rainin' ", "first", "came" and even "aint"; and you need the recording above all because that long middle-line demands Dylan's own pronunciation, by which "but what's worse" becomes three equal fur-mouthed jerks and that "what's" rhymes gleefully with "hurts". You really have to hear Dylan doing it.

Leopard-Skin Pill-Box Hat is also a minor song, though far from a bad one. It's a good joke and a vehicle for showing Dylan's electric lead-guitar-work, and that's really all. The joke goes right through the song, and it's a truly clever idea to use an extended joke about a leopard-skin pill-box hat (which really is what it's about) in conjunction with a traditional, if rocked-up, blues structure.

Right from the opening line, Dylan takes advantage of this structure. He uses a repetition of his first line *as if because the blues do that* in such a way as to make it a put-down, the repeated full description of the hat suggesting its owner's smallness of mind:

I see you got your brand-new leopard-skin pill-box hat
Yes I, see you got your, brand-new leopard-skin pill-box
hat.

There are other smiles within the song—little flashes of malice and mockery—which don't depend on the blues structure but which ride along happily enough on its waves:

Well I asked the doctor if I could see you:
It's bad for your health, he said . . .

and:

> Well I saw him makin' love to you
> (You forgot to close the garage door)
> You might think he loves you for your money but
> *I* know what he really loves you for! :
> It's your brand-new leopard-skin pill-box hat.

The best thing in *Leopard-Skin Pill-Box Hat*, though, utilizes the blues structure devastatingly. It comes in the second verse, while Dylan is still disparaging the hat; he marries the long downward trail of the standard blues third-line to this:

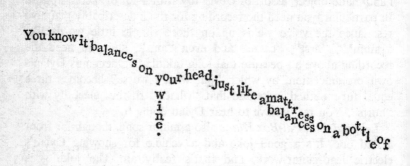

It would be hard to find a better instance of words, tune and delivery working so entirely together.[7]

The other song on "Blonde On Blonde" that memorably draws on the blues—and rather more seriously so than does *Leopard-Skin Pill-Box Hat*—is *Pledging My Time* (the progression of which, incidentally, is echoed by Dylan's *It Hurts Me Too* on the "Self Portrait" album) which for this reason is dealt with not here but in Chapter Two.

Then there is *Obviously Five Believers*, which sounds as if it belongs on the "Highway 61 Revisited" album rather than "Blonde On Blonde" (just as the thing aimed at in *Outlaw Blues* was actually achieved on the later *From A Buick 6*) and is very much a rock song. It gives us a totally relaxed, in-command Dylan—so much so that he rightly hands over the harmonica part to Charlie McCoy, and the words don't matter one iota. The most that is really required of them is that they shouldn't interfere—and indeed they don't. In fact they include lines already made familiar (and thus undemanding and undistracting) at the beginning of the album. The album starts with *Rainy Day Women Nos. 12 & 35,* with its simple pun chorus lines:

> But I would not feel so all alone:
> Everybody must get stoned

and the first finish of the album (by which I mean that the final side is in an essential way separate from the rest), falling on *Obviously Five Believers,* echoes that phrase quite explicitly:

> Guess I could make it without you honey if I
> Just did not feel so all alone.

As for the major songs in the "Blonde On Blonde" collection, they strike me as being *One Of Us Must Know (Sooner Or Later); Memphis Blues Again; Visions of Johanna* and *Sad-Eyed Lady Of The Lowlands.*

Whereas the last two of those are important primarily because of their words, and whereas *Memphis Blues Again* is important for its lyric at the same time as being a superlative piece of rock music, *One Of Us Must Know* doesn't seem to me to say anything important. Its greatness is to do with vague but dramatic impressions it carries in its music and its overall structure. It is manifestly, magnificently alive—like some once-in-a-lifetime party (and indeed in that the lyric impinges at all, it sounds as if it is being delivered at a party, because the voice rises and falls against a backdrop of bubbling noises and motion). The music offers itself, in fact, in waves, so that this impression, inextricably linked to the party impression, makes the song a rock equivalent, at least fleetingly, of the party Scott Fitzgerald describes in *The Great Gatsby,* where

> ... the orchestra is playing yellow cocktail music, and the opera of voices pitches a key higher. Laughter is easier minute by minute, spilled with prodigality, tipped out at a cheerful word. The groups change more swiftly, swell with new arrivals, dissolve and form in the same breath; already there are wanderers, confident girls who weave here and there among the stouter and more stable, become for a sharp, joyous moment the centre of a group, and then, excited with triumph, glide on through the sea-change of faces and voices and color under the constantly changing light.

One Of Us Must Know reminds me of that—not in terms of its people or its social orientation but as regards its rhythms, its movement: its life. The song is a great one, it seems to me, just in that it breathes with a kind of majestic sexual life; it holds your attention with a symphonic sort of warmth. You don't have to even hear the words—what Lawrence would call one's solar plexus gets attuned to the music and the movement before one is conscious of its having happened. The music never stops rising and falling like some great big beautiful boob; and to complement this, ordinary words, signifying little on their own, are caressed into a loving but subservient eloquence by Dylan's voice. Dylan singing the line

But you said you knew me an' I believed you did

and words like "personal" and "understood" come across as merely part of the musical whole. A truly great song.

It is difficult to suggest quite why, beyond the fact of its being an exciting rock-music performance, *Memphis Blues Again* should be regarded as at least as great as *One Of Us Must Know*. Yet it can at any rate be said that it shares with *Visions Of Johanna* and *Sad-Eyed Lady Of The Lowlands* a greater-than-average duration and, far more pertinently, a general high seriousness of intention. It also offers all those qualities noted earlier as being characteristic of "Blonde On Blonde" songs.

In Chapter Seven, the song is discussed in terms of drugs imagery. Accepting, now, that drug references can be detected anywhere and can assume however much importance the listener requires of them, it is true to say that in *Memphis Blues Again* as in many other songs the images are not of lasting interest because they "stand for" this specialist drugs jargon—they are of lasting interest despite that. In other words, Dylan's imagery is not basically a code to be cracked and put back into ordinary language: it is in its own right an *extra*ordinary language. And in *Memphis Blues Again* its emphasis is visual.

The narrator is someone just trying to get by in modern America: someone trying to get by, that is, without shutting off or closing up; someone who sees a lot happening around him but can't discern any pattern to it nor any constant, but only meaninglessness; someone who, in this situation, stays more outwardly

206

vulnerable than he needs to because he retains a yearning, however vague, for some better kind of world.

All this comes through to the listener from disconnected visual glimpses: that is how the imagery works. The song begins with this:

> Oh that ragman draws circles
> Up an' down the block
> I'd ask him what the matter was
> But I know that he don't talk

and the visual dominance is such that we get a picture to cover the third and fourth lines—they don't just pass over as abstract reflection. We glimpse the narrator standing disconsolately, aware that there is no point in making the attempt to communicate.

The same process of visualization—if that is a word—applies throughout the song. The narrator is there in front of us, avoiding "some French girl who says she knows me well", confronting Mona, believing the railroad men, thinking about Grandpa, hiding under the truck, winning his argument with the teen preacher, staggering around stoned and telling us that we just get uglier, smiling at black-haired Ruthie, and sitting patiently on Grand Street ("where the neon madmen climb")

> Waiting to find out what price
> Ya have to pay to get out of
> Going through all these things twice.

It is only with the heartfelt cry of the chorus,

> Oh! Mama! Can this *really* be the *end*?!
> To be stuck inside of *Mobile* with the Memphis *Blues*
>   again!

that the visual predominance dies away. We only picture Dylan saying "Oh! Mama!"—we don't picture Memphis Tennessee or Mobile Alabama at all. They are not part of the visual language; they are symbols, words that stand for other things—hope and despondency, potential and restraint. They are effectively abstract ideas.

This song is interesting too in the way that Dylan, very typically, handles his moral point. He operates this simply by bestowing an implicit blessing on some things and frowning implicitly on

207

others. It is a question of drawing to the listener's attention that some things strike the artist as enhancing and others strike him equally as restrictive.

The narrator himself, in fact, is made to represent certain values, certain virtues (and since we can associate the narrator directly with Dylan, this is easy enough—and a useful instance of how Dylan uses his personal legend to assist his art). These amount principally to a frank and sensitive openness to life, even at the expense of sophistication and propriety:

> ... An' I said Oh! I didn't *know* that! ...

> ... Ev'rybody still talks about
> How badly they were shocked;
> But me I expected it to happen,
> I *knew* he'd lost control! ...

which is contrasted with the machinations of the senator

> Showing everyone his gun,
> Handing out free tickets
> To the wedding of his son

and to the neon madmen of the modern city—the ones who have settled into it all—and to the claustrophobic suburban ladies who furnish him with tape, and so on.

The humour that breaks out beyond the histrionics of hamming up "Oh! I didn't *know* that!" is also engaged in the central process of moral evaluation. The narrator only adds to our awareness of his virtue when he raps out

> Y'see, you're just like me.
> I hope you're satisfied.

Who wouldn't be?

To a certain extent, the language of *Visions of Johanna* has been dealt with in the latter part of Chapter Three; and any amount more could be said. What should follow here is therefore doubly difficult to sort out.

The mixture of "serious" and "flippant" language; the mixture of delicacy and coarseness; the mixture of abstract neophilosophy and figurative phraseology; the ambiguity that begins with the song's very title—because Johanna is not just a girl's name but also the Hebrew for Armageddon; the humour; the intensive

208

build-up of the song's scope—all this is pressed into the service of a work of art at once indefinable and yet precise. It is, for me at least, quite impossible to say what the song is "about" and yet it impresses most people as saying a good deal, and in doing so it engages a great many of Dylan's distinctive strengths.

The effects are precise in the sense that the glimpses we get (as Chapter Three suggested with particular reference to the first verse of the song) are very strikingly accurate re-creations of experience.

The character-sketches, if they can be more than very approximately called that, are very accurate too; for instance, look at

> ... Little boy lost, he takes himself so seriously;
> He brags of his misery, he likes to live dangerously ...
> He's sure gotta lotta gall
> To be so useless an' all
> Muttering small talk at the wall
> While I'm in the hall—

or

> In the empty lot where the ladies play blind man's bluff
>   with the keychain
> An' the all-nite girls, they whisper of escapades out on the
>   D-train
> We can hear the night-watchman click his flashlight,
> Ask himself if it's him or them that's insane ...

Because the atmosphere there, utterly unequivocal, rebounds so incisively off phrases like "the empty lot", "out on the D-train" and "the all-nite girls", that nightwatchman comes across as vividly as any character in Dickens. Indeed that "click" that Dylan provides him with is precisely the kind of tiny detail the recording of which compromised such a large part of Dickens' touch. Dylan gives us the same sort of cartoon-precision, has shown us instantaneously the nightwatchman's mannered essentials. We don't need to know what clothes he wears, or the colour of his hair, or the shape of his nose. He is real and we have truly seen him.

But the idea of Johanna is what dominates the song. In putting *this* across, Dylan's judicious weighting of language, his economical fusion of simple words and simple tune, is amazing:

> And these visions, of Johanna,
> They've kept me up, past, the dawn ...

But these visions, of Johanna,
They make it all, seem so, cruel ...

So the broadness of the song's scope is suggested by its very possession of this fixed focal point. In effect, it is because the narrator's mind returns again and again to the single situation of his
relationship with Johanna, that he is able to be so receptive—to
give an *equal* receptivity—to everything else he comes across. Thus
it is with an equal and splendid impersonality that the song can
focus one minute on the coughing heat-pipes in Louise and her
lover's room—where they are entwined and oblivious—and can
focus next minute on casual speculation about the essential function of museums. Since Johanna, or the effect of Johanna on the
narrator, is so much the centre of everything, the outer circum-
ferences are all equitably regarded and rendered: all seen dis-
passionately as equally significant and insignificant: "Jellyfish
women"; the secret of the Mona Lisa smile; the sounds of the
night; they all flow with the same detachment through the narrator's mind, until

The harmonicas play the skeleton keys in the rain

(a beautiful line—that connection between harmonica sounds and
skeletons is a flash of real imaginative genius and fiery intuitive
observation)

And these visions, of Johanna,
Are now all, that remain.

To turn from *Visions of Johanna* to *Sad-Eyed Lady Of The
Lowlands* is not only, as earlier implied, to turn from one major
song on "Blonde On Blonde" to another; it is also to turn from
a success to a failure—and a failure no more easily explicable than
most things to do with Dylan's work.

It is unsuccessful, and rather grandly so, inasmuch as it is
offered on the album, as something of extraspecial importance, and
yet no one, subsequently, has, after any thought, really accepted it
as such. It takes up the whole of the fourth and final side of the
double-LP, despite lasting only about one minute longer than
Desolation Row, which slots in with three other songs on a single
side of "Highway 61 Revisited". Nobody now regards *Sad-Eyed
Lady* as a more important song than *Desolation Row*. It's long, it's

attractive, it's puzzling and ambiguous—but it isn't one of Dylan's great songs. No one that I know of plays it very often, except in so far as plenty of girls use Dylan's voice as sexual, fur-lined wallpaper and his voice does come over beautifully from that point of view.

All the same, the intention behind the song was clearly a major one, and the consequent recording is obtrusive enough to merit giving it a special attention.

It is as well to begin by recognizing a few ambiguities. The chorus of the song is full of them:

> Sad-eyed lady of the lowlands,
> Where the sad-eyed prophets say that no man comes,
> My warehouse eyes, my Arabian drums—
> Should I leave them by your gate,
> Or, sad-eyed lady, should I wait?

As a concentration of drugs jargon, that is noted in Chapter Seven; but the "warehouse eyes" juxtaposition, at the very least, is of more general impetus and impact than that. It is a fine enough encapsulation, perhaps, to compensate for the slightly indolent vagueness of those figurative "drums" and the corresponding "gate". Yet perhaps it is even a little *too* encapsulated: it is almost just a diagram, from which the listener has to fit the bits together by himself: a sort of Poetic Language Kit that needs to be built up at home. As for the rest of the chorus, I think it's fair to say that the line preceding "warehouse eyes" means absolutely nothing. It's just there for neatness' sake (which inevitably means that it comes across as not artistically neat at all)—for mood-setting repetition and rhyme. And the title-line itself stands for—what?

Of course, Dylan *could* have meant anything: it could stand for his grandmother; or, as Weberman suggests, for the concept of oligarchy; or indeed it could stand for Chaucer's Wife Of Bath. Within the logic of the song as a context, however, the possibilities are a great deal more limited. Either the sad-eyed lady is just that, or she is America.

It shouldn't matter. The lady's sad eyes are just as much warehouses as the narrator's; Dylan passes his myriad perspectives in front of those eyes, and what the song tries to communicate is the world which therein confronts them—the world that makes them sad. It shouldn't be important, therefore, whether they belong to a woman or to some equivalent of the Statue of Liberty, some symbol for America. Either way, "she" is, by the logic of the song's format, merely a convention—a sort of camera.

The failure of the song is that it gives our "shouldn't" no support; that while the above fairly suggests the argument urged by the song's structure, it is contradicted by the logic of its ingredient parts. So much so that in the vain hope of cutting down on our perplexity in response to the whole, we *do* find that the identity of the title person, or title symbol, matters to us.

The camera-shots, the perspectives: do they really create more than wistful but nebulous fragments? Do they add up to any kind of vision, as the whole presentation, duration and solemnity of the song, imply that they should? Surely, in the end, one's reply is No.

The only thing which unites the fragments is the *mechanical device* of the return to the chorus, and thus to the title; because there is nothing to suggest a particular significance to that title (as say, there is in *Visions of Johanna* and *Memphis Blues Again*), its intended function of holding things together virtually fails. It is, in the end, not a whole song at all, but unconnected chippings, and only the poor cement of an empty chorus and a regularity of tune give the illusion that things are otherwise. The structure makes the song seem a complete entity; the sense of the song denies it.

All the same, these disunited parts are interesting, and the spread-eagled "Blonde On Blonde" recording offers many of the features of Dylan's artistry. It uses many of his patented trademarks. It may be a failure, yet it is none the less not unrepresentative of Dylan's talents. It is, then, worth glancing at his use of language in the song.

Dylan delivers it like slow-motion waves, unfurling the phrases with a strung-out concentration that is at once committed, intense and yet mellow. He breathes out the lines—lines full of alliterative emphasis, melting and echoey atmosphere, and obscured, nebulous pictures:

> The kings of Tyrus with their convict list
> Are waiting in line for their geranium kiss
> And you wouldn't know it would happen like this
> But who among them, really wants, just to kiss you?

212

With your childhood flames on your midnight rug
And your Spanish manners and your mother's drugs
And your cowboy mouth and your curfew plugs
Who among them do you think could resist you?
Sad-eyed lady of the lowlands? ...

The fourth line there offers a much cheaper cynicism than Dylan normally exhibits; and the rhyming eighth line is unusually weak. The other six lines of that verse are more demanding.

The opening couplet gets much of its force from its elaborate alliteration and internal rhymes—and how nicely the tune holds back fittingly on the word "waiting" in line two. The power of the *imagery*, though, is fundamentally untraceable—for it is basically surrealistic, and thus not susceptible to rationale or analysis. For me, "the kings of Tyrus" is hardly visual at all; "their convict list" is not really visual either—but it is distinctly atmospheric: it increases my sense of sadness, it suggests perhaps an irretrievable past. The "waiting in line" gets disregarded almost entirely: it is just the outstretching hand that presents that marvellous "geranium kiss". Why try to explain the impact of that? And it is only natural, correspondingly, to give up on "your cowboy mouth and your curfew plugs"—which yields perhaps less unadulterated impact but a great deal of unadulterated aesthetic pleasure. The singer's 'ru-u-u-ug" and "dru-u-u-ugs" is perhaps a necessary device for lending the relevant couplet its impression of parallels, but beyond that "midnight rug" makes those "flames" literal and visual, and is in itself evocative enough: and that sixth line

And your Spanish manners and your mother's drugs

brings in, with a skilful kind of equipoise, pleasantly conflicting ideas of elegance and tragedy—and thereby lends both a harmony and counterpart to the misty moods of the whole verse.

Some lines in other verses operate in much the same essentially surrealistic ways—

With your mercury mouth in the Missionary Times ...
And your matchbox songs and your gypsy hymns ...
To show you where the dead angels are that they used to hide ...

yet some lines operate a great deal less intensively. In the first place there are lines and lines of largely explicable simile, where the listener's problem is merely to gather from them what could conveniently be called the moral slant. Is this sort of thing intended as praise or condemnation or neither (or indeed both)?:

> ... your eyes like smoke and your prayers like rhymes
> And your silver cross and your voice like chimes ...

If they seem morally neutral it is only because they are uninspiring; as the similes grow more distinctive—largely through becoming instantly-recognizable cliché, paradoxically enough—they lose their neutrality. By the time we have had "your face like glass" (a classically back-handed compliment) and we reach "your saint-like face and your ghost-like soul", we can't fail to be aware of Dylan's/ the narrator's severity. His condemnation comes so powerfully through the line just quoted that the question which follows— ostensibly reverential rhetoric—comes across as a fairly heavy sneer:

> Who among them do you think could destroy you?

(and if it is still possible, from the meagre evidence the page can give, to regard that line as complimentary in intention, listen to Dylan's delivery of "destroy you"; he is positively back on 4th Street there, assuming the tone of *that* song's final verse).

Other lines, bereft of similes, join in the condemnation of the lady (which makes her, of course, at once, more than the camera that the song's structure pretends she is). Notably, there is the concluding verse's second line, with its clever and derisive piece of shorthand description of

> ... your magazine husband who one day just had to go.

Yet if, within the song, there are these many and varied attractions and insights, then it is, in the end, no less necessary to insist that they have been bundled up together, and perhaps a bit complacently, without the unity either of a clear and real theme or of cohesive artistic discipline. *Sad-Eyed Lady Of The Lowlands* shows eloquently, one might conclude by adding, that to consider Dylan's "use of language" or his "imagery" is only useful where such consideration is modified by a due attention to questions of organ-

214

ization and disciplined handling. The one aspect of Dylan's work is very much, and rightly, dependent on the other.

In contrast to that of "Blonde On Blonde", Dylan's surrealism is deliberately stripped down to a chilly minimum on that sombre, central song of "John Wesley Harding"—*All Along The Watchtower*. Really, this is impressionism revisited, and no longer a reflection of summer tension in the city but of wintertime in the psyche instead. And by the time of "Nashville Skyline" and "Self Portrait" we find, not unexpectedly in view of their terrain, no trace of surrealistic imagery at all. The images for those two albums rest as firmly in logic as would be consistent with imaginative expression: they are founded in the logic of traditional rural life, logic dependent on that life's unvarying rhythms and verities— seasons, the process of agriculture, growth, replenishment and death.

> Turned my skies to blue from grey ...
> Tonight no light will shine on me ...
> Once I had mountains in the palm of my hand
> And rivers that ran through every day ...

And the impetus of those lines is less a matter of image-coining than of the use of idiom—idiom that is a natural product of rural culture. Those lines, moreover, if we regard them as holding images, comprise the sum total of the imagery on the "Nashville Skyline" album—with four rather special exceptions. First, that awkward, uncharacteristically saccharine "Whatever colours you have in your mind/I'll show them to you and you'll see them shine" (which fails to sound like Dylan, and stands out of the song in which it occurs—*Lay, Lady, Lay*—in the same way that the chorused phrase "Take me down to California, baby" stands out in the basement-tape song *Yea Heavy And A Bottle Of Bread*). Second, that imagery which is integral to deliberately selected cliché, as with "You can have your cake an' eat it too", which is again from *Lay, Lady, Lay*. Third, the images that are images only in the sense that they yield snapshots of the narrator-predicament—as with, for instance, "If there's a poor boy on the street" (from *Tonight I'll Be Staying Here With You*) and *Shake*

215

me up that old peach tree! (from *Country Pie*). The fourth and final exception is again from *Lay, Lady, Lay*—an exceptional song! —and is here:

> His clothes are dirty but his, his hands are clean
> And you're the best thing that he's ever seen ...

At first glance, that is strikingly Laurentian—and then one notes a reversal of the expected moral weighting. Surely the Noble Workman has honourably *dirty* hands—and in the west, clean hands belong only to the no-good gamblin' man. But it is plainly *not* a "John Wesley Harding" style double-edged comment from Dylan here. It is plainly a statement of praise. And in fact it takes its ethic not from the mid-west (nor indeed from Lawrence) but from the Bible: from the 24th Psalm, which is a Psalm of David:

> Who shall ascend into the hill of the Lord?
> Or who shall stand in His holy place?
> He that hath clean hands, and a pure heart.

A SECOND AFTERWORD: ON THE CIRCULAR INTERPRETATION OF "ALL ALONG THE WATCHTOWER":

If *Desolation Row* can be seen as a circular song, with its parade going on for ever (see this Chapter, page 186) so too can the song that is, among other things, a far more economical—and far more chilling—restatement of the same theme: *All Along The Watchtower*, from the "John Wesley Harding" album.

All Along The Watchtower can be said to end, as Richard Goldstein argued, in a *Village Voice* review, with an emphatic full-stop—indeed, a terrifying full-stop. Just three clean, razor-sharp verses, with an end that comes across as signifying the end of *everything*:

> Outside in the distance
> A wild cat did growl
> Two riders were approaching
> The wind began to howl.

As Goldstein says, the suggestion of menace in those lines is far too ominous and powerful to allow them to be concluded felicitously with a series of dots. Yet there is an alternative interpretation—that which envisages the song going on for ever. Such an interpretation does not disregard the menace in the song: it sees the end as lying in the very *endlessness* of the nightmare vision offered (an endlessness emphasized by the then *recurrent* helpless cry "There must be some way out of here!").

NOTES

[1]As a matter of fact, *Masters Of War* also provides an example of Dylan's using an "echo-image": that is, where the wording used to give one visual picture deliberately echoes other pictures, other moods—even another poet's voice:

> An' I hope that you die, and your death will come soon,
> *I will follow your casket on a pale afternoon* ...

The poet there, of course, is Eliot; and in recalling him, Dylan moderates his song's mood of anger with the Eliot tone of underlying wisdom and sadness.

[2]There is another sound-image from an early song that I find particularly attractive—but probably just because I am English, and not American. I'm thinking of "grabbed hold of a subway car", which tumbles out of the very early *Talkin' New York*. Actually, of course, it's a *visual* image that *sounds* nice: the appeal is in the colloquialism rather than in the image itself. For me, it is the best kind of Americanism: a phrase that is totally unEnglish in the implicit self-conception of its user's relationship with the world. It carries an utterly inoffensive arrogance. The first such colloquialism I came across (while hitching home from Paris in 1965) still impresses me. I was riding with several people including a man who said he owned a U.S. record label called "Bullfrog". He said to the driver: "If you see a Bureau de Poste, pick it up." A sort of American Maoism.

[3]Another Dylan song that in the sense just discussed resembles *The Times They Are A-Changin'* and contrasts with *When The Ship Comes In*, is the much more obscure (discrographically speaking) *Paths Of Victory*. Its language is total platitude: not a single fresh analogy breaks up the flow of cliché: "The trail is dusty/And my road it might be rough/But the better roads are waiting/And boys it aint far off—/Trails of troubles,/Roads of battles,/Paths of Victory/We shall walk." An instantly forgettable and rather tiresome song—and yet the theme is the same in basics as the theme of *When The Ship*

Comes In. How erratic the standard of Dylan's use of language still was at the end of 1963!

⁴See also, in this connection, the second afterword at the end of this chapter.

⁵The lines immediately following that "Titanic" have their applicability too:

> Everybody is shouting
> Which Side Are You On?

Which Side Are You On? was an intensely political song composed by one Florence Reece (then aged 12), the daughter of a miner in Kentucky. (The tune, incidentally, as Alan Lomax explains it, was a variant on the English *Jack Munro,* the title phrase replacing "lay the lily-o".) It later became a national union song. It is cited also in Duberman's political play *In White America.* Dylan, interviewed by *Playboy* in 1966, made his attitude clear:

> Songs like *Which Are You On?* and *I Love You Porgy,* they're not folk music songs: they're political songs. They're already dead.

⁶A comparable example is "You walk into the room/with a pencil in your hand", from *Ballad Of A Thin Man.* That yields a visual incongruity by means of its juxtapositioning; it also uses the "pencil" as a symbol—so that the two lines give us not only the man's entrance as others see it but also his own attitude (because, that is to say, to come in "with a pencil in your hand" is plainly to be unreceptive to real life—to wish to be an observer and not a participant).

⁷There is in fact another attempt at a similar effect in another "Blonde On Blonde" song, *Most Likely You Go Your Way And I'll Go Mine.* Lack of balance is treated there too, in middle-eight lines for which tune helps words by seeming to falter and totter appropriately in the delivery of lines which include "But he's badly built/An' he walks on stilts/Watch out he don't/Fall on you . . .": but in this case it is a more studied co-operation and its success is correspondingly more limited.

6

The Use Of Cliché

*Dylan approaches a cliché
like a butcher eyes a
chicken*

—Richard Goldstein

With "Self Portrait" it might seem more true to say that Dylan
approaches a cliché like an elderly lady strokes her cat. Be that
as it may, for the other albums Richard Goldstein's remark is a
useful starting point. There are indeed moments in Dylan's songs
where, with a sudden flash, the knife comes down:

> You say my kisses are not like his
> But this time I'm not gonna tell you why that is ...

But this way of doing it (and with this intent)—setting up the tired
old bird and then killing it in front of us—is comparatively rare.
Usually there is no explicit butchery. Dylan simply *displays* the
clichés, holding them up in relish of their obvious absurdity, and
allowing them to fall over, squawking in the mud, of their own
accord:

> Well Frankie Lee he sat back down
> Feeling low and mean
> When just then a passing stranger
> Burst upon the scene.
> Saying Are You Frankie Lee, The Gambler,
> Whose Father's Deceased?
> Well If Y'are There's A Fella Callin' Ya Down The Road,
>   An' They
> Say His Name Is Priest.

If this were all that was involved, Dylan's handling of cliché would be funny, but only that. The *richness* of the humour comes from the deeper purpose it serves: the celebration of human foibles. The clichés—not merely of speech but often of posture too (both coming down to clichés of *thought*, essentially)—give us swift but uncannily accurate glimpses of an oh-so-fallible humanity; and the contexts in which these glimpses are placed give us the reasons for celebration.

As early as *Talking World War III Blues* (from Dylan's second album: "The Freewheelin' Bob Dylan") we come across this neo-Shakespearean expansiveness of perspective, this generosity of oulook.

> Well I seen a Cadillac window up town
> There was nobody around
> I got into the driver's seat
> An' I drove down 42nd Street!
> In ma Cadillac!
> Good car to drive.
> After a war.

It is all so well pressed into service there. The exaggerated hesitancy in the delivery of the first two lines; and then the rhythm of the third line, tum-ta-ra-tiddle-tum-ta-ra, begins to sketch the ridiculous vanity of the man in the picture; and this gets added force from the pride of announcement of the fourth and fifth lines. The vulnerable self-centredness comes out in the full balloon of the cliché, "Good car to drive", and is at once sardonically deflated, as the full context of the situation is brought into focus: "After a war".

For the context in which we see this likeably inadequate man indulging his childish Cadillac daydream is supposedly the aftermath of a nuclear war. He is the only man left; and in this truly staggering situation, we see his comically foolish response. I say *supposedly* the aftermath of a nuclear war, because plainly, like the Wood in which Bottom and Company rehearse inside *A Midsummer Night's Dream*, it is not intended as a realistic setting. It is a consciously fanciful one.[1] And the fancy assists Dylan's *celebratory* purpose.

Like Bottom, the man in Dylan's picture is indeed *comically* foolish, and the comic element comes from the sympathy we're invited to feel for him. His vulnerability is as important as his self-centredness; his enacted childish fantasy is child*like* too; his response to the situation is as understandable as it is inadequate. In context, then, this fallibility is worth celebrating because it is the assertion of his very humanity—and holds up the victory of life over the (albeit fanciful) nuclear destruction.

Dylan gives us many such pictures—many other sympathetic sketches of human foibles, human weakness, people who wrap up warm in absurd but plausible self-deception.

These sketches flash past us without warning, in the most unexpected places, the most unexpected songs. In *Maggie's Farm*, for instance (1965)—where suddenly, after three verses of bitter complaint explaining why the narrator "aint gonna work on Maggie's Farm no more", the half-figurative language of the exposition gives way to this genuinely compassionate summary of Maggie's ma:

> Well she talks to all the servants
> About Man and God and Law
> Everybody says she's the brains behind pa,
> She's sixty-eight but she says she's fifty-four
> Ah! I aint gonna work for Maggie's ma no more.

So, as we see, she's an impossible puffed-up old battle-axe rasping out dreadful philosophic homilies, and doubtless she takes advantage of her hick sons and workmen most unscrupulously (you can just see them all going about their labours muttering sullenly, and darkly telling this new hand, Dylan, that they reckon she's the brains behind pa). But all the same we smile for her on catching her at that little impotent touch of feminine pretence, patting her hair into place a bit girlishly and claiming to be "only" fifty-four. Dylan uses the cliché of the posture to advantage, and the compassion evinced very much contradicts the common idea that not until much later could Dylan feel for ordinary people and that his sympathy could extend only to the outcasts with their admirable lawless honesty. It also contradicts Steven Goldberg's assertion (see Chapter Nine) that Dylan's compassion never tempers his vision until the "John Wesley Harding" LP.

The same kind of manifest human vanity that Dylan warms to in *Maggie's Farm* is shown in abundance in *Leopard-Skin Pill-Box Hat* ("Blonde On Blonde", 1966). Here too the use of cliché expresses Dylan's smiles, and here too his attitude is a maturely balanced one. He doesn't go soft on the dumb girl who wears the hat, any more than Holden Caulfield goes soft on the dumb girls he dances with in the crummy New York club where they hang out; but as with Caulfield's, Dylan's put-down is infused with a friendly tolerance (which is also expressed in the very *chattiness* of the tone):

> Well I see you got a new boy-friend

—how well Dylan brings out her dumbness just by using, and savouring, that "boy-friend"—

> You know I never seen him before
> Well I saw him makin' love to you
> (You forgot to close the garage door):
> You might think he loves you for your money but
> *I* know what he really loves you for!:
> It's your brand-new Leopard-skin Pill-box Hat.

It would be comparatively easy to use the cliché *merely to* prise open the sensibility which would deal in it as mental currency (as, in the verse just quoted, he uses "You might think he loves you for your money but ..." to expose the way her mind works: Does He Love Me For Myself? Does He Love Me For My Money? Or Does He, tut, tut, Just Want My Body??). But Dylan goes beyond that. He doesn't just expose the empty-headedness, the women's magazine mentality, and leave it in front of us so that we can sneer (or gloat; or sniff). The exposure is a part of an open acceptance of life-as-it-is. A quite opposite tone to, say, this characteristic one of Eliot's:

> The red-eyed scavengers are creeping
>   From Kentish Town and Golders Green

Even in the elevated love-vision of *Love Minus Zero/No Limit*, in which Dylan exalts his magnificent raven-woman, he has the time and tolerance to infuse his observation of ordinary mortals as much with compassion as with detractive comment:

> In the dime stores and bus stations
> People talk of situations
> Read books, repeat quotations,
> Draw conclusions on the wall ...

That finely-set condemnation—using to the full the shoddy and sad associations yielded by "dime" in that first line—is clearly tempered by a corresponding sadness *for* them: a sympathy revealed, albeit obliquely, in the last line quoted above. We're invited to register that their only *opportunity* for self-expression is in diffident and furtive graffiti: and this is one reason why, when it *does* come out, the self-expression is such a poverty-stricken thing.

In other songs, Dylan uses the clichés for a more simple comic effect: they help to establish an image of Chaplinesque naïveté for the narrator—and since we see Dylan himself, tousle-headed and jerky, as the narrator, the clichés contribute to our seeing a Dylan of comic innocence:

> Mona tried to tell me
> To stay away from the train-line
> She said that all the railroad men
> Just drink up your blood like wine
> An' I said *Oh!* I didn't *know* that! ...

The term "cliché", I'm aware, is being stretched to fit, but essentially it does and the point, I think, remains valid. *"Oh! I didn't know that!"* is given us in consummately *archetypal* wide-eyed-American-innocence—given us as a common expression we have knowingly heard mouthed before often and oft: and in this sense it functions as cliché. The full comic effect comes, as usual, from the context; and in this instance the exposition of naïveté stems from our seeing that while Ramona's advice is figurative speech, it gets taken at face-value (and with so much boyish enthusiasm too).

Later in the same song—*Memphis Blues Again*, from "Blonde On Blonde"—Dylan plays for a very similar effect, except that this time the contrast between the two levels of conversation glimpsed is not merely a contrast of figurative and literal language but also of the sophisticated and the hick.

> When Ruthie says come see her
> In her honky-tonk lagoon
> Where I can watch her waltz for free
> 'Neath her Panamanian moon
> An' I say Awh! C'*mon* now!
> Ya know ya know about my debutante ...

The figurative—which is to say, in this case, the surrealistic—

language surrounding Ruthie all suggests a sophisticated personal elegance in her. The words iridesce around her like a rich man's party—almost as if she had stepped, suitably unreal, out of a Leonard Cohen song. The very name, "Ruthie", fits perfectly the ethos of the lagoon, the fanciful moonlight waltzing and the necessarily sophisticated sensibility that would alight on "Panamanian" (and it is *her* Panamanian moon!). And all this contrasts so beautifully with the inarticulate, ignorantly sceptical, masculine world of "Awh! C'*mon* now!" A platitudinous but robust rejoinder.

Elsewhere, the same contrast of sophistication and the lack of it used more one-sidedly—in direct condemnation of sophistication; and thus the platitude—which is to say, the ready-made, unit-constructed, automatic language—is used on the other side: as a symptom of what is under attack. In *Bob Dylan's 115th Dream* (1965) these lines set the scene:

> ... I went into a bank
> To get some bail for Arab
> An' all the boys back in the tank ... ;

then comes the economically-written confrontation:

> They asked me for some collateral
> An' I
> Pulled down ma pants ...

And actually the values invested in that are more complex than a first glance might show. On the one hand, Dylan has, in this story-situation, nothing to offer *but* his masculinity: it really is offered as "collateral", and as such echoes that old Code of the West (where men were men and bank-tellers weren't). Then again, the setting is effectively a modern city, and the hillbilly is new to the place. His response is characteristic: an exposition of the assumption that any unfamiliar multisyllabic words must mean something obscene (an assumption nearly all schoolkids subscribe to).

So on one level—embracing, incidentally, everything worth saying in *Midnight Cowboy*—those very few lines give us an accurately-placed slam at the city's values (You need help? Have you got any money?). And overriding that what we're offered is the Laurentian confrontation between Life—impulsive and raw and with its cock out—and Anti-Life, properly dressed and properly spoken, standing behind a glass partition.

Dylan is equally capable of mocking *these* values, where he finds them over-simplified and tired: when, to return to the point about cliché, he finds them adhered to via automatic thought (i.e. non-thought). Hence, in *Motorpsycho Nitemare* (1964), when the narrator comes to beg a sleeping-place for the night from a curt and intransigent boor of a farmer, we are shown the farmer eyeing him suspiciously, and then we get this:

> Well by the dirt 'neath my nails I guess he knew I wouldn't lie,
> He said "I guess you're tired", (He said it kinda sly) ...

Oh that good old working-man's dirt beneath the nails!

Just as Dylan can thus use cliché to lampoon an attitude or ethic, so, naturally, he can use it to lampoon a kind of song. But he does it respectfully: the respect is the equivalent of the compassion that infuses his comic glimpses of people in the songs cited earlier.

The supreme example is *Peggy Day*—so lightly done, such an *attractive* song in the midst of the lampooning. It holds a *delicate* mockery, and yet the clichés are clear-cut enough.

> Peggy Day, stole my poor heart away
> By golly, what more can I say—
> Love to spend the night with Peggy Day.

The economy there is amazing, especially since it's in the nature of the language he's pinning down to be generalized to the point of vagueness—that is, to be highly *un*economical. By golly, what more need you say?

That song is from "Nashville Skyline", of course—and on "Nashville Skyline" Dylan uses cliché in a new way (a newly-detached way); yet his purpose is again the characteristic celebration of human fallibility.

It is in *Tell Me That It Isn't True* that we see what's being done, fully poised, to best effect.

> They say that you've been seen, with some other man
> That he's tall dark an' handsome, and you're holding his hand
> Darlin' I'm a-countin' on you:
> Tell me that it isn't, true.

225

Dylan is using the clichés—but without the slightest hint of condescension—to render, and very poignantly, the love song of an ordinary man. It isn't lampooning a familiar kind of song (although he allows and *uses* an element of that) and equally, it isn't giving us the Dylan of, say, *She Belongs To Me*—an intellectual's love-song to a marble-perfect woman.

It is done *so* masterfully. The first verse establishes the tone and the level at which it is pitched: it's simple language—the language in which the lover's *feelings* register with himself; but the simplicity results from a real artistry on Dylan's part, and he makes it free of any fortuitious clumsiness.

This is emphasized, lightly enough, by the judicious *balance of* the middle-eight lines:

> I know that some other man is, holding you tight;
> It hurts me all over—it doesn't seem right

The one line balances the other so quietly and neatly; the second line has those two concise self-diagnoses which, correspondingly, balance each other. (And oh! the sureness of touch which lets fall that diffident "doesn't *seem* right!")

Thus, given all this judiciousness—given it as inseparable from the simplicity of the whole monologue—we can accept that lovely "All of these awful things . . ." That *is* amusing (for yes, of course, we're invited to smile)—and yet it also impinges as sincerely eloquent. The clichés and the corresponding inarticulacy are used with this intelligence of compassion in showing us the simple but genuine feelings of the ordinary heart.

So too, in the context of the whole song as it unfolds, we see in these lines from the second verse the fine life-celebration of Dylan's *wit*:

> They say that you've been seen, with some other man
> That he's tall dark an' handsome, and you're holding his
> hand . . .

That "tall dark an' handsome" yields far more than merely the reminder of the cliché's existence. It isn't just popped in for good measure—for an extra smile. Because it echoes down through the rest of the song it never leaps out at us in a distracting way; and because it is immediately and directly allied to "and you're holding his hand" it shows us, in a darting glimpse, the full vulnerability

226

of the lover. Knowing his rival only from rumour, he is unsettled and diffident and so vulnerable that the real and the storybook world mix in his mind—as they do for those flimsy girls who live in the land of *Red Letters* and *Valentine* while working and painting their nails at city office-desks; and as they do equally for the heirs of Krebbs: lost young men who live in, say, Nebraska and swallow up comic-strip stories of the Wild West. Yet Dylan's exposition of the consciousness of the lover in *Tell Me That It Isn't True* is, of course, immeasurably more delicate than any attempted paraphrase could be.

Delicacy is the keynote of the song, and on the printed page it can't come across adequately: you need the shy tracery of the tune and you need Dylan's acutely responsive delivery in order really to appreciate the song for the remarkable achievement it is.

The Ballad Of Frankie Lee & Judas Priest, finally (which needs and offers far *less* delicacy but radiates at least as much poise as the one just discussed) is the Dylan song in which the function of the cliché is perhaps most strikingly, immediately clear. Certainly the cliché is sustained and dominant as in no other Dylan song; and it provides, of itself, an authoritative study on Dylan's use of cliché.

NOTES

[1]His use of the war-aftermath *as* an unreal setting can readily be taken also as a felicitous criticism of a protest movement which would handle it as grim realism, and handle it therefore unimaginatively—and thus make the setting itself a cliché.

7

Theories—Anyone Can Play

Play Dylan's records and welcome in the Theory Squad. His work is better-than-average hunting ground. Everyone can rush in on Dylan and by darting in and out of his songs—taking a line here, another there as evidence—come up with an all-embracing theory "explaining" what it's all about.

Some artists come much nearer to escaping this sort of thing. Once you call Wordsworth a Romantic Poet, or Zola's novels Realism, the labels almost protect them from more complex envelopments.

We all make these attempts at envelopment, and even the Wordsworths and the Zolas can't avoid us entirely. It's a forgivable impulse, and easily accounted for: we don't like disconnection. We like to believe that all is ordered and balanced inside our heads, so we rush to make links between our likes and dislikes, without much heed to whether such links are illusory. A man who likes George Bernard Shaw and loathes Edward Albee will almost certainly make the assumption that Shaw would have hated Albee too. And if the man's wife loves Mozart and has a passion for the sea, she will find the sea in Mozart's music.

Everyone makes these connections and Dylan's work is especially inviting. He leaves you plenty of scope because he deals in ambiguities and piles up strange and fresh word-associations which seem to "demand" explanation, and he offers more questions than answers. "Explaining" him is fun, and he can be most things to most men.

To Steven Goldberg, of the City University of New York Sociology Department, "Bob Dylan is a mystic". (See Chapter Eight.) In the summer of 1967, in London, I spent three hours on the phone listening to an expert on the Jewish faith explain to me that Dylan's work can't be understood without an intimate knowledge of ancient Jewish texts. From other perspectives, Dylan is simply a

228

dope-fiend, simply a surrealist, simply an impressionist, simply a man obsessed by apocalypse/sex/homosexuality/alienation, simply a political sell-out, simply a businessman.

This chapter sets out some of these theories. None of them originates with me, but in the telling I've developed all but No. 3, and have wandered very haphazardly between putting the theories as eloquently as possible and stressing their absurdity both in the telling and in explicit commentary. None of what follows seems to me necessarily wise or profound or fundamental, nor necessarily baseless or irrelevant. It's just an interesting game. Anyone can play.

1. THE THIEF TO BOSS THEORY

Dylan starts out with his integrity intact and changes, over the years and with success and wealth piling up for him, into a businessman. But not only does he sell his soul—and for *power*—he documents the whole process in his songs. Look at the songs properly and you'll find the signposts just as clearly through the changes as you will in the honest early days. And the changes signed in the songs are from attacks on power (*Masters of War*) to the wielding of power (*Tiny Montgomery*; *Minstrel Boy*); from being with the losers to being a winner; from being an outsider around the commercial world of pop to becoming its dominant and supersuccessful leader; from being the thief to being the boss.

The change doesn't come where the early-60s folk-fans put it —doesn't stem from Dylan going electric. That, on the contrary, showed Dylan still the honest man: it was a change that kept Dylan true to himself. "You say I've let you down; you know it's not like that," he sings, and means it. In the same song comes the scorn-laden accusation that "You just want to be on the side that's winning ..." and it's plainly not addressed to himself.

Dylan is still on the side that's losing. In a world turning further and further right-wing, Dylan starts out singing left-wing protest songs. His second and third albums are full of them. When he rejects the explicit protest formula, he is still, as an artist, subversive —still standing up against the tidal-wave of totalitarianism.

He's still with the losers on "Highway 61 Revisited" and *Desolation Row* is still a political song—a kind of updated *Grapes of Wrath* through which protest is still being enunciated.

As late as the first side of the "John Wesley Harding" album, the anguish of a soul in protest, albeit the death-throes of that protest, is still there. *All Along The Watchtower* is a more desperate, and consequently much more economical, revisit to *Desolation Row*.

Dylan the beautiful loser lasts as long as that, and if you trace it back to the beginning its gets clearer and clearer. He hasn't been "bent out of shape by society's pliers". So he stands up squarely for the losers—hoboes; circus freaks; the maid in the kitchen; Lee Harvey Oswald; the poor white duped into killing Medgar Evers as much as Evers himself. "To live outside the law," he later writes, "you must be honest." He identifies with these people. He dresses like a ragamuffin, travels America like a hobo. So he identifies also with *The Chimes Of Freedom*, which are

> Flashin' for the warriors whose strength is not to fight
> Flashin' for the refugees on the unarmed road of flight ...
> Tollin' for the luckless, the abandoned an' forsaked,
> Tollin' for the outcast burning constantly at stake ...
> Strikin' for the gentle, strikin' for the kind ...
> ... for each unharmful gentle soul misplaced inside a jail

(that beautifully ambiguous "misplaced"!); Dylan starts out speaking, in fact, for

> ... every hung-up person in the whole wide universe.

But from being the freedom-fighter, the thief, he moves into a tainted phase as master-thief—he becomes too good at it, too successful as champion of the luckless; his ego starts to call. He realizes and records the change:

> If I was a master-thief perhaps I'd rob them

he sings, on *Positively 4th Street*; and he changes again, this time towards the acquisition of greater power: so well might the chimes of freedom *toll* for the outcast. He moves from thief through master-thief to master. He sells his soul, as most idealists and rebels do. He joins the side that's winning—and joins from a position of strength.

He registers the feeling of wanting to change in his unreleased *Tears of Rage*:

> Why'm I always the one who must be the thief?

and in the album "John Wesley Harding" he announces the emergence of the new Dylan.

First he praises Harding not for his honesty or valour but because "He was never known to make a foolish move". In the next song Tom Paine, symbol for the Liberal Establishment *and* the New Left rebel, fails him and ends up saying "I'm sorry sir". Then, dreaming he saw St. Augustine, Dylan admits to finding himself "amongst the ones that put him out to death".

Next comes that last cry of conscience, in *All Along The Watchtower*, before, like for Macbeth, the dream-prophecy comes to real fulfilment. Succumbing to Judas Priest's dollar-bills, the honest man enters the palace of temptation

> With four-and-twenty windows
> And a woman's face in every one

which is, as the song says, where he dies of thirst. The old Dylan, the drifter, escapes; and in *I Pity The Poor Immigrant* he is allowed his last stand as narrator. The *new* Dylan is the immigrant

> Who falls in love with wealth itself
> And turns his back on me.

The song that follows is called *The Wicked Messenger* (the old Dylan, that is, as seen through the eyes of the new) and is about how he gets taught a lesson. It ends:

> And he was told with these few words
> Which opened up his heart:
> "If you cannot bring good news then don't bring any."

And from then on—silence. The voice of conscience has been drowned and the man who, for power and money, gives the public what it wants—"good news"—takes over, on the cheerful *Down Along The Cove*, the reassuring *I'll Be Your Baby Tonight* and the bland "Nashville Skyline" and "Self Portrait". Good news music. And by the time of "Self Portrait", Dylan has been seen to be the master of so many modes of music. Master Protest Man; Master Rock Star; Master Country Artist; Master Folk Singer; perhaps, in the future, Master Niteclub Personality too.

2. THE TRANSVESTITES/QUEERS/INCEST/SCATOLOGY OBSESSION THEORY:

Dylan is obsessed by sexual deviation and shit. A large number of his songs, appearing on the surface to be "about" women and love are really just expressive of these obsessions.

Think, for a start, of the number of times in Dylan songs that Queen gets mentioned: Queen Jane, Queen Mary, the Queen of Spades, ye gifted Queens, the motorcycle-black-madonna-two-wheel-gypsy queen, queen for queen.

Then there are a lot of more or less explicit transvestite/homosexual references scattered throughout his work. The title *Temporary Like Achilles* could deal with Dylan's temporary refuge in a homosexual relationship. Part of the lyric goes

> He's pointing to the sky
> An' he's hungry like a man in drag

and, taking up the phallic suggestion of that "pointing to the sky", the chorus includes the ambiguous question

> Honey, why are you so *hard*?

In *Million Dollar Bash*, there is the energetically suggestive delivery of the line "Well the big dumb blonde" and its telling follow-up (in the sheet music version, though not actually on the recording) "With gorgeous George"; and maybe the line "With his cheese in the cash" should end "in the *Cash*"—.

The Ballad Of A Thin Man has Mr. Jones propositioned, or mock-propositioned, by a sword-swallower (meaning cock-sucker?) who kneels (confirming the idea?) and "clicks his high-heels".

In *Bob Dylan's 115th Dream* he sings

> I went to a restaurant
> Lookin' for the cook
> I told them I was the editor of
> A famous etiquette book
> The waitress he was handsome
> He wore a powder-blue cape
> I ordered some Suzette, I said
> Could You Please Make That Crêpe?

Perhaps also the beautiful couplet at the end of *Absolutely Sweet Marie*:

> And now I stand here lookin' at your yellow railroad
> In the ruins of your balcony—

is a conscious reference to Genet's "Balcony".

The most sustained homosexual statement, however, is in another "Blonde On Blonde" song, *Just Like A Woman*. It isn't just the fact of the title, but that none of the description of the "woman" in the song is about real femininity. Everything mentioned is external, as much disguise or theatre-prop as real:

> Everybody knows
> That Baby's got new clothes
> But lately I see her ribbons and her bows
> Have fallen from her curls ...
> With her fog, her amphetamine and her pearls ...

And yes, the song does refer to "Queen Mary", and does carry the passage

> Please don't let on that you knew me when
> I was hungry ...

the last line of which can be cross-referenced to its more explicit twin in *Temporary Like Achilles*. And it is in the context of all this that the title does begin to seem ambiguous, especially with its enclosing chorus, which, last time around, runs:

> Ah you fake just like a woman, yes you do
> You make love just like a woman, yes you do
> Then you ache just like a woman
> But you break just like a little girl.

That "fake", of course, makes the most sense for the homosexual interpretation, and the "little girl" very little sense. (Switch to transvestite theory proper to handle that?) But in this connection there is another point which favours such an interpretation: namely, that if it *was* a song about a *woman*, it would be a most uncharacteristically bad song from Dylan. Either way you take the song, its chorus is empty and ponderous enough, but if the song is not

233

about homosexual relations, then that embarrassingly twee contrast between "woman" and "little girl" is easily the most tired thing in the whole of Dylan's output.

The incest theory is a great deal weaker and I can't present it with any objectivity. It relies on one absurd, perverse falsification, one misleading rumour, one small section of *Tears Of Rage* and one verse of *Highway 61 Revisited*.

The falsification is the claim that Dylan's frequent use of "Mama"—in *It's All Right Ma (I'm Only Bleeding)*, *Memphis Blues Again*, *Crash On The Levee*, *Tombstone Blues*, *Quit Your Low-Down Ways*, *Poor Boy Blues*, *Mama You Bin On My Mind* and more besides—is *a literal* use and implies an Oedipus complex. Ha ha.

The misleading rumour part is that before the release of "Self Portrait", it was reportedly gleaned from somewhere that one of the songs on the album was about "family troubles"—an American euphemism for incest. The main trouble with this is that the *release* of "Self Portrait" has contradicted the rumour.

One verse of *Highway 61 Revisited* could be said to be describing just such "troubles":

> Now the fifth daughter on the twelfth night
> Told the first father that things weren't right
> My complexion, she said, is much too white
> He said come here, step into the light
> He says hmm, you're right
> Let me tell the second mother this has been done
> But the second mother was with the seventh son
> And they were both out on Highway 61.

Finally though, there is *Tears Of Rage*. Ignore the obvious evocation and you get your incest "evidence" here:

> Oh what daughter beneath the sun could treat a father so
> To wait upon him hand and foot and always answer no?

That's a pretty crude interpretation though—crude in the sense that it's so very reductive and attributes a kind of brutishness to Dylan's lines that Dylan doesn't ever actually trade in.

When Dylan is crude, it's a different thing altogether. *4th Time Around* gets most of its energy from pornographic innuendo; so do a number of songs from the Basement Tape (the unreleased collection of work cut with The Band in 1967). But there is a poise and a precision and an economy and a wit that keep these songs up in the air. You can't graft the same sort of innuendo on to the lines from *Tears Of Rage* quoted above without their losing all poise, without destroying all precision and wit and dissipating any economy the lines possessed beforehand.

In the context of the acetate collection and the qualities which sustain Dylan's Mailerish crudity, *Please Mrs. Henry* is a very interesting song. In fact it constitutes the case for the Dylan-scatology-obsession theory.

> Well I've already had two beers
> I'm ready for the broom
> Please, Mrs. Henry, won't you
> Take me to my room

(the gents; or in the rather revolting American slang-euphemism, the "little boys' room"—with "Please Mrs. Henry" suggesting a little-boy vulnerability on the narrator's part)

> I'm a good ol' boy
> But I bin sniffin' too many eggs

(farting)

> Talkin' to too many people
> Drinkin' too many kegs
> Please, Mrs. Henry, Mrs. Henry please!
> Please, Mrs. Henry, Mrs. Henry please!
> I'm down on my knees

(that last line not only enforcing the picture of his asking but also emphasizing his desperation to get there)

> An' I aint got a dime

(you have to put a dime in the slot) ... And so on and so on (every line fits), right down to

> I'm starting to dream
> My stool's gonna squeak

(stool=turd)

> If I walk too much farther
> My crane's gonna leak

(penis is gonna leak)

Look Mrs. Henry

(a cry of increased, ultimatum-pitched desperation)

There's only so much I can do.

But of course, though it's nice and—unlike the incest theory on *Tears of Rage*—doesn't actually spoil the song, maybe that interpretation is really just a load of ...

3. THE ANCIENT JEWISH TEXTS THEORY

I have nothing against this theory at all—I have nothing against ancient (or modern) Jewish texts—except that it's obvious nonsense to claim that Dylan *can't* be understood without a specialist knowledge of the subject. Such a knowledge might get you something *more* from Dylan's work (just as I'd get rather *less* from his work if I knew nothing about pop music, or about English literature); but getting more and getting less is very different from Understanding and Not Understanding. What's involved isn't a code, it's creative writing.

Beyond that, I can't make much comment. The Cabbala is a secret system of theology, metaphysic and magic, a pantheistic doctrine derived from Neo-Platonism and Neo-Pythagoreanism which, in interpreting the Bible, takes advantage of the fact that each Hebrew letter stands for a number and which attaches a mystic significance to numbers.

Dylan's use of numbers—*Highway 51*, *Highway 61*, *Rainy Day Women Nos. 12 & 35*, the fifth daughter on the twelfth night, the first father, the second mother with the seventh son—may well be deliberately synchronized in some way to the system of the Cabbala. But on the other hand alternative explanations appear to make just as much sense, even if they're less mysterious.

Highway 51 would take Dylan "from up Wisconsin way" (relatively near to Minnesota, his home-state) down the St. Louis-Memphis-Mississippi blues country right to New Orleans. Highway 61 runs down a similar vertical, from Minneapolis, a little further west than 51, and dips through Missouri and Arkansas en route to, again, New Orleans. As for *Rainy Day Women Nos. 12 & 35*, well, they're nice numbers to put together regardless of symbolic potential—like the numbers littered down the lines of the unreleased *Barbed Wire Fence*. The niceness could be their sole *raison d'être*. "The fifth daughter on the twelfth night" noticeably re-uses 5 and 12, which might tend to confirm some special meaning; but you don't need specialist knowledge to see that "the first father" means God—and indeed the song begins explicitly enough with God addressing Abraham.

4. THE DRUGS IS ALL THERE IS THEORY

This theory doesn't assess the importance of drugs to Dylan's vision or as a source of imagery for expressing that vision. It confines itself here (if "confines" is the right word) to proposing that Dylan's songs are very often dominantly *about* drugs. It runs like this (only more so), from plausible references down to barrel-scraping absurdities:

The first and obvious drugs song is *Mr. Tambourine Man*. The fairly explicit chorus comes first after a verse that tells us of the deadness of Dylan's old, straight world. (*My Back Pages*, the song from the previous album in which he renounces his explicit political world, is laden with images of death: "spoke from my skull", "ancient history/Flung down by corpse evangelists".)

The chorus of *Mr. Tambourine Man* leads then into the celebratory pleas for initiation:

> Take me on a trip upon your magic swirlin' ship
> My senses have bin stripped, my hands can't feel to grip . . .
> I'm ready to go anywhere, I'm ready for to fade
> Into my own parade; cast your dancin' spell my way,
> I promise to go under it.

The chorus comes back, is succeeded by an impressionistic portrait/encouragement for others, is repeated again and again leads back (so that the words, as well as the music, are in a way circular—as of course is the symbol, the tambourine, itself) to the initiatory supplication:

> Then take me disappearing through the smoke-rings of
> my mind

(circles again)

> Down the foggy ruins of time, far past the frozen leaves,
> The haunted, frightened trees, out to the windy beach
> Far from the twisted reach of crazy sorrow
> Yes, to dance beneath the diamond sky with one hand
>   waving free
> Silhouetted by the sea, circled by the circus sands

(and again)

> With all memory and fate driven deep beneath the waves
> Let me forget about today until tomorrow

And then, for the last time, the chorus returns.

That song came out on the fifth album—"Bringing It All Back Home"—and signed the way to the two which followed and which came from a Dylan well into the drugs scene, using its slang with a strange and tugging eloquence. On "Highway 61 Revisited" the drugs songs are *From A Buick 6*, *It Takes A Lot To Laugh, It Takes A Train To Cry*, *Like A Rolling Stone*, *Barbed Wire Fence* (unreleased but recorded at the same time—and a great piece of rock music), *Subterranean Homesick Blues* and the tremendous *Just Like Tom Thumb's Blues*.

From A Buick 6 boasts a graveyard woman who is a "junk yard angel". The second verse, using the mainlining slang of pipes, rivers and highways (i.e. veins), runs:

> Well when the pipeline gets broken and I'm
> Lost on the river bridge
> I'm cracked up on the highway and
> On the water's edge
> She comes down the thruway
> Ready to sew me up with thread

and the song carries the simple complementary chorus

> Well if I fall down dyin' you know she's
> Bound to put a blanket on my bed.

The same slang—railroads, like rivers and highways, can always stand for veins—get utilized heavily in *It Takes A Lot To Laugh, It Takes A Train To Cry*.

In *Like a Rolling Stone* we find "the mystery tramp" and

the slightly menacing "Say, do you want to, make a deal"; in *Subterranean Homesick Blues* we find a lot more.

> Johnny's in the basement
> Mixin' up the medicine

and the pusher,

> The man in the coon-skin cap
> By the big pen
> Wants eleven dollar bills
> You only got ten.

And so on, and so on.

In *Barbed Wire Fence* perhaps as elsewhere "the woman I got" is a drug, the love of his life:

> This woman I got she's, killing me alive
> She's makin' me into an old man and man I'm not even twen'y five!

More explicitly, the song includes this:

> The Arabian doctor come in 'n' gives me a shot
> But he wouldn't tell me what it was that I got.

This idea is echoed and developed in *Just Like Tom Thumb's Blues*:

> I cannot move, my fingers are all in a knot
> I don't have the strength t' get up an' take another shot
> And my best friend my doctor won't even say what it is I've got.

There are two released versions of this song by Dylan—the quiet and reflective version on the "Highway 61 Revisited" album and a recording from his concert in Liverpool in May 1966, released as the B-side of the *I Want You* single. This second version is a supreme underlining of the drugs milieu—an aching, eloquent, stretched-out treatment, with swirling, free music against a desperate voice that squeezes every word and tugs it out like an emptied syringe.

The drug emphasis doesn't just run through the verse

part-quoted above. It weighs in at the very beginning. The first line of the song runs

> When you're lost in the rain in Juarez

—which is ambiguous: the "rain" being a term of the heroin effect of things dissolving/melting/falling in front of your eyes. The last verse takes up this lostness—which every other verse has also illustrated in disconnected episodes—and gives a summary of the whole story:

> I started out on burgundy
> But soon hit the harder stuff
> Everybody said they'd stand
> Behind me when the game got rough
> But the joke was on me
> There was nobody even there to call my bluff
> I'm going back to New York City
> I do believe I've had enough.

But Dylan hadn't had enough. "Blonde On Blonde" is at least equally drug-orientated. I've heard it claimed that every verse of *Memphis Blues Again* is soaked in it. Certainly the chorus evokes a connected feeling of take-me-outa-here—and thereby echoes the more innocent *Mr. Tambourine Man*.

Things get hardest in verse seven—and by this time Dylan is a long way from the magic swirling ship of *Mr. Tambourine Man*, with its promise of dancing under diamond skies "far from the twisted reach of crazy sorrow". The gap is emphasized by contrasting the reassuring circularity of *Tambourine Man* with the plunging straight line that *Memphis Blues Again* takes as its structural shape:

> Now the rainman gave me two cures
> And then he said, jump right in
> The one was Texas medicine
> The other was just railroad gin
> And like a fool I mixed them
> An' it strangled up my mind
> An' now people just get uglier
> And I have no sense of time.

240

At the end of the song, he leaves us with this moral-of-the-story-self-portrait:

> ... here I sit so patiently
> Waiting to find out what price
> Ya have to pay to get out of
> Going through all these things twice
> Oh! Mama! Is this *really* the end
> To be stuck inside of *Mobile* with the
> Memphis *Blues* again

Rainy Day Women Nos. 12 & 35 is at least as explicit, but a contrast. The tone has the opposite of dark undercurrents. The music and the tune make clear the mood and the device of the pun is just as light-hearted. It's ultra-simple and runs like this:

> They'll stone you when you're ...
> But I would not feel so all alone:
> Everybody must get stoned!

The other drug-laced songs on "Blonde On Blonde" return us to the more diverse slang and to imagery. There are direct statements, though these are rare—"your Spanish manners and your mother's drugs" in *Sad-Eyed Lady Of The Lowlands*; the peddler in *Visions of Johanna*; Baby's amphetamine in *Just Like A Woman*. But with those same songs we are back in Dylan style. *Sad-Eyed Lady Of The Lowlands* ends each chorus with this:

> My warehouse eyes, my arabian drums
> Should I leave them by your gate? Or,
> Sad-eyed lady, should I wait?

"Warehouse eyes" evokes the dilated pupils and the exaggerated taking-in function a trip produces; "arabian drums" means amphetamines, the "drums" evoking the racing heartbeat and that "arabian" of course echoing the "doctor" of *Barbed Wire Fence*.

With *Visions of Johanna* and *Just Like A Woman* we are back with "the rain" and in *One Of Us Must Know* (*Sooner Or Later*) back with the "snow". The first of these songs has Louise holding "a handful of rain/Tempting you to defy it"; the second—as in *Just Like Tom Thumb's Blues*—has the singer "lost inside the rain"; in the third, he explains to the girl the song addresses that "I couldn't see when it started snowin'".

Another girl not a million miles from the drugs scene is
Absolutely Sweet Marie:

> Well your railroad gate you know I just can't jump it ...
> Well I waited for you inside of the frozen traffic ...
> Well six white horses

(consignment of hard drugs)

> that you did promise
> Were finally delivered ...
> The Persian drunkard

(cf. the Arabian doctor again?)

> he follows me.

(If you take up that "follows me" and link it to the "six white
horses" you are back to Dylan's *first* album and the older drugs
world of the blues men whose songs he was at that time singing.
In *Highway 51 Blues* he sings

> I got six white horses followin' me
> An' there's six white horses followin' me
> Waitin' on my buryin' ground.)

After the "Blonde On Blonde" album came a number of relevant
songs from the 1967 unreleased Basement Tape: *Nothing Was
Delivered*; *The Mighty Quinn*; *Please Mrs. Henry*; *This Wheel's
On Fire*; *Too Much Of Nothing*; *Yea Heavy & A Bottle Of Bread*;
and *You Aint Goin' Nowhere*.

By this time, though, the evidence is getting thinner, and the
most interesting of it suggests that drugs were becoming, like
explicit politics before them, a subject for renunciation.

On *Yea Heavy & A Bottle Of Bread* he says:

> ... pull that drummer out from behind that bottle
> Bring me m' pipe ...

which suggests—if it suggests anything—a headlong rush back to
soft-drugs-only: a return, perhaps, towards Burgundy.

Too Much Of Nothing is pertinent simply by its title, which,
taken in a drugs context, signals another distinct cooling off.
Perhaps the song's chorus, too, carries the renunciation message:

Say hullo to Valerie
Say hullo to Marian
Send them all my salary
On the waters of oblivion.

Certainly that *could* suggest an offer of help to get addict-friends
unhooked. And "Valerie" and "Marian", coupled like that, does
manage—though I couldn't say why it does—to suggest that the
people involved are losers.

Similarly, in *This Wheel's On Fire*, "he" wants to stop "her"
from fixin' (Fixin' to die??): he says "I was going to confiscate
your lace"—"lace" being, like the "tape" in *Memphis Blues Again*,
used to bind the arm that gets injected. The conviction—which is
hostility to drugs by now—implied by that very definite and
authoritative "confiscate" goes aptly with the somewhat dire
warning in the chorus of the song:

Just notify my next of kin that
This wheel shall explode.

Then there is the conversation-song *Nothing Was Delivered*—
a conversation between verse and chorus, between the would-be
scorer who has had a bum deal and the pusher-who-isn't-really-a-
pusher. The former, hard-edged, slow, inarticulate, a little paranoid,
demands his fair deal with empty threats. The latter, with exactly
the kind of bland compassion we now associate sometimes with
Dylan himself, replies with the simple case for *renouncing* "deals",
fair or otherwise, from there on in:

Verse: Nothing was delivered
But I can't say I sympathize
With what your fate is going to be
Yes, for telling all those lies
Now you must provide some answers
For what you sell has not been received
And the sooner you come up with those answers
The sooner you can leave.
Chorus: Nothing is better, nothing is best:
Take heed of this and get plenty of rest.

And the music accentuates the contrast very simply. The verse
is hesitant, a bit jerky, rather tired—the chorus is calm, confident,

soaring and smooth, and set to a very *logical* fragment of melody.

All the same, if Dylan is by this point arguing for, or at least announcing his own, renunciation, he still allows himself lapses. In *Please Mrs. Henry* he asks that lady:

> Why don'cha look my way 'n'
> Pump me a few?!

and *The Mighty Quinn,* in the context of his other work, could be another of Dylan's pushers, happy in his job and generally welcome:

> Ev'rybody's in despair
> Ev'ry girl and boy
> But when Quinn and Eskimo gets here
> Ev'rybody's gonna jump for joy

and perhaps also the last line of the last verse is not, after all, "doze" but "dose":

> There's someone on everyone's toes
> But when Quinn the Eskimo gets here
> Ev'rybody's gonna wanna —

The Basement Tape song which the Byrds cut as a single, *You Aint Goin' Nowhere,* is just as big a lapse from the renunciation position, despite the possible implications of the title—and with this song, in fact, we're back to the old hypodermic language:

> Rain won't lift
> Gate won't close

The "gate" is the puncture; when it "won't close" it means the bleeding won't stop. And the chorus? (All the Basement Tape songs have a chorus—a thing Dylan tended to avoid in the earlier years of his composing.) It runs like this:

> Whoo-ee! ride me high!
> Tomorrow's the day my bride's gonna come
> Uh huh, are we gonna fly
> Down in the easy chair!

"High"-flying in an armchair? He has to be on a trip.

All this may vary a lot in plausibility, but at least the songs so far covered are from the years ('65–7) when Dylan was known

244

to be moving very fast—his years of frantic confusion. In other words, they're from the years when drugs and Dylan are most likely to have come together heavily. In 1966 he told *Playboy* he wouldn't advise anybody to use hard drugs (which isn't, especially for someone with Dylan's position, the same as saying he'd advise anybody not to) but that "opium and hash and pot—now those things aren't drugs: they just bend your mind a little. I think everybody's mind should be bent once in a while." In 1969 he explained to *Rolling Stone* that when he'd been on the road (which, concentratedly, was 1965–66: that was the heavy period) he was on drugs, on "a lot of things. A lot of things just to keep me going, you know? ... I had to start dealing with a lot of different methods of keeping myself awake, alert ... And I don't want to live that way any more."

After that period came the big pause, which began with an after-touring rest and was extended, so the official story goes, by his motorcycle accident. It seems just as likely that during this time Dylan was "silent" because he was undergoing a drugs cure course. Any summer in Europe you'll meet Americans on vacation who claim to know some nurse who worked at some addiction centre where Dylan took his cure. And if you like, you can add to that a kind of "ah! so!" from the fact that his long-time friend Johnny Cash is an ex-heroin addict.

It doesn't matter a tinker's fart, of course, to Dylan's art, but it does have some relevance to the drugs-is-all-there-is theory. It even makes it plausible when this theory's supporters widen its scope a little and go on beyond these middle-'60s years to the time of "John Wesley Harding".

Dylan renouncing, warning people off, can be said to surface again on this album, in *As I Went Out One Morning*. The italics here are mine, but should make the point:

> I spied the fairest damsel
> That ever did walk in chains
> I offered her my hand
> She took me *by the arm*
> *I knew that very instant*
> *She meant to do me harm*.

But the trouble is that besotted with the theory, or maybe just with *having* a theory, its supporters then extend it wildly in both directions—forward so that it stretches all the way up to the last track on "Nashville Skyline" (and probably, by now, on through to "New Morning" also) and backwards through all his early albums.

Still on "John Wesley Harding", you see, there's that old faithful hypodermic jargon back on the second side's *Dear Landlord*:

> When that steamboat whistle blows ...

On "Nashville Skyline", you just aint bin listening if you haven't found the drug talk on *Country Pie, I Threw It All Away, Lay, Lady, Lay*, and *Tonight I'll Be Staying Here With You*. Taking those in reverse order, you get:

> I can hear that whistle blowin'
> I can hear that station-master too

and:

> Whatever colours you have in your mind
> I'll show them to you

(with my drugs)

> and you'll see them shine

(when you're high) and:

> Once I had ...
> ... rivers that ran through every day

and:

> Saddle me up a big white goose ...
> Tie me on 'er an' turn me loose ...

(get me a large fix of cocaine)

> Little Jack Horner's got nothin' on me

(Jack=fix).

I've been told too that when, at the beginning of *To Be Alone With You*, Dylan says to Bob Johnson, the producer, "Is it rolling, Bob?" that is *really* Johnny Cash (still in the studio after his duet on *Girl From The North Country*) asking Bob *Dylan* whether the drug he's just taken is starting to take effect.[1]

The theory goes rushing back to the "Freewheelin' Bob Dylan" album too. The version of *Girl From The North Country* on *that* includes the line "If you go when the snowflakes fall" which, as ever, means not actual snow (that would be too, too, naïve) but cocaine. And in fact there's an early recording, never released, of Dylan singing the standard *Cocaine* with its specific refrain:

Cocaine—
All around ma brain—

Then there's the six white horses (already mentioned) on *Highway 51 Blues* and innumerable songs about highways, railways, rivers and inclement weather.[2]

But by this time, the theory is in total collapse. Every folk singer/bluesman cuts a version of *Cocaine,* just as every night club singer does *Bye Bye Blackbird*. It's just one of those things. And in the context of Dylan's early work, highways really are highways. Those songs are from the traditional-hobo-Guthrie world, not the modern urban junk-yard.

NOTES

[1]The suspicion of a drugs element on "Nashville Skyline"—a suspicion largely encouraged by *hearing* the album when mildly stoned —can, however, also be "explained" biographically. i.e. Dylan had earlier pursued a systematically severe policy of drugs-use—enough to go far beyond that dabbling stage which necessitates repeated use of soft drugs to recall a stoned mood. Dylan had gone far enough to have assimilated any drug pay-off into his everyday range of perceptions, so that when producing relaxed, informal work like that on the "Nashville Skyline" album, such a range of perceptions automatically obtains—in contrast to the determinedly ascetic "sobriety" of "John Wesley Harding".

(The work on the basement-tape recorded between "Blonde On Blonde" and "Harding" is very interesting in this respect—interesting, in fact, beyond the scope of this Theories Chapter. Its songs form a very clear link between the two radically different albums. They have the same highly serious, earnest sense of a quest for salvation which characterizes the "John Wesley Harding" work, and at the same time they are soaked in the blocked confusedness of the earlier LP. Thus *Tears Of Rage,* for example, is an almost exact half-way-house between a song like *One Of Us Must Know (Sooner Or Later)* and, say, *I Dreamed I Saw St. Augustine.*)

So with "Nashville Skyline", the hint of drugginess comes back —back into Dylan's jokes, for instance, in the song *Country Pie*. Yet obviously, in no instance does it form a central purposive impulse and the references to drugs are kept strictly at a name-dropping level ("Little Jack Horner got nothin' on me! ") and never get anywhere near being a *raison d'être* for any of the album's songs.

²including: *Baby I'm In The Mood For You*; *Ballad For A Friend*; *Black Crow Blues*; *Bob Dylan's Dream*; *Chimes Of Freedom*; *Down The Highway*; *Farewell*; *I'll Keep It With Mine*; *It's All Over Now, Baby Blue*; *Honey Just Allow Me One More Chance*; *Let Me Die In My Footsteps*; *Long Time Gone*; *Man Of Constant Sorrow*; *Paths Of Victory*; *Poor Boy Blues*; *Quit Your Low Down Ways*; *Ramblin' Gamblin' Willy*; *Rocks & Gravel*; *Standing On The Highway*; *Talkin' New York*; *Tomorrow Is A Long Time*; *Train-A-Travelin'*. For more information on where these songs crop up, see Appendices A–C.

8

Lay Down Your Weary Tune: Acid, Mysticism and Self Portrait

Steven Goldberg's thesis that Dylan is a mystic, and that the mystical experience "pervades all that Dylan has written in the past six years",[1] was left out of the Theories chapter because it deserves more consideration than inclusion there would have permitted. It also needs linking to a more inward approach to drugs than the Theories chapter offered.

Drugs and mysticism go together in the West simply because most of us are far from "natural" mystics. We need drugs to open Blake's doors of perception (as the title of Huxley's exploratory book acknowledged). The very word "high" suggests the connection—to be high all the time would be to hold on always to a transcendent vision. It is being high, not the brute possession of drugs, which totalitarian law-and-order should make illegal, because as it is their Dream Police let the Blakes through the net.

Dylan is not a natural visionary in the sense that Blake is. Being an artist, he has vision beyond the scope of most of us, but that vision has not encompassed mysticism, as Goldberg says it has, unaided. There is plenty of evidence of everyday concerns in his work—his early self-immersion in the blues, his absorbed concern for music generally, and his songs of socio-political comment: songs full of the signs of competitive ego, surface ideology and Western logic, and infused with Old Testament concepts of vengeance. Dylan's mysticism must have come through drugs.

It follows that, to agree with Goldberg's assertion that Dylan "is a mystic", you don't have to claim him as a Blakeian genius or imply that his mind is essentially Eastern and thereby cut off utterly, in spirit, from the minds of the overwhelming majority of his audience. Goldberg, however, does support that last implication. He must, he says, "admit to scepticism concerning how many of Dylan's youthful followers have even the vaguest conception of what he is singing about". But Goldberg doesn't even mention drugs—yet for Dylan "the mystical experience" can also be called "the acid experience", and more than a small minority of his followers have been through that. In the context of Goldberg's theme, drugs keep Dylan close to his audience. The West has a million mystics now.

This sort of claim provokes more in the way of antagonism than abhorrence at the prospect of mass drug addiction explains. We, who think ourselves so much finer than the Victorians, adhere still to their mistrust of the painless and the instant—and yet we adhere so inconsistently. We still like to believe in "love at first sight"; we accept as valid the instant conversion of Paul on the road to Damascus; we trust photographs which snatch up scenes and situations in a fraction of a second; and yet we have learnt to use the label "instant" as a derogatory term—even where it misleads and oversimplifies to use it at all.

Acid only works "instantly" in that it clarifies: what it clarifies is a wealth of experience and feeling acquired as slowly as life itself unfolds, assembled and blended gradually over the years.

Huxley's idea as to the way such a drug works seems compellingly plausible. He suggests that we operate "normally" with a brain that filters the information we receive, obscuring much of the actual, so that we glean only a narrow apparition of reality. For Huxley, mescalin rolled back the filter. Acid appears emphatically to do the same. It is in this sense that it clarifies: it allows the receipt of perceptions and the distillation of experience unwarped by the blinkers of the everyday brain.

What Goldberg urges as the broad outline of Dylan's mystical vision corresponds closely to what are apparently common denominators in many people's unfiltered worlds. It is in this context that Goldberg's article holds such interest: in this context that it makes sense for him to attribute "the mystical experience" to Dylan.

He writes of Dylan's "preparing to become an artist in the Zen sense" and explains:

... he was searching for the courage to release his grasp on all the layers of distinctions that give us meaning, but, by virtue of their inevitably setting us apart from the life-flow, preclude our salvation. All such distinctions, from petty jealousies [and

Dylan warns us of those in *I Am A Lonesome Hobo*] and arbitrary cultural values to the massive, but ultimately irrelevant, confusions engendered by psychological problems, all the endless repetitions [when "you're sick of all this repetition/ Won't you come see me Queen Jane", Dylan sings elsewhere] that those without faith grasp in order to avoid their own existence—all of these had to be released.

Acid releases. The barriers and masks we construct in "coping" with our "psychological problems" drop away. We release our grasp.

Goldberg's article continues:

The strength, the faith, necessary for this release was ... a major theme of Dylan's for ... three years. In *Mr. Tambourine Man*, an invocation to his muse, he seeks the last bit of will necessary for such strength.

That seems at once pertinent and yet unfaithful to the mood of that song. Dylan is not, in *Mr. Tambourine Man*, asking for the willpower needed to give him "the strength, the faith": he has the faith already. It shines through the song with a celebratory optimism directed at what he anticipates finding upon the "magic swirling ship". Yet the very next line of the song shows the pertinence of Goldberg's commentary, as Dylan sings "my senses have bin stripped".

But why, having reached this point, does Goldberg still not mention drugs? Why hide behind that vague phrase "an invocation to his muse"? It is more than obvious that in *Mr. Tambourine Man*, drugs are the focus of Dylan's "invocation".

The acid-mystic equation is strengthened further when Goldberg goes on to discuss Dylan with respect to form. Here:

Dylan faces the same problems that face all artists. His creations must give form and order to apparent chaos. In an attempt to catch the tune of a universal melody, mere awareness of the melody is not enough. For we all possess the potential to hear the tune; many of us do hear it but are incapable of communicating even a hint of its beauty. Only a supreme talent can hope to translate the experience into art. It is not enough for the poet or composer merely to relay random sounds, for such sounds

251

have beauty only in their universal context. The artist must create a new form on a smaller scale that, if it will not mirror the holy chord, will at least provide harmony for it. Dylan is like the chess grand master; there is one correct way to play chess, but this way is far too complicated for any person or computer to comprehend. So the master does not attempt merely to extract a few moves from a plan he can know but cannot understand: he creates his own imperfect strategy with its own imperfect form, in order to suggest a chord that can only be sensed.

Vague and even irritating though that might be, with its telling mixed metaphors, it does, paradoxically, make "clear" Goldberg's conception: a conception which is badly served by language.

But it isn't only that such things as his language hints at correspond convincingly to the vision that acid can bring. Such a correspondence must, in the end, drop into the background. Mystic or not, acid-head or not, Dylan the man makes no odds to his art—that has to stand up alone. The main reason for paying attention to Goldberg's article is that his comments can illuminate Dylan's work, not his mind.

On the "Highway 61 Revisited" album, for instance, Goldberg offers a refreshingly positive commentary:

Goldberg writes:

By the time Dylan wrote the songs that were to appear ... [on this album] his talent was rapidly achieving parity with his vision. He now felt more at home with that vision and was less obsessed with detailing its every aspect. This enabled him to return partially to the subject of man. About the only redeeming virtue of Dylan's pre-visionary songs had been an attractive empathy towards the outsider. While Dylan was not to achieve the complete suffusion of vision with compassion until "John Wesley Harding", in "Highway 61 Revisited" he did begin to feel that the eternally incommunicable nature of the religious experience did not render human contact irrelevant. If his attentions were not loving, at least he was attempting to reconcile man's existence with his vision. ... *Like A Rolling Stone*, which is probably Dylan's finest song and most certainly his quintessential work, is addressed to a victim who has spent a lifetime being successfully seduced by the temptations that enable one to avoid facing his own existence.

Goldberg goes on:

Dylan's poetic talents are at their zenith in "Blonde On Blonde". Vision overwhelms him less than before, and he concentrates on finding peace through the kinds of women he has always loved: women of silent wisdom, women who are artists of life, women who neither argue nor judge but accept the flow of things.

Dylan had suggested the premise of this album in *Queen Jane Approximately* on "Highway 61 Revisited" ... here one finds not only Dylan's everpresent sense of irony and humour, but also his use of overlapping levels of meanings. As one enters this song more and more deeply he becomes aware first of its concern with the fashionable ennui that periodically affects us all, then its representation of disgust with oneself and the games he thinks he must play, and—finally—its subtle description of the endless repetition to which so many of us chain ourselves.

Visions of Johanna ... and *Memphis Blues Again* ... fuse all the themes we have discussed so far and indicate Dylan's imminent discovery that the mystical experience must give way to a life infused with mysticism and compassion, lest even the mystical experience be perverted into an excuse for evasion.

There are no "messages" in Dylan's song; neither is there ideology. The flight of a supreme imagination, the ability to tap into the highest levels of truth, preclude the artist's accepting the simplistic artificiality that is necessary for ideology's goal of widespread acceptance. If an artist is capable of no greater vision than the rest of us, then of what value is he?

Goldberg's ideas force him to dismiss far too easily what he calls "Dylan's pre-visionary songs", but much of his commentary seems both acute and honestly appreciative—and seems particularly so when he comes to deal with Dylan's seventh (and greatest) album:

Goldberg writes:

In "John Wesley Harding", Dylan reiterates his belief that compassion is the only secular manifestation of the religious experience; any code which demands more than pure compassion is generated in the imperfection of experience and does not flow only from a vision of God. Indeed, while change in Dylan's universe is the natural form of egotism: it is an individual's

253

setting himself apart from the flow ... "John Wesley Harding" is not a political philosophy and our attempting to view it as such is to drain it of the wisdom it has to offer. This album is Dylan's supreme work; it is his solution to the seeming contradiction of vision and life. His vision continues to preclude a political path to salvation, but finally overcomes the exclusion of humanity that had plagued his previous visionary songs ... the creative manifestations of a life infused with God, gentleness and compassion replaces bitterness and cynicism. Where once there was confusion, now there is peace. Dylan has paid his dues. He has discovered that the realization that life is not in vain can be attained only by an act of faith ... To the children of Pirandello, drowning in their ennui and relativism, Dylan sings:

> There must be some way out of here
> Said the joker to the thief
> There's too much confusion
> I can't get no relief ...
>
> No reason to get excited
> The thief he kindly spoke
> There are many here among us
> Who feel that life is but a joke
>
> But you and I we've been through that
> And this is not our fate
> So let us not talk falsely now
> The hour is getting late

The only way in which any of us can hope to play the thief, can ignite the faith of another and rob him of his confusion, is through love and compassion. For better or worse, all wisdom is eventually distilled into a few lines; even the unfathomable mysteries of the Bible must finally reside in the compassion of the Golden Rule. Dylan concludes *Dear Landlord* with a prayer for true compassion ...

Dylan's art is capable of igniting ... faith. In any age that is a considerable artistic achievement; in the lonely world of the contemporary young, it would seem almost a miracle.

To me, however, the most interesting part of Goldberg's article in his citing of *Lay Down Your Weary Tune* as a signal of Dylan's changing from politics to mysticism.

This song was published in 1964—the year of the "Another Side Of" album, which also had a signal-song, *My Back Pages*. But Dylan's recording of *Lay Down Your Weary Tune* has never been released (except on bootleg tapes).

It isn't amazingly astute of Goldberg to point it out as signalling some change—a song more strikingly different from Dylan's earlier output would be near impossible to imagine. All the same, it's a song that has received less attention than almost any other in the whole of Dylan's repertoire, so that it's of interest that Goldberg should focus on it at all. And no other song could enforce, for me, so strong a sense of the acid-mystic equation's validity. Goldberg cites it in terms of mysticism; I would cite it as Dylan's first acid song—the first concentrated attempt to give a hint of the unfiltered world, and a supremely successful *creation*. Goldberg refers elsewhere in his article to Dylan's having "heard the universal melody". Nothing could better substantiate the spirit of such a claim than *Lay Down Your Weary Tune*—one of the very greatest and most haunting creations in our language.

What strikes home immediately is its distance from what we know as acid-rock music. There is more here than the evocation of a feeling or mood: the song's chorus posits a philosophy through compassionate incantation and the verses deal with an enchanted existence, wholly realized.

The tune, in A Major, runs through a simple 14-bar structure which, after its initial chorus statement, is repeated nine times—though always with delicate variation.

By the device of having one self-renewing tune to serve both chorus and verses, Dylan adds to the sense of unity which covers the whole song, and its images, as Harunobu's umbrella shields his lovers in the snow. We find enforced an impression of perfect balance not only between verse and chorus but between the opposites focused by the words—between the night that has gone and the morning announced by its breeze; between the trees and the earth to which their leaves descend; between the ocean and the shore; between the rain that sings and the listening winds.

The melody seems to entwine itself around us, in allegiance to the associations of "wove", "strands", "waves", "unwound", "unbound", and "winding strum" in the lyric. And by its very impingement as a strong melody—a melody that seems all-pervading—it urges the felicity of Dylan's analogies between nature's effects and the sounds of musical instruments. As it flows through each line, with a graceful and liquid precision, the melody nurtures and sustains in us an awareness of how involving and creative such analogies are made to be. The tune, in fact, offers itself as an embodiment of "the river's mirror"; its water smooth does indeed run like a hymn.

In contrast, the solo guitar accompaniment involves itself less with the verses than with the chorus. Based on the three simple chords of A, D and E, it does offer a strength in its strings. Paradoxically, it achieves this strength through strumming: and this maintains a rhythm that is at once flexible—responsive to Dylan's voice—and insistent—almost marching (as on a pilgrimage)—in its beat.

It's only necessary to say of Dylan's voice on this track that, expressive as ever of distilled, unspecified experience, it displays and utilizes interpretatively a fine sensibility, totally engaged. Handled by anyone else, it would not be the same song.

If only Dylan's recording gives us the complete creation, it's equally pertinent to lay the stress of that assertion elsewhere—to say that the words of the song have a complexity that demands such a voice as Dylan's. In the context of the whole song, the words are as central as the music and the performance.

Never before or since has Dylan created a pantheistic vision—a vision of the world, that is, in which nature appears not as a manifestation of God but as containing God within its every aspect. The nearest Dylan comes to such a view elsewhere—and it isn't really very close—is in *When The Ship Comes In*. There, many aspects of nature are seen as indicators of a deity's feelings: the rocks, sun, sea-gulls and so forth function as signs that God is on Dylan's side. In *Lay Down Your Weary Tune*, though, the pantheistic vision is complete.

Underlying an exhilaration so intense as to be saddening, there is a profound composure in the face of a world in which all elements of beauty are infused with the light of God. Rejecting, here, the Wordsworthian habit of mixing poetry with explicit philosophizing, so that it is explained, in a prose sense, that the divine light shines through everything, Dylan registers the same convic-

tion with true poetic genius—making that dissembled light a felt
presence throughout the song.

Contributing to this achievement is the selection of words which
not only work as images but also as symbols: and the first verse
sets the pattern for this process.

> Struck by the sounds before the sun
> I knew the night had gone

The night, there, is both real and metaphorical: and so is the
morning that follows. Dylan uses the same symbolism in *When The
Ship Comes In* (and that song calls to mind *The Ancient Mariner*
by the supreme English pantheist Samuel Taylor Coleridge), which
looks forward to the triumph of righteousness when

> ... the mornin' will be a-breakin'.

This in turn relates closely to the chorus of *I Shall Be Released:*

> I see my life come shinin'
> From the west unto the east

(where morning breaks)

> Any day now, any day now
> I shall be released.

It is, of course, a conventional metaphor, but a none the less
effective one in the context of the song we're discussing, because
its very conventionality prevents it from obtruding. The song
would be much less powerful if the symbols were not contained
within their corresponding realities—the symbolic within the real
night, and so on.

(A far more original means of expressing the same antithesis
between hope and despair, in *Memphis Blues Again*, cleverly
avoids comparable obtrusiveness by its very centrality to the song:

> Oh! Mama! Can this really be the end:
> To be stuck inside of Mobile

—despair—

> With the Memphis Blues again.)

The morning Dylan sings of in *Lay Down Your Weary Tune* is heralded by a breeze: and again, Dylan accommodates the conventional associations—associations of freshness and change.

The "bugle" at once alters the complexion of the line. It places the morning more specifically—because the bugle is not commonly a secular instrument—within a context of salvation.

In the following verse, this religious complexion is supported by the "organ" with its obvious associations with worship (it is plainly not Al Kooper's electric organ that Dylan is using here). The connotative effect of this support is later confirmed by the "trumpet", by "like a hymn" and "like a harp".

The pantheistic idea is also implicit in the narrator's rejection of all distinctions, which works on more than one level. In the first place, each part of nature focused is given equal weight: to no part is any directly qualitative adjective or adjectival phrase ascribed. The nearest Dylan comes to such ascription is with the "clouds unbound by laws" and the rain that "asked for no applause"—and these confirm the idea of God as an evenly-distributed presence by suggesting a moral gulf between divinity in nature and the reductive inadequacy of man. The perception of this gulf is upheld by the last line of the chorus, which, were the implicit made explicit, would read "No *human* voice can hope to hum".

The song also rejects evaluative distinction between the various facets of nature by uniting them all in the central motif of the orchestra: each "instrument" contributes towards an overall sound; each is concerned with the one divine melody.

This all-important unity is substantiated by a wealth of onomatopoeic words within the song—strum, hum, bugle, drums, crashin', clashed, moaned and smooth. It is further developed, becomes multi-dimensional, because the narrator creates an impression that, in response to this enchanted world, his senses (and therefore, vicariously, ours also) mix and mingle. An open acceptance of Baudelairean *correspondances* is involved.[2]

What, to begin with, constitutes the strength of strings? Their sound? Their physical vibration? Their vertical parallel lines? Their tautness? Their recalling of classical Greece (the lute of Orpheus, the melodious divinity of Jan's irresistible music)?

The *emotion* experienced as dawn appears corresponds to the *sound* of drums: and mingling such as this helps the verse achieve its haunting pull on the listener—an effect far beyond the simple dynamics of alliteration in that

> ... breeze like a bugle blew
> Against the drums of dawn.

"The ocean wild" produces an image of movement—a thing felt as well as seen (and the cadence of that phrase as carried by the melody emphasizes the sensation)—and corresponds not only to the sound but also to the physical act of playing the organ. The correspondence between ocean and organ depends also for its total effect on the similarity of sound between the two words and on the striking antithesis between an ocean's being clean and sharp and an organ's seeming musty and somehow imprecise; yet at the same time the antithesis is resolved by the impression of depth (again, metaphorical as well as real) common to both.

A part of the sense-mingling achieved by the line "the cryin' rain like a trumpet sang" is almost surrealistic. However fleetingly, we get a visual image of the rain becoming a trumpet. This belies the effect of that cryin' because to transform itself (from silver-grey to gold) into a singing trumpet, the rain must pour out, if not upwards, horizontally, like musical notes on a sheet of manuscript. It is no small tribute to Dylan's achievement that we can accept, in passing, this strangeness of effect without finding it a distraction or otherwise inappropriate.

Again, the cadence of the melody works perfectly: the notes that carry the words "rain like a" ascend with a distinctive regularity that enacts the pressing down of consecutive trumpet stops. Not only that, but the "a" is held, extended, so that the "trumpet" emerges on resolving notes and we can accept the image readily because the music that presents it returns us to base. To produce the "trumpet" image on homecoming notes lends it a certain familiarity. The image remains striking, but not incongruous.

The cadence is equally co-operative in the first line of that same verse, where it enacts what the words describe: it allows a graceful unwinding of the voice from the cushioning effect of that "unwound", where the second syllable lingers, in the air, and dissembles into the cascading fall of "beneath the skies".

There is, in fact, not one phrase in the lyric that fails to gain an extra power from the cadence—which shows how delicate and responsive Dylan's variations are within the structure of his "simply" and economical 14-bar melody.

None of these devices depend for their effectiveness on the listener pushing them through the kind of identification-parade which I have attempted above. Being poetic devices, they work inwardly and unseen. The song only demands of its listener the kind of open responsiveness to nuance which allows free play to the overall effect of the work.

I have already suggested that this overall effect is enough to mark out *Lay Down Your Weary Tune* as a major achievement in the poetry of our language. It remains to be added that the song is enriched in another way too: it is strongly reminiscent of the Elven songs that celebrate Lothlórien in Tolkien's *Lord of The Rings*; and there is much in Dylan's vision which corresponds to Tolkien's description of Lothlórien itself.

The sanctuary of the Elves (and, in the story, the temporary refuge of the travellers), Lothlórien is the one domain that Sauron cannot touch, unless he can acquire the

> One Ring to rule them all, One Ring to find them,
> One Ring to bring them all and in the darkness bind them.

Like Dylan's world in *Lay Down Your Weary Tune*, Lothlórien is uniquely beautiful and pastoral. ("Pastoral", of course, is most pointedly applicable to the Dylan song in that conceit which opens the fourth verse. The idea of leaves forsaking the branches—arms—of their first love for the welcoming breast of the earth is a surprising one for Dylan: surprisingly traditional. It seems to have escaped from a poem by, say, Wordsworth, or Thomas Hardy—or even Matthew Arnold.)

Like Dylan's world, too, Lothlórien is a paradise, spiritual because real. Colours and sounds are ennobled and enhanced; and that there is an ethereal quality which caresses everything is no denial of the intense reality. It is an extra quality, endowed by the light—which, though Dylan never mentions it, seems somehow unusual in his world also.

That *Lay Down Your Weary Tune* does echo Tolkien is first apparent when Legolas sings "a song of the maiden Nimrodel, who bore the same name as the stream beside which she lived long ago ... In a soft voice hardly to be heard amid the rustle of the leaves above ... he began:

> An Elven-maid there was of old,
> A shining star by day:
> Her mantle white was hemmed with gold
> Her shoes of silver-grey.
>
> A star was bound upon her brows,
> A light was on her hair
> As sun upon the golden boughs
> In Lorien the fair.
>
> Her hair was long, her limbs were white,
> And fair she was and free;
> And in the wind she went as light
> As leaf of linden-tree.
>
> Beside the falls of Nimrodel,
> By water clear and cool
> Her voice as falling silver fell
> Into the shining pool."

There are nine more verses to that song, but those first four are sufficient to illustrate the echoes. Not only can you hear Dylan's voice breathing the right kind of delicate life into the lines above; not only does that fourth verse, in particular, constitute a similar (if much simpler) sort of writing, as regards mood and focus and technique—but beyond that, it's interesting (perhaps significant, even) that the whole of the Legolas song fits Dylan's tune.

There are less precise connections, but none the less real ones, between the Dylan song and this:

> I sang of leaves, of leaves of gold, and leaves of gold there
>   grew:
> Of wind I sang, a wind there came and in the branches
>   blew.
> Beyond the Sun, beyond the Moon, the foam was on the
>   Sea ...

That is a part of the song of 'Galadriel, tall and white; a circlet of golden flowers ... in her hair, and in her hand ... a harp." And there we come across the similarity that exists even between Dylan's song and Tolkien's prose.

Lastly, it is Tolkien's prose that is of interest—the prose that gives us the description of the land of Lorien, largely through Frodo's eyes. This brings us back, in fact, to Steven Goldberg's thesis and the mystic-acid equation. I am not suggesting that Tolkien took LSD but it remains true that just as Dylan's vision in *Lay Down Your Weary Tune* corresponds closely to Frodo's perception of the land of Lorien, both correspond, in turn, to what an acid vision can offer, by transforming an ordinary world into an earthly paradise:

... Frodo stood awhile still lost in wonder. It seemed to him that he had stepped through a high window that looked on a vanished world. A light was upon it for which his language had no name. All that he say was shapely, but the shapes seemed at once clear cut, as if they had been first conceived and drawn at the uncovering of his eyes, and ancient as if they had endured for ever. He saw no colour but those he knew, gold and white and blue and green, but they were fresh and poignant, as if he had at that moment first perceived them and made for them names new and wonderful. In winter here no heart could mourn for summer or for spring. No blemish or sickness or deformity could be seen in anything that grew upon the earth. On the land of Lorien there was no stain.

He turned and saw that Sam was now standing beside him, looking round with a puzzled expression ... "It's sunlight and bright day, right enough," he said. "I thought that Elves were all for moon and stars: but this is more Elvish than anything I ever heard tell of. I feel as if I was inside a song, if you take my meaning."

... Frodo felt that he was in a timeless land that did not fade or change or fall into forgetfulness ... he laid his hand upon the tree beside the ladder; never before had he been so suddenly and so keenly aware of the feel and texture of a tree's skin and of the life within it. He felt ... the delight of the living tree itself.

... Frodo looked and saw, still at some distance, a hill of many mighty trees, or a city of green towers; which it was he could not tell. Out of it, it seemed to him that the power and light came that held all the land in sway. He longed suddenly to fly like a bird to rest in the green city.

Frodo, like Dylan, stood unwound beneath the skies and clouds unbound by laws: without confusion, in the discovery of release, attuned to the holy chord.

Steven Goldberg contends that Dylan returns to this position from "Nashville Skyline" onwards. Goldberg was writing before the release of "Self Portrait", but his account includes predictions about "the future", and no doubt he'd be happy for his remarks to extend to "Self-Portrait" as much as to "Skyline". This is his concluding paragraph:

> It is only in the light of all that came before that ... "Nashville Skyline" can be truly understood. Perhaps this is a failure of the work; certainly one would think so if he insists that any great work of art must stand alone. Alone, "Nashville Skyline" is a tightly written, cleverly executed series of clichés that would seem to be merely a collection of nice songs by a Dylan who has gotten a bit mentally plump. As the final step in Dylan's search for God, however, it is a lovely paean. Dylan's acknowledgement of the joy of a life suffused with compassion and God. If this does not make the album particularly illuminating for the man who is unaware of Dylan's cosmology, to others it is evidence that he has finally been able to bring it all back home. He has heard the universal melody through the galaxies of chaos and has found that the galaxies were a part of the melody. The essence that Dylan has discovered and explored is a part of him at last. There will be no more bitterness, no more intellectualization, no more explanation. There will only be Dylan's existence and the joyous songs which flow naturally from it.

It seems to me that with *Wigwam* (from "Self Portrait"), and *only* with *Wigwam,* is there any real basis for applying these last remarks of Goldberg's to Dylan's recent work. *Wigwam is* reminiscent of *Lay Down Your Weary Tune.* It does come across as an attempt to create, in a small way ("his own imperfect strategy with its imperfect form", as Goldberg would have it), the music that was merely sensed in the earlier song. Dispensing with words as if because they seem too clumsy, too "unknowing", *Wigwam* glows with an exhilaration and a majesty that is purely musical and yet is music for the spirit and of the spirit—and which corresponds emphatically to the majesty and exhilarated feeling apparent in *Lay Down Your Weary Tune.* Its scintillating choir of brass comes over like a pure, bright light (and that is an inbuilt Baudelairean *correspondance* as impressive as any in the earlier song) that comes from all around. And in this way, *Wigwam* runs parallel to *Lay Down Your Weary Tune* also in taking us back to Frodo's glimpse of Lothlórien quoted earlier—and particularly to that striking sentence "A light was upon it for which his language had no name".

Moreover, taking up another point made by Goldberg—that with "John Wesley Harding" Dylan has arrived at the resolution of the gap between his vision and humanity, discovering, as it were, the bridge of compassion—we can see in *Wigwam* another vital resolution: the bridging of the moral gulf between divine nature and man—the gulf to which, in the midst of its pantheism, *Lay Down Your Weary Tune* pointed. In *Wigwam* a human voice (which is Dylan's mind externalized) *does* hum the tune. And the precise alignment of that voice with the choir of trumpets enforces our impression that the tune is indeed intended as a hint of "the universal melody".

But what of the rest of "Self Portrait"? Like "Nashville Skyline" it does indeed give us "a collection of nice songs". But for me at least, saying more than that involves leaving, not embracing, Goldberg's conclusions.

The difficulty with "Self Portrait" is not the usual one of trying to set down in words responses to experience not readily accessible to words. With "Self Portrait" the problem is to decide what responses need explaining—or even holding on to.

The same problems applied for many people when Dylan took up rock music in the mid-sixties—but the necessary adjustments were comparatively easy to make at that time, in those circumstances. Once you got into rock music, then plainly Dylan's was the best there had ever been; and in any case it was as much a means as an end in itself. It was a logical move—it fitted what was happening outside, amongst the audiences.

For people accustomed by training, and perhaps by inclination too, to check their responses against applied "critical" ideas—for people like me, in other words—the adjustments necessary in coming to terms with "Self Portrait" were very much larger. Dylan is demanding more and almost certainly contributing less with this album.

At first hearing, much of the work is trite, rutted and simplistic: and that, in itself, has enormous and perplexing impact. Here is an apparently third-rate collection of work from a man who, rightly or wrongly, has been given an almost total trust for the past seven or eight years. How should we respond?

There are, of course, people who don't face these difficulties—those who simply listen and enjoy; and Dylan has always been on their side, against classification, with those who, in his view, "know too much to argue or to judge".

All the same, the question "How should we respond?" has been a common one—and it seems to me that those who haven't felt the need to ask it of themselves are those whose concern is disproportionately connected with Dylan's *music*, and not with the other huge factor in his art—the words.

For the rest of us who have long been Dylan listeners, the asking of that first question, "How should we respond?" invites another; because people's trust in Dylan's integrity has been so great, it brings up to consciousness the terrible shadow of doubt that may have been around, submerged, for ages: "What If We Have Been Fooled?"

It's a pretty paranoid query, but it does tend to come up—and so some people "drop" Dylan from "Self Portrait" onwards, just as others have been doing annually with each freshly-directed album since 1964 and the non-Protesting "Another Side Of Bob Dylan".

Others again don't drop Dylan but have to shelve or pervert their own previous conceptions of what Dylan is and what he isn't, in order to make "Self Portrait" fit. And Dylan would be glad of that too.

The result is characteristic. Dylan's "simplest" album provokes more conjecture about its purpose, its value, its omens and its creator than any of his earlier works. There is much more to speculate on in "Self Portrait" than in an album as complex as "Blonde On Blonde". *That* album does not so generally call people's critical equipment into question.

Shall we say, then, that "Self Portrait" is a good album—is of major importance and value in that it *does* make us question so much in ourselves? The shadow surely comes back—for don't we have to smother the feeling that *any kind of bad album from Dylan* would be labelled as good on this account? Dylan, of course, would say that if we didn't screw ourselves up with this useless desire to divide things into good and bad, our problem would not exist. For me at least, screwed up or not, it just isn't that easy. My reactions to the album, after all this time, are still equivocal and contradictory.

None the less, my equivocation has, since the days just after "Self Portrait's" release, at any rate changed *balance*: it is now a question mainly of shaking off the old disapprovals. These still seem to me worth stating, and before offering a more composed critique, I set them out below.

In the first place, it isn't true that, as the reviewers would have it, Dylan shows himself a happy man on the album. It doesn't have a fraction of the warmth of "Blonde On Blonde". The voice that goes back patiently through *Like A Rolling Stone*—Dylan's "quintessential work", as Goldberg calls it—from the Isle of Wight concert, does more than take out the bitterness:

> (scrounging around

instead of

> SCROUNG*ing*!

and

> invisible no-o-ow

instead of

> in VIS*ible now*!)

and replace it with bland and humble understanding. It is the blandness of defeat: and the hoarse, shouted, descending chorus-line that breaks through just once at the end is like a rattling of chains. And this feeling of defeat spreads across everything on the album.

It produces a self-deprecation which damages Dylan's art. What can his *Blue Moon* demonstrate but that he can bring to something mediocre a balancing mediocrity in his handling of it? He seems to be trying to make us believe—presumably to get us off his back—that he is no better a singer than Roy Orbison and no better a composer than the boring and cautious Rogers and Hart.

266

From similar motives, perhaps, Dylan takes no composing credit for *Days of 49*, which the record label puts down as "Traditional". And yes, it is traditional—but only the great artist that Dylan is pretending not to be could have pulled off the brilliant delivery of "And over Jake they held a wake" or drawn out the ironic ambiguity of this:

> They call me a bummer an' a ginsop too
> But what cares I for praise?

And the earlier Dylan would have claimed the credit. (Even Arthur Big Boy Crudup's song *That's All Right, Mama* appears in the Bob Dylan songbooks; and on the first LP, Dylan takes arranger's credit at least for *Man Of Constant Sorrow*, *Pretty Peggy-O* and *Gospel Plow*.)

This self-deprecation is not always as acceptable as on *Days of 49*, however. It eats into the selection of work put on the album, not least in the selection of the Isle of Wight tracks. That concert included some beautiful performances, among them a magnetic *Will Ye Go Lassie* and a fine re-working of *One Too Many Mornings*: yet for "Self Portrait" Dylan chooses no such highlights. He chooses instead a clumsy, hurried, off-hand performance of what's possibly his most trivial song: *The Mighty Quinn*; *Minstrel Boy*, the encore song that was, at the time, clearly intended as a once-only number and which, with the repeated plays an album yields, soon loses its "wit" and grows ponderous; and a version of *She Belongs To Me* that is markedly inferior to the "Bringing It All Back" LP version, to the 1965 BBC-TV version, to the 1966 concerts version, and to the marvellous, introspective version cut at the same time as the "Bringing It All Back Home" album but never issued (except on a bootleg LP). And as these songs appear on "Self Portrait" they don't even recapture that pure liquid sound that they seemed to possess that night at the Isle of Wight Festival.

Much of the rest of the album gives us Dylan, the man who invented the nine-minute rock song and who turned all the assumptions of Tin Pan Alley upside down, accepting all these assumptions wholesale: using all the most obvious popular-music formulae for leading into middle-eights, returning to the tonic note and so on. And going with this is the surely unnecessary *reliance* on sheer numbers of musicians (there are, if you include the back-

267

up singers, fifty of them on the album). Dylan told *Rolling Stone* in 1969 that he had only ever done solo recordings because the right musicians hadn't been available at the right times in the early days—but even if true, that isn't synonymous with saying that if they *had* been available he would have used fifty of them, and relied on them so much. Anyone who has ever appreciated how much music Dylan can suggest on his solo recordings will be only too conscious of what is *missing* because of all the "Self Portrait" musicians.

This self-assassination of power, the corresponding refusal to write any thoughtful lyrics, and the self-portrait in oils that shows a Dylan with sightless, empty eyes—all this testifies to a sense of defeat, not a sense of joy.

Dylan even gives up on the integrity of the packaging. We could, perhaps, have seen this coming from the back cover of "Nashville Skyline", in that it featured that "poem" by Johnny Cash which purported to sum up Dylan and only succeeded in showing up Cash.

> ... And know
> The yield of rend; the break
>   of bend
> The scar of mend
>   I'm proud to say that I
>   know it,
> Here-in is a hell of a poet.
> And lots of other things.
> And lots of other things.

(If only that was consciously a parody of Hemingway.)

The cover of "Self Portrait" is, in some ways, worse, with its unreadably florid script and that back-of-album shot which is conceived and coloured like one of those scenic photographs that pretend to be windows in tarted-up cafés.

The packaging of the album is symptomatic, but doesn't, of course, hold any key. The sense of listless defeat on Dylan's part comes most clearly through his voice. It conveys, especially in the "happiest" songs, a constant impression of a sort of choking caution (just listen, for instance, to the voice on *I Forgot More*) —an impression that Dylan, in complete negation of what Steven

268

Goldberg maintains, has walked, Godlessly, close to "the valley of the shadow of death" and *dare not now explore* beyond the simplistic verities acknowledged by Nashville Tennessee. It is not so much mental plumpness as an exhaustion of courage—as if the Dylan of "Self Portrait" has placed himself under house-arrest because the old Insanity Factory is too close to his gates. And while this kind of rest/retreat is understandable enough in the *man*, it doesn't do much for his art.

Such were the early, largely hostile reactions: and though a shadow remains of them, they seem now unintelligently niggardly. How could the overall impressions have been so warped by prior expectations? Why did so much *worrying* go into initial responses? Why was it not possible simply to recognize that here was another admittedly minor collection of work, like "Nashville Skyline"—but a minor collection capable of yielding a great deal to the relaxed listener? Where the album first seemed too simple, it now seems infinitely complex and subtle—with nuances of performance on Dylan's part more delicate and faultless than ever before. What makes it a *minor* achievement is that it looks backwards, not into the future; that the jokes don't always work (as for instance in the case of those "bom! bom!"'s at the start of *Copper Kettle*); and that the skilled use of language has been almost entirely discarded in favour of the simple joys of music-making—as if any such choice need have been made. Yet for all that, this "minor achievement" offers an incredible richness.

In the first place, "Self Portrait" does *not l*ack warmth—and if "warmth" is any criterion, it's worth remarking that this album offers much more of a glow than the much, and rightly, admired "John Wesley Harding". In the second place, what seems at first like damaging self-deprecation on the album can as plausibly be understood as egolessness. As Bill Damon put it (in *Rolling Stone* magazine, September 3rd, 1970):

With all of its unity and inclusiveness, "Self Portrait" is too complex to have a point of view ... It is Eastern in its egolessness ... Dylan does remind us on this album of all the ways we have known him ... But Dylan's image serves only his music. It is an elusive, chameleon-type image anyway ... Which Dylan is it? Only the song will tell ... [*and the second version of "Alberta" and "Little Sadie" shows that*] there is no way to sing or feel about a story, and the second time around Dylan unbinds us from the moods of the first.

And thus the cover portrait, which, as Geoffrey Cannon says, could be of anyone.

Effectively, it disembodies Dylan; a strategy he's followed in different ways for years now. The empty eyes of the portrait stare at, or maybe past, you ... He will no longer assert his own self. "There is no eye—there is only a series of mouths" said Dylan in 1965.

And apart from all this, it's a nice painting in lots of ways, enjoyable for its colouring and its childlike technique, a relief from image-building photography, and interesting also because—like the painting Dylan did for The Band's first album, "Music From Big Pink"—it owes a lot to the pen-and-ink sketches of Woody Guthrie.[3] Quite a throwback.

On one level, the whole album is a throwback. It is not, as Richard Williams maintained, "an attempt at the Great North American Album", but it is a deliberate package of Golden Oldies, from folk to country to chart-busting pop.

I Forgot More Than You'll Ever Know is a "country classic", and Dylan sings it like Roy Orbison might try to. Among other appearances, the song was featured back in 1962 on the "Sound Of Johnny Cash" album; and a comparison between the Dylan and Cash versions is less than usually unflattering to the latter. On their *Girl From The North Country* duet, Dylan outshines Cash spectacularly: Dylan's voice carrying every scar he's ever sustained, the other stuck together with pebble-dash virility. And the contrast is as marked on their unreleased duet on *One Too Many Mornings*. On *I Forgot More* there is less of a gulf. Cash, as usual, leans heavily on the clichés and breathes heavily in between them; Dylan is more delicate and more judicious, but it's a long way from being his best performance. "Choking caution" really does deaden it.

With another song on "Self Portrait", though, this gulf of contrast between Dylan and Johnny Cash shows up again. *In Search Of Little Sadie* and *Little Sadie* are based on an older song, a song Cash recorded under the name *Transfusion Blues* when he was with the Tennessee Two on the Sun label and which he changed into his *Cocaine Blues* on later CBS recordings (one in a studio, one in front of a prison audience). The story-line of the song has remained much the same—it tells of an escape, an arrest, a trial, a jailing.

This time to call the comparison unflattering to Cash is to be far too kind to him. Where he plods through a tired, lifeless narrative, congealing in his artificial Manliness, Dylan ditches the worst platitudes, transforms others—by his timing—into wit, and fills his narrative with creative idiosyncrasy.

Geoffrey Cannon's review of "Self Portrait" mentions another contrast, too, between the Dylan *Sadie* songs and their Johnny Cash equivalents. He points out that while Cash sings "overtook me down in Juarez, Mexico" (a place, incidentally, mentioned by *Dylan* in more than one earlier song of his) Dylan has

> They overtook me down in Jericho

which gives, says Cannon, "an echo of his persistent references to places of abstracted myth. Cash places the arrest: Dylan puts it anywhere".

At the same time, Dylan's use of "Jericho" provides a clue to something else: one of the little witticisms in the (obviously spontaneous) performance is the way Dylan's voice goes *up* as he sings the word "down—"; and this is exactly what Elvis and the Jordannaires did with the same word in their beautiful version of *Joshua Fit De Battle of Jericho* on the "His Hand In Mine" album of 1961.

The titles Dylan chooses are interesting too. Is it coincidence that he uses so much more energy *In Search Of Little Sadie* than for *Little Sadie* herself? Or is it a deliberate compliance with that cliché which so often happens to be true—to travel hopefully is better than to arrive. Or again, perhaps, Dylan is in effect suggesting the opposite—saying that *In Search Of* is a portrait of his early-days approach (the approach of his first album), a treatment relatively naïve and uncertain, while *Little Sadie* shows the Dylan of experience, no longer searching but thoroughly *au fait*. I prefer *In Search Of*.

In any event, whatever the titles may or may not signify, what both the *Sadie* recordings do is discredit any idea that the "Self Portrait" Dylan is but a shadow of his former selves. *In Search Of* is quite unsingable—yet Dylan is there, unpredictable but right, on every single note, and combining as only he could a self-mockery with a straightforward self-expression. And *Little Sadie* is a triumphant instant revisit.

The other Oldies on the album are Gordon Lightfoot's modern classic *Early Mornin' Rain;* Dylan's *Woogie Boogie*—in that it's one of those tunes that bear the stamp of the late 1950s in general conception and get composed more by the piano, because of the physical facts of its keyboard, than by any particular person; a comparable piece would be *Honky Tonk,* which was a million-seller in the fifties and which, later, Buddy Holly used to fill up an album track innocuously, much as Dylan does with *Woogie Boogie* itself; *Like A Rolling Stone*; *Copper Kettle*; *Gotta Travel On*; *Blue Moon*; Paul Simon's song *The Boxer*; *The Mighty Quinn*; *Take Me As I Am* (*Or Let Me Go*); *She Belongs To Me*; and two of the Everly Brothers' hit songs, *Take A Message To Mary* and *Let It Be Me*.

In concept, Dylan's *Living The Blues* is an Oldie too. It's less like the Guy Mitchell-Tommy Steele hit *Singing The Blues* than people say, but it's far from new. The structure is Tin Pan Alley traditional, and whereas the version Dylan sang on CBS-TV in '69 (a much faster version than the album one) drew heavily and splendidly on Fats Domino pianowork, the "Self Portrait" performance draws correspondingly on Jerry Lee Lewis. Not the Jerry Lee of *Great Balls Of Fire* and *High School Confidential*—though Dylan bows briefly to that in his earlier *Down Along The Cove*—but the Jerry Lee Lewis of his old B-sides and his country work: of *Fools Like Me* and *Cold Cold Heart*.

Neither did *It Hurts Me Too* originate with Dylan. Elmore James did it years and years ago; others, including Mayall (whom Dylan met while on his British tour of 1965), have done it since. Dylan's version is fascinating: in the first place because it seems to provide an example of where Dylan's concern for the *music* as against the words—a characteristic, as already noted, of the whole "Self Portrait" album—leads him near to neglect of his own vocal delivery (as if, having got the *sound* he wanted for his voice, no *interpretative* function was demanded of it). In the second place, *It Hurts Me Too* is fascinating in that, despite being technically of a standard basic structure, it appears to flow on and on in a beautiful free-form that is unimpeded by any structural considerations. It appears such a modest track—it is actually a sizeable achievement, the guitar-work *so* good, and the melody so full of illusions.[4]

Finally, Dylan's own *Belle Isle* ("a model of nonlinear narrative", as Bill Damon called it) must also come into the effective Oldies category. It is deliberately unoriginal in story, language, structure and overall ethos.

This preponderance of Oldies is natural enough, whether or not you accept the album's title straightforwardly and even if a musical autobiography wasn't really necessary to give us a picture. We already knew, from the earlier albums, where Dylan's musical backgrounds lay—and only some of them are brought up to focus by "Self Portrait". But it's nice to have the songs (and that remark, really, when everything else that can be said about the album *has* been said, will remain a fair summary of its significance, for me at least). And it's no surprise to find among them traditional folk material as well as modern country music and pop songs of the not-too-distant past.

Indeed, it's all very methodically set out. *Days of 49* is a Yankee song; *Copper Kettle* is Appalachian (and belongs to the same folk tradition as the old Southern song *I've Been A Moonshiner*, which shares the same theme, and which Dylan recorded—calling it *The Bottle Song*—on a demo tape in about 1962–63); *Belle Isle* comes of a sympathetic understanding of Gallic folk tradition (and in fact there *is* an island called Belle-Ile off the coast of Brittany); and *It Hurts Me Too* captures the essence of traditional country blues.

When Dylan comes to the more modern pieces, he keeps his concern for the songs themselves—he makes no big switch towards honouring singers instead: and this consistency is part of the egolessness. As Bill Damon wrote, "Dylan attains such astonishing unity with the music that in the end it makes little difference who wrote (any of the songs)."

Damon is, I think, right, in that context; but it is of considerable interest to *note* who wrote which songs, and to try to assess why the selection of songs is as it is on "Self Portrait".

I Forgot More seems to have been selected as a tribute to a song-writing formula on which Dylan must have been partly nurtured—his performance, and the arrangement chosen, carry an appropriate tinge of reflective nostalgia. (Almost as if Dylan was expressing his regret that one of the effects of his own earlier writing has been to make the "I Forgot More" song-formula seem so very dilapidated.)

Early Morning Rain is certainly a tribute to Gordon Lightfoot's *writing*. It's clearly a song Dylan would like to have written, and it is out of a due respect for the song that he gives us a version so much finer than Lightfoot's own. He hasn't, in any virtuoso sense, taken it over: *he* adapts to *its* demands completely—and in doing so conjures up a mood he has never dealt in before. Perfect understanding of the poetry of Lightfoot's lines produces an intensely personal kind of reflection, and an appreciative ruefulness lights up simple glimpses, as for instance, the long-held "roar" is made to express the ruefulness and the engines' sound simultaneously; and when he comes to the matching "high" in the line, Dylan seems to hold two notes at once: a low-pitched resonant note that sustains the sound set up by the "r's" in "silver bird" (themselves, of course, extensions of that "roar—") and with it, a lighter sound that gives us the force of meaning of the phrase "on high" itself. Similarly, later in the lyric, his voice *creates* the final take-off of the plane. (Bill Damon's article cites this last instance in illustration of what he calls Dylan's "astonishing unity with the music"; and he illustrates the point also with reference to a line in *Copper Kettle*, where Dylan's voice snaps hollow on the word "rotten" in "Don't use no green or *rotten* wood".) In *Early Mornin' Rain* such instances could be multiplied—as where, in giving us "She's a woman now at last", Dylan's voice enacts an appropriate coming-to-rest. All through the song, in fact, Dylan's delivery has a sensitivity and an intelligence of control that justify the term "perfect". It is a far from *tired* Dylan at work here. He shows us how much the phrase "musically alive" can signify, making *Early Morning Rain* into the great song he must have seen it could be. If Gordon Lightfoot the singer feels outclassed, Lightfoot the composer must feel more than flattered.

Dylan's double-tracked version of Paul Simon's *The Boxer* is far from the same kind of tribute—if indeed it's a tribute at all. Perhaps, like *Blue Moon*, the track on the album that immediately precedes it, it is included just to call a halt to pointless myths of rivalry. Rodgers & Hart songs epitomize what people have liked to consider the very antithesis of Dylan's kind of writing. Perhaps just to put paid to that—because it must seem to him an illusory classifying perspective, and because to do so is a part of the

274

attempt at egolessness—Dylan sings Rodgers & Hart. Similarly, Paul Simon and Dylan are supposed to be locked in mortal artistic combat, the one collecting just as many accolades as the other. So Dylan chooses one of Simon's few unpretentious songs (he could, instead, have picked *Homeward Bound* and tailored *that* to suit him equally well) and made it very clear that, in the words of *Country Pie,* he aint runnin' any race.[5]

Whether such an object-lesson was really called for, and whether it would have occurred but for the fact that Dylan also, presumably, simply *likes The Boxer,* is another matter; in any event, his recording is well worth having, whatever the motive for its inclusion. The performance he gives, with the two voices (one old, one new) apparently wandering apart yet coming together so cleanly on that "and *cut* 'im", shows how Dylan can actively educate, or re-educate, his listener in matters of timing. On a first play, the thing that hits you is what sounds like an incredible amateurishness—a raggedness that could easily be put down to indifference. Given more time, the apparently ragged comes across as the absolutely right, as an intended precision; and thus he revises the listener's idea of what timing can comprise.

Dylan also improves the song, widening its scope at a stroke with the simple single word change from:

> And he carries a reminder
> Of every glove that's laid him down

to:

> Of every blow that's laid him down.

To take account of "every blow" is to glimpse the boxer more inwardly—to comprehend that outside the ring as well as inside it, his life is a series of defeats.

The other thing the same recording proves, once and for all, is that the Dylan voice of 1962-63, the voice used on the "Freewheelin' " album, can still be used at will—and was, correspondingly, used *at will,* rather than "naturally", in the early days as well: all of which shows that the legitimate distinction between personal and artistic sincerity has always been understood and appreciated by Dylan—if not by a good many of his followers (especially the old ones). At any rate, that old voice still exists. He could use it all the time—if he cared to (just as he cared to give it us in scoops on "Desolation Row"—scoops that were something to latch onto when we first listened to "Highway 61 Revisited" and missed that old voice so, and didn't much like, say, *Tombstone Blues* for the lack of it). It is the "underneath" voice on *The Boxer*. You can nearly separate it—bring it up for inspection, if you want to—by adjusting your stereo speakers properly. A real self-portrait from Dylan.

The inclusion on the album of the two Everly Brothers' hit songs also helps the case—if it's worth helping—for saying that "Self Portrait" is a straightforward title. And with the Everlys, it's tribute-time again.

The Everlys are forgotten heroes of the fifties: forgotten not because they don't now have international hits or make big appearances any more, but because people take too much for granted the achievements they pulled off—the achievements their old hits represent.

They topped the U.S. charts first in 1957 (*Wake Up Little Susie*) and from then until some time after their feud with Mr. Bryant, in the early to middling sixties, they had many, many more smash successes. They were very commercial and they were very good. At a time when most people "found a sound" by accident, they developed one deliberately and intelligently, always bridging what gap there was between pop and modern country music; and at a time when pop's understanding of music was near retarded, the Everlys were consistently alert and curious. They handled their own arrangements and they had taste.

A couple of years ago, Dylan wrote *them* a song, called *The Fugitive*—which for some reason never seems to have been put out. His recording of their two hits on "Self Portrait" repeats the same compliment. It's a fitting acknowledgement of their deserved stature and their influence.

There is, though, a distinction to be made between *Let It Be Me* and *Take A Message To Mary* as they are given us on "Self Portrait". With the first, Dylan does nothing in the way of a transformation. It's a perfectionist's re-drafting of the Everlys' version in effect; probably in intention it is simply a repeat: just Dylan singing their song the way they indelibly made it. He stays very faithful to their wistful and solid world.

With *Take A Message To Mary*, Dylan departs from the idea of the Everlys' rendition, and transforms the song (though his

276

new "driving beat" stands in place of the Everlys' old one). The music is transformed, and also (again Bill Damon has said it first) the song is brought "back to the Code of the West".

The music follows the "Nashville Skyline Rag" principle of giving a fresh instrument dominance for each verse. While Dylan's distinctive pronunciation of "Mary" takes us back to earlier albums, the piano in the second verse has a new and wonderfully *light* ironic life of its own: and the two elements combine to give a sudden, celebratory sense of re-birth.

Yet there is also a contrasting, fleeting moment in the song in which Dylan cashes in on its essential pop aura to implant a strange, distracting notion in the listener. That is, when he sings ". . . this cell is cold" he sets us a most odd contradiction—an almost erotic suggestion of warmth—by the whispered echo of the same words by a breathy girl chorus: it is as if, for a moment, the girls are there with him in the cell. It's a funny idea to throw in.

Perhaps with this one Dylan is at least aware of paying tribute to the talents of the song's composers, Boudleaux and Felice Bryant. This would be logical enough. The Bryants wrote dozens of the songs that came out of Nashville and into the transatlantic charts. Like Presley's early favourites, Leiber and Stoller, the Bryants were one of the elite writing teams whose tunes and phrases got repeatedly embedded in the minds of everyone who grew up with the pop music of the times. It only indicates a slice of their output to note that the Byrants, between them, wrote

> *Like Strangers*
> *Love Hurts*
> *All I Have To Do Is Dream*
> *Problems*
> *Bird Dog*
> *Sleepless Nights*
> *Nashville Blues*

and

> *Bye Bye Love*

They've probably sold more records than Bob Dylan.

Boudleaux Bryant also wrote *Take Me As I Am (Or Let Me Go)*, which appears on "Self Portrait"—and which offers a title not inappropriate to Dylan: it sounds like one of his mottoes from way-back-when. And his recording of the song re-drafts the presentation of that motto, removing from it the big contradiction, the huge inconsistency, that used to apply. On the old tracks where Dylan was saying Accept What I Am, Tolerate, he said it without any tolerance at all, delivering the message with a bitter impatience. (The only exception, I think, is *All I Really Want To Do,* the first song on "Another Side Of Bob Dylan", 1964). With *Take Me As I Am* that paradox has gone. Gently, he restates, having learnt to practise what he pleads for:

> You're trying to re-shape me in a mould, love
> In the image of someone you used to know
> But I won't be a stand in for an old love—
> Take me as I am or let me go.

For "someone you used to know" read "someone I used to be"; the old love is a younger Dylan.

With the Isle of Wight revisits to those two key songs of 1965, *Like A Rolling Stone* and *She Belongs To Me,* Dylan is *not* eradicating his earlier self, but rather is relying on the "Self Portrait" listener's knowledge of them. This at any rate has to be true of the 1969–70 *She Belongs To Me.* It's lightly done and not meant to replace—just a playful flip of an old coin that is everybody's property and still in circulation. *Like A Rolling Stone,* I think, is more than that. Some people think of the song still as the one with which Dylan really threw down the gauntlet of the change to his rock music; and perhaps Dylan was using it again at the Isle of Wight in that kind of way. By now that's not very important. The point is that, whatever the emphasis of intent, the version on "Self Portrait" takes off from the old version, builds its free-flying melodic decorations on the solid edifice of the 1965 achievement. And as such, it still improves with each playing.

The Mighty Quinn doesn't; and it falls a long way short of the other Dylan version of the song—the one on the 1967 Basement Tape. Yet in fact *both* versions give us the impression that "Quinn" is one of those songs that got away: we are never going to get the *real* Dylan version of it.[6]

In contrast, "Self Portrait" gives us a very fine version of that strangely familiar song, *Gotta Travel On.* As Frank Zappa would say: see the way it builds up? In one sense it is the archetypal song of the album, in being "just a nice song" in a collection of

278

same. Yet it's also one of the many tracks on which Dylan's delivery is incalculably subtle. Listen, in *Gotta Travel On*, to the way that phrasing, timing and pronunciation become one, one stroke of genius, as Dylan's delivery bends around the repeated lines.

> That chilly wind will soon begin ...

As elsewhere, the voice enacts it—*creating*, as it weaves around the words, the whispers of the wind itself, and using an instinctive distortion (though, characteristically, a slight one) of that short-i sound that runs all through the line. Dylan even sustains it on the second syllable of "chilly", instead of intruding with the cosy—and thus contradictory—sound that the "y" suffix usually carries. And, in another verse, when he comes to the repeat of

> That lonesome freight at 6.08

he pulls off a similar feat in switching to a different rhythm to cover the line: a sort of jerky clockwork rhythm (except that it's more subtle than that) which gives us the shunting movement of the freight train starting off and at the same time takes up the suggestion of timetabled regularity made by that specific "6.08".

All The Tired Horses, in further contrast, gives no Dylan voice at all; and the lyric is ultra-simple. Putting it generously, it is three lines long:

> All the tired horses in the sun:
> How'm I s'posed to get any riding done?
> Mm—mm—m-m-mm ...

but there is one thing more in the words than that: there is the fact that on the record—though this isn't possible on the page—"riding" is pronounced by the two girl singers (one is Maeretha Stewart) in the same way as "writing": and doubtless, coming at the beginning of an album for which Dylan has himself written little, that effective pun is intentional. (It isn't the first time he has relied on being able to put two separate meanings into one sound in a way that the printed page does not allow. In *The Lonesome Death Of Hattie Carroll*, for instance, the line that on paper is simply "... slain by a cane" becomes, on the record, superimposed with the Biblical allusion of "... slain by a Cain".)

Yet even with its mere three lines—indeed, partly *because* it has only three—*All The Tired Horses* provides, if one wants it to, plenty of scope for speculation as to what Dylan is doing: especially since it is with this song that the album is launched. But let's not go back to all those fears and doubts.

On one level the song is "but a joke". You hear the intro, you are surprised by the girls' voices, and you wait for Dylan's to come in. When it becomes obvious that this isn't going to happen —say as it comes around for the fifth time—you still wait for the words to change, or the tempo to switch, or something. Instead, it keeps on going—fourteen times through altogether—and then fades out. And actually, though the recording fades out, as all recordings must, the song goes on for ever, because the last chord of each verse only gets resolved by the first chord coming round again.

On another level, it's a very neat reversal of the way pop songs are commonly built. Where the norm (well represented elsewhere on the album) is for a lyric, and thus a vocal track, that varies to rest on the structural solidity of an unchanging melody and accompaniment, in *All The Tired Horses* all the variation, development and embellishing occurs within the orchestral arrangement. The voice track, seeming weird because it remains emphatically—relentlessly—up front, provides the unchanging solidity.

Then again, it offers the framework of a Round, with Dylan having written only one part out of the four. And to accommodate this, of course, the song is *musically* four lines long, not three. The first two lines of the lyric count for eight bars, and so do the "mm's". How appropriate that at the beginning of the album that is primarily concerned with music, not words, we should be given the opportunity to substitute for the usual kind of collaboration demanded of us as listeners, the kind of *musical* collaboration that is involved in writing in the other three parts of the Round in our heads.

Perhaps, however, the main function of *All The Tired Horses* is to give us, right at the outset, an object-lesson in tolerant non-classification (and it certainly helps to have one when you first begin to listen to the "Self Portrait" album). The song gives the impression of being Dylan's most concerted attempt to produce a song it is impossible to classify—a song that really does elude even the most determined critic-listener in a way that he is forced to become aware of—a song that it truly *isn't* possible to call either good or bad. And as such it sets the tone (though it doesn't indicate the scope) of the whole double-album.

Finally, there is *Belle Isle,* which, with *Wigwam* (to get back to classifications), is for me the highlight of "Self Portrait".

Like others already mentioned on the album, *Belle Isle* has been seen in the context of a link to an earlier Dylan recording: in this case, a link to the beautiful *Boots Of Spanish Leather*—and certainly they are both love dialogues. And since the latter ends with an estrangement the other can be considered an imagined spiritual reconciliation: a neatening up of existential history. Susie Rotolo, meet Wise Old Father Dylan! But that's no interpretation, it doesn't lead anywhere. Neither song really casts any light on the other—and anyway, what light needs casting? *Belle Isle,* granted its traditional Gallic pattern of story, is self-sufficient and self-contained. Like an island, in fact.

It's hard to avoid words like "exquisite" in assessing the song: and yet it isn't that shallow. While the tune flows out lightly and gracefully, like a gown billowing out around the maiden in the story, the accompanying strings are sombre: more sombre than any ostensibly appropriate, atmospheric Gallic mist. And while Dylan treats the subject and the tradition it springs from with respect and yet, simultaneously, with a sympathetic mockery, there is also a tone in his voice which takes up the almost foreboding suggestion in the strings. There is some darker presence around the edges of the Romance.

This only disperses for a little while near the end (before the strings impinge again to bring it back) when the full sunshine of Dylan's comedy bursts through:

> Young maiden I wish not to banter:
> 'Tis true I come here in disguise;
> I came here to fulfil my last promise
> And hoped to give you a surprise!
> I own you're a maid I love dearly,
> And you've bin in my heart all the while ...

That first line is so joyously funny because through the archaisms it *is* graceful, and the poise is kept so beautifully all the way through to that "banter": and Dylan singing "banter" is the aural equivalent of A Sight To Be Seen (especially since "you've bin in my heart all the while" comes in later to emphasize the closeness of incongruity). The second line, with its force falling so gleefully on "disguise", makes it radiantly clear just how far into the traditional Gallic story-world Dylan is taking us, while the third line has a well-contrived calming influence—its words float down in a gentle spiral—so that the imminent absurdity of what follows doesn't overbalance and come too soon. The fourth line brings the fall—that ludicrously bad distribution of syllables, the awfulness and corn of the rhyme and the consequent bathos of the hope expressed, which is itself accentuated by the rush of syllables given over to its expression: it has all been perfectly timed. It is brilliant clowning: the best thing of its kind since that "unbalanced" line from *Leopard-Skin Pill-Box Hat*: "You know it balances on your head just like a mattress balances on a bottle of wine". And the *Belle Isle* achievement is much more subtle than that—much more complex.

Moreover, Dylan doesn't leave it there like some broken Humpty Dumpty. With the lines that follow, all is restored. That "I own" enacts the first flourishing towards a restoration, as Dylan's voice gently hams up a bewildered search for the right note; the hush through "you're a maid I" begins to get it back; the slowing-down on "love" gives the necessary foothold; "de-e-ear-ly" acts as one last wobble; "And you've bin in my heart" is oh-so-nearly back in balance, and the eventual resolve of the voice's note with the music, which comes at the end of "all the while", announces the achieved restoration of the balance. So then, as the firm emphasized beat comes down on the word "me" in the line that follows—

> For me there is no other damsel

—where the voice and the music are precisely synchronized, Dylan re-sets the tone of the song, right there at the end:

> For me there is no other damsel

In re-setting the tone there, and in the music that follows to close over the song, Dylan draws all its elements together: the sombre quality, the humour and the traditional Romance. The sum of these united parts is, in *Belle Isle*, mystery. And mystery, as Dylan said in 1966,

> is a fact, a traditional fact ... traditional music is too unreal

to die. It doesn't need to be protected. Nobody's going to hurt it. ... All these songs about roses growing out of people's brains and lovers who are really geese and swans that turn into angels—they're not going to die.

Likewise *Belle Isle*.

Postscript

"Self Portrait" also keeps up Dylan's demonstrable independence of the Underground which he did so much towards initiating. "John Wesley Harding" is in this sense an effective gesture of distancing; so is "Self Portrait". It is very much out on its own. It looks back at things instead of "being progressive"; it even, in a sense, affirms the existence and significance of hits, charts, commercial pop.

In addition, it maintains Dylan's rejection of the *language* of the Underground. Up until "John Wesley Harding", his work had been scattered with the familiar phrases: hung up, where it's at, and so on, along with much hip drugs-terminology. With "John Wesley Harding" this language disappears. "Nashville Skyline" showed a careful reliance on the language "of ordinary men"; and "Self Portrait" is consistent with this change of track.

In this connection, it's interesting to compare what Dylan told Nat Hentoff in his *Playboy* interview of 1966 with parts of Patrick Thomas' piece on Doug Kershaw (violinist on Dylan's *Blue Moon*) in 1969.

Dylan explained to Hentoff that he'd been unhappy prior to the emergence of *Like A Rolling Stone* because: "I was singing words I didn't really want to sing. I don't mean words like 'God' and 'mother' and 'President' and 'suicide' and 'meat-cleaver'. I mean simple little words like 'if' and 'hope' and 'you'." With "Nashville Skyline" and "Self Portrait" Dylan is reconciled to those words.

Patrick Thomas quotes this exchange with Doug Kershaw in Nashville:

Kershaw: But anyway, what need is there for this sort of language? (The four-letter Underground sort) Just how many people would I want to show this kind of thing to? (Indicating an Underground magazine) Are you married?

Thomas: No.

Kershaw: You got any kids?

Thomas: No.

Kershaw: Well, I'm married and I've got two kids. Now I wouldn't show this to my kids. You wonder why Dylan's down here. You saw his little boy, didn't you? . . . Well then I think you should know why he's here. He's grown up. Just what's this big difference between here and San Francisco. Do you really think the people are that different between here and there? You think people aren't poor here? You think people don't go out on their wives here?

Thomas appends this comment (he's referring to "Nashville Skyline", then the newest Dylan album):

In the light of this, the "new" Bob Dylan lyrics, which wring out responses from words like "suitcase" and "rumours" are simply the recognition of the fact that not all Americans feel the dead weight of thrice-throttled, TV-choked English.

And he contrasts this "new" Dylan language with "the constant overstatement of urban vernacular".

"Self Portrait" maintains the gulf. More than ever before, Dylan is using ordinary language; and more than before also, his bent is towards a dignity of expression which involves *understatement*.

Later in his work, though, his language "relaxes" again—and in the 1971 song *George Jackson* Dylan says "shit" very deliberately indeed. I hope Doug Kershaw can see why that's O.K.

NOTES

[1]"Bob Dylan & The Poetry of Salvation", *Saturday Review* (U.S.A.), May 30th, 1970.

[2]*Il est des parfums frais comme des chairs d'enfants,/Doux comme les hautbois, verts comme les prairies,/—Et d'autres corrompus, riches et triomphants,/Ayant l'expansion des choses infinies ..."* And certainly, drugs like acid, or even hash, can give those of us less sensitive than Baudelaire an equivalent multi-sensual awareness.

[3]It is also very similar to the picture on the mantelpiece on the front cover photograph of the "Bringing It All Back Home" album.

[4]The illusions, the tricks of the melody and of the voice that manages them, are reminiscent of another country-blues recording: Leadbelly's priceless *Boll Weevil Song,* where in the clinching repeat of the chorus line "Lookin' for a ho-o-ome", what sounds like a conventional drop of a fifth at the end is actually a brilliantly handled falling sixth.

[5]This attempt at "egolessness" is not peculiar to the "Self Portrait" album, and neither is his corresponding opposition to classification —and one doesn't need to accept Steven Goldberg's thesis that Dylan is a mystic to see it. He has been making the same stands for years. It is just that the conception behind "Self Portrait" has enabled him to make the attempt more comprehensively.

[6]The theme the song so obliquely treats of, and one which the Anthony Quinn film it refers to was based, is that of "the noble savage"—and in this connection there is an interesting (if hard to pin down) similarity between another Dylan song, the unreleased *Seven Curses* (1963), and the climax—if it can be said that there is one—of Voltaire's *L'Ingénu,* which, as its title suggests, shares the "noble savage" theme.

9

New Morning?

Dylan's popularity has clearly waned since the "Nashville Skyline" album and the disappointing Isle of Wight concert performance of August 3rd, 1969. It seems to me curious that this decline should so closely have corresponded to a decline in Dylan's standard of output—and not only because Dylan has been so badly misjudged before (and never more so than during his tour of 1966, with all those audience walk-outs from what were, in retrospect, the very greatest ever moments of pure rock music; it's amusing, now, to think back to the evening the tour was at Sheffield, where, after the concert, a friend of mine heard someone else say: "Well, Bob Dylan died tonight."). The parallel of declines is also curious because within the rock music world there is usually no correlation at all between a drop in standards and a drop in public love. Chuck Berry's popularity has largely been in retrospect; certainly, measured by sales and hits, it was at the time far too short-lived and too slight to match his long-sustained creative peak. Similarly Elvis Presley, in Britain at least, was at his most popular during the least good of his four Good Periods.[1]

But in Dylan's case there does seem a correlation. It would have been, perhaps, impossible to sustain for any really substantial length of time the level of popularity that Dylan has "enjoyed", and ten years has proved too long; but if a declining popularity has been operant since "Nashville Skyline", a decline in standard of output has run parallel to it—beginning, perhaps, from that moment towards the end of "John Wesley Harding" when he sings:

If you cannot bring good news then don't bring any.

In the long run of things, of course, this parallel is doomed, because once the peak of fashionability is lost, it is inevitably irretrievable, whereas no similarly obvious or definite pattern can be predicated for standard of output in the future.

As for what's already happened in this direction, what's involved is, as I see it, twofold. In the first place Dylan has largely lost, somehow, that amazing urgency of communication—that arresting quality, that abrasive "presence"; and in the second place I don't think that he has recently had anything much to say. Obviously the two are connected, though one is a matter of delivery, of performance, while the other is a matter of vision.

In any event, the two have given us a Dylan on record who has sounded abstracted and tired and not really "there" by his own earlier standards (think, for instance, of *It Hurts Me Too*) nor markedly on top of what's happening (*One More Weekend*) and with little to put across anyhow.

The latter deficiency has been made manifest, it strikes me, in several ways. There has, first of all, been a gradual change in Dylan's use of cliché—a change from the obvious sharpness brought to bear on, say,

> You say you told me that you
> Wanna hold me but you
> Know you're not that strong ...

to the drearily presented platitudes of *Take Me As I Am* and *If Dogs Run Free*. On the pleasant, slight *If Not For You*, the cliché is knowingly offered—as if Dylan were back in 1966—and carried to the point of self-ridicule:

> Winter would have no Spring,
> Couldn't hear the robins sing;
> I just wouldn't have a clue—
> Anyway it wouldn't ring true—
> If not for you.

Yet even here the emptiness is as prominent as the confession of it. When, later on in the "New Morning" album, we come to *The Man In Me*, there is—in consequence of this sort of emptiness—an added dimension, of irony (which, again, Dylan's own awareness of does not dissolve) in the lines

> The man in me will hide sometimes
> To keep from being seen
> But that's just because he doesn't want to
> Turn into some machine ...

Too late??? In any case it's a reasonable response to feel that the artist in Dylan ought not to be so much in hiding. I'm not, of course, arguing that no artistry is shown by *The Man In Me*; it's masterly cut. But it has no commitment. It would have been just as "shapely" and far more alive if it had emerged from "Blonde On Blonde". And really it's a pretty pointless joke to have a middle-eight lyric that so closely parallels the *My Fair Lady* song *On The Street Where You Live*: "But Oh! what a wonderful feeling/Just to know that you are near." And when, in *Winterlude*, he strokes us with

Winterlude, this dude, thinks you're fine

we're likely to feel we've had enough songs now from "this dude" and that we'd prefer to return to those of the genius whose best talents lurk so perversely under this blithe and stereotyped personality.

It may even be not unduly pessimistic to suggest that Dylan has lost control over this latest (and most irritating) persona—lost control, that is, to the extent of letting two different selves get accidentally mixed up. This happens, I think, in *Sign On The Window*. To rhyme "Build me a cabin in Utah" with "Have a bunch of kids who call *me Pa*" would be immaculate, with all that doubt about this formula-for-happiness shown up in Dylan's delivery of the lines, *if*, when he came to the word "Pa", the note was laid down *firmly,* like a trump card. That would be the "real" Dylan way. Let's at least say, it would be the old way— and however stylized, and therefore however *personally* insincere, it would have flawless *artistic* sincerity. But, as has never happened before on any of his released material, Dylan quite simply delivers it wrong. He gives the word "Pa" a wobble on the voice—a really awful Flanders & Swann type of tremolo-gentility. It's embarrassing. And I think it happens because of this entanglement of the dude and "the real Dylan".

Another way in which Dylan's lack of anything to say shows itself is in his conformity to what's become a general trend: namely, his careful gathering up of whole clusters of ever-more-famous, ever-more-eminent session musicians. No one could deny their abilities, but it's pertinent just to recognize that Dylan's earlier records show how unnecessary these extra battalions are for him and for his art.

It's also true that the whole trend reveals, right across the scene, a huge disparity between the tiny amount the 1960s stars have left to communicate, and the vastness of their access to the best studios and the very best supportive facilities, as a result of their previous (more primitively-achieved) attainments. There they all are—George Harrison, Eric Clapton, Crosby, Stills, Nash, Young, Kanter, and more—all laying down increasingly trivial material, decorated and supported by increasingly exquisite, "professional" accompaniments. And Dylan is right there with them.

It become, before long, a spurious sort of panacea and, since it relies more and more on the ordinary listener possessing extraordinarily good stereo (or, imminently, quadrophonic) equipment, it is debatable whether, under these conditions, technology is the servant or the master of the music. Certainly, one's awareness of the technology—the ever-present sense that it is *there*—impinges on the music: and it should do so the more acutely when the message of the music purports to be anti-materialistic. At the very least, it seems ironic when, as happens on the title track from "New Morning", it's all used to extol the virtues of watching rabbits in the great outdoors. If taking up the electric technology for his city/confusion songs of the mid-sixties was logical and apt, then relying on even more of the same technology while his songs are country straightforward is likely to be judged correspondingly inappropriate. And that there should be this gap between, if you like, medium and message, can only enforce the impression that the message is inconsequential. (It implies, for one thing, that it has hardly impinged on the artist himself—because if it had, more concentration would have made for more unity in its interpretation.)

This aspect of the albums from "Nashville Skyline" onwards leads us into noticing a further sense in which Dylan has little to say. That is, in specializing in songs of rural simplicity he has at the same time given himself, again and again, a Happy Family Man role as singer/narrator.

Even in "New Morning's" rock song, *One More Weekend*, there is a facile combination of country-sounding slide guitar and noticeably cosy lyrics:

> We'll go some place unknown
> Leave all the children home;

Honey why not go alone
Just you and me . . .

It compares very directly with the "Blonde On Blonde" song
Leopard-Skin Pill-Box Hat:

If you wanna see the sunrise
Honey I know where
We'll go out and see it sometime
We'll both just sit there and stare

and the change in the later song (which parallels the earlier in
its structure and music too) to a married-couple-situation is far
from artless. Nor are the details of the realization. That "Honey"
for instance, which comes immediately after the situation reveals
itself, so that it half-suggests "honeymoon"—while the whole pro-
posal does urge, of course, precisely a second honeymoon. No
wonder it's a slightly weary track.

It's been said earlier in this book that this Happy Family Man
role, irrespective of how it applies to Dylan's private life, is un-
convincing in his art; that you don't render a vision of happiness
by insisting that you're happy, or simply by using your most bland
voice. Yet this was what Dylan attempted—and what he failed
with—on "Nashville Skyline" and "Self Portrait". On "New
Morning" it is there again: yet with a significant difference.

I've touched on the self-awareness of this fault that shows up on
tracks like *If Not For You*; and it seems to me that the accompanying self-effacement, sometimes self-apology, goes very much
further. In other words, the situation on "New Morning" is much
more complex.

There is indeed an obvious continuation of the family-man-
countryman syndrome. It's there in the title track, in *Day Of The
Locusts*, in *Time Passes Slowly*, in *Winterlude*, in *One More
Weekend*, in *The Man In Me*, and—in so far as such a persona
is associated with the upholding of exactly the kind of traditional
ideas which it apparently celebrates—in *Father Of Night*.

Yet Dylan draws back from this persona as he doesn't really
do (despite the self-parodying little smiles) on the two previous
albums. And he draws back in several different ways.

For one thing, Dylan used the album, in certain respects, to
"answer" or even appease, hostile criticism of the two that had

come before. He waited till he had a cold to do the recording, so as to make his voice a bit rougher again. He went back to a much heavier "city" sort of backing. And he brought back into play some of the old "Blonde On Blonde" imagery (almost, thereby, imitating himself—which is a trap many distinctive writers eventually fall into, from Wordsworth to Mailer): trying to reach the floor and the door in *If Not For You* just like in *Temporary Like Achilles*; the parallel already noted between *One More Weekend* and *Leopard-Skin Pill-Box Hat*; that specially-for-the-fans touch in *Day Of The Locusts* where, after that lovely pun

> The weather was hot
> nearly ninety degrees

he gives us the sort of flash that belongs in, say, *Memphis Blues Again*—or even right back in *Dylan's 115th Dream*:

> The man standing next to me
> His head was explodin'
> Woh I was prayin' the pieces
> Wouldn't fall on me ...

And then the old crossword sign in *Winterlude* just like in *One Too Many Mornings*; the *déjà vu* allusion to chaos in *The Man In Me,* when

> The stormclouds are ragin'
> All around my door ...;

and the blatant nostalgia of that line in the middle of the flawed but fabulous *Sign On The Window*: "Sure gonna be wet tonight on Main Streeeeeeeet ..."; plus, perhaps finally, what is in effect a reassurance (the nearest he gets to the sort of secret message that Weberman is constantly looking for) that yes, after all, he still remembers his roots, when he ends *I Went To See The Gypsy* with this utter *non sequitur*:

> So I watched the sun come rising
> From the little Minnesota town
> From that little Minnesota town.

On top of all this, there is a marked expression of explicit doubt about this family-man-countryman role. Thus the element of self-

parody is far more apparent than on the two preceding albums—
to the extent, indeed, that birds become "birdies" (echoing, in
the process, Jerry Lee Lewis' track *Living Loving Wreck*), and
the wife-and-children become merely a possible formula to try
out:

> Build me a cabin in Utah
> Marry me a wife; catch rainbow trout;
> Have a bunch of kids who call me Pa . . .

And to clinch it, this is followed not only by a patently unconfi-
dent remark (and made less positive still by its being repeated, as
if for self-reassurance):

> That must be what it's all about
> That must be what it's all about

but also by the capping touch of genius—that intentionally in-
genious little "Oh-oh-oh-oh!" which Dylan puts over the end of
the riff that follows.

Running underneath all this, there is, throughout the album,
a subtle but sustained "falsification" of the rural/patriarchal ideas:
a persistent kind of Midas touch which deliberately makes the
picture an idealized and therefore *not* a real one.

If this corresponds to any of the earlier Dylan material, it is
(with the exception of *I Threw It All Away*, with its figurative
mountains and rivers) to *much* earlier Dylan—material like *Lay
Down Your Weary Tune*.

In "New Morning" it shows in going not to "the hills" at the
end of *Day Of The Locusts* but to the American hills most arti-
ficialized by Tin Pan Alley—"the Black Hills of Dakota". It
almost suggests Dylan rushing off to Doris Day; it makes his
escape to the hills just a story, by making it just a joke—mere
literary allusion.

Then, just as the next song, *Time Passes Slowly*, takes up this
story *in* the hills (it begins "Time passes slowly/up here in the
mountains") so also it takes up the unreality suggested in the
previous track.

> We sit beside bridges and walk beside fountains

warbles Dylan, and plainly, as he's begging us to notice, there

292

aren't any fountains up mountains. The very word, as his delivery emphasizes, suggests the Ideal, not the real. It offers a kind of exquisite, ethereal, pastoral conceit: a sort of Greek Mythology-land, an Elysium. And equally plainly, the intention is not to generate or display massive enthusiasm—Dylan isn't exaggerating the pleasantness of the countryside as if he were penning an advert for rural holidays—but rather to present something unreal; something not there.

Then comes the strange and fragmentary *I Went To See The Gypsy*, and out of its disjointed but compulsive evocation comes what is a simple phrase yet decidedly an odd one if you take the song in isolation:

> Outside the lights were shining
> On the river of tears. . . .

Its context is outside the song but clearly within the album as a whole: for the function of the line is to ally and associate with the Elysian motif established in the earlier songs.

The same track also lets drop the remark—and it's made with some emphasis—that the Gypsy can "bring you through the mirror". Literary allusion again; and for me at least, it points straight to Lewis Carroll's lovely *Through The Looking Glass*.[2] And reminding me of the Alice book, of course, means that I infer from Dylan's line that he is yet again suggesting an unreality —an unreal world; and the ambiguity of the line (which way can the Gypsy bring you through?) only makes its suggestion the more persuasive.

Following that is "Winterlude", wonderful "Winterlude", in which the unreal becomes dominant and pretty explicit. The title itself implies that the album is all a show, like, in this sense, *A Midsummer Night's Dream*; the rhythm is waltz-time (with all the associations *that* must bring to mind in the average Dylan admirer); the clichés focus on a kind of dream-world of romance —which therefore denies any corresponding "real life" romance —the kind that comes to us more usually by courtesy of school-girl comics or The Dixie Cups (especially with that "chapel"; the Dixie Cups won a gold record for *Chapel Of Love*):

> . . . my little apple
> Winterlude let's go down to the chapel

And it's not only a waltz, it's a skating song. It's *Dylan On Ice*, in other words, which apart from being unlikely in the sense of being a long way from what we'd ever have expected in the old days, offers an obvious further suggestion of the unreal and the precarious. Ice is merely a covering—a sheet hiding and transforming something else; and alongside this, the lyric reveals—and rather in the manner of some showman-promoter's floodlight—the snow on the telephone wires and on the sand … the shifting sand.

After that, there is the uncertainty of tone (a bad thing making it a bad track) on "If Dogs Run Free", which can only endorse the unreality being presented, with its blatantly hollow mysticism:

> In har-mo-ny
> With the cosmic sea
> True love needs no
> Com-pan-y

and

> Across the swamp of Time,

made more hollow still by being pitched against a horrific and lasciviously plastic New York Night Club background—which is likely to remind us of Frank Zappa's *America Drinks & Goes Home*.

Matching the waltz-time of *Winterlude*, the second side of the album begins with the title track, *New Morning*, which is, except for the two-line middle-eight, a fox-trot. And with this song, we're back to those country bridges and the intentional things-aren't-what-they-seem touch of

> a country mile, or two …

and this same characteristic illusionary quality is taken further still—right from the obvious theatrical mystique of the title—on *Sign On The Window*.

Further, the whole theme of the track that follows, *The Man In Me*, is keep-it-all-hid.

As for *Three Angels*—well, it impresses us straight away as being not only explicitly surrealistic but also as echoing that classic of *false* religiosity, Wink Martindale's *Deck Of Cards*. It also echoes a short but noticeable passage from Genet's *Our Lady Of The Flowers*:

> But neither of the two seemed to care whether Divine was absent or present. They heard the morning angelus, the rattle of a milk can. Three workmen went by on bicycles along the boulevard, their lamps lit, though it was day. A policeman on his way home, where perhaps he would find an empty bed (Divine hoped so, for he was young), passed without looking at them.

It's an expertly improbable, supposedly awkward, and ludicrously didactic tale about the everyday world—"the real world", as we so often call it—which passes like a pageant below the gaze of the narrator and his three rather ungainly angels. And Dylan's making them ungainly—keeping them perched up on poles, wearing

> green robes, with wings that stick out

—is another wry confession of his intent.

The cumulative effect of all this carefully established unreality is to make "New Morning" something very different, in its vision, from any of the other Dylan albums. After all the bland smugness of "Nashville Skyline" and "Self Portrait"—which, as I've argued earlier, hinted strongly at a failure of nerve, an unwillingness on Dylan-the-artist's part to go outside his own gates or explore any but the most truistic verities—"New Morning" seems to me to express a new strength: a new optimism-through-doubt.

On "Self Portrait", that is, the courage of the artist appeared to have failed so utterly that only insistent claims of a most conventionalized happiness could be "allowed out", as it were. On "New Morning" that courage has returned to the extent that Dylan-the-artist can feel himself able to question, to keep behind, even to deny, the lasting validity of those previous claims.

"New Morning" doesn't offer us the same complacent countryman persona: it queries it. The happy-family-man comes under a delicate but unwavering scrutiny; and so does the whole post-'67 hip ethic of retreating to the country.

It is in this sense, and not any other, that the title of the album can be taken as a kind of promise for the future. It's not a new morning in the sense that this album gives us a Dylan who has, as it were, turned over a completely new leaf and returned to giving us irreproachable, progressive work of a "Blonde On Blonde" standard. But it does offer a promise that the artist in Dylan is ready again to explore what really lies around him—around us.

NOTES

[1] I take his first Good Period to be the very early, Sun-inspired, country-blues material cut in '55 and '56; the second to be the period immediately after, at first a kind of transformation period—*One Sided Love Affair*, for example, or *I Want You I Need You I Love You*—and then the fully-fledged rock sound of 1958 (and the smouldering ballads of the same time, which are just as tough in sound-concept), which includes the tracks not issued till his Army days (like *A Big Hunk O' Love*) and spilling over on to the 1960 album "Elvis Is Back". The third, and least impressive, Good Period is I suppose that launched with *It's Now Or Never* and disintegrating after *His Latest Flame/Little Sister*. The fourth phase seems to me to be spasmodic and recent—a series of recordings made after the huge and appalling block of musical films churned out in the '60s. This phase includes the "From Elvis In Memphis" and "Elvis Country" albums and the *If I Can Dream* single.

[2] It was noted in an earlier chapter that Dylan's work recalls Carroll's elsewhere—particularly with the "John Wesley Harding" song *The Drifter's Escape*.

10

Bob Dylan's Art: Conclusion

The best thing about this whole question is that this can't possibly be a real conclusion: Dylan's art is not concluded.

I have merely tried to open up some aspects of that art as we have it up to the time of writing. Much has emerged during the course of this book's growth, and more will emerge soon afterwards, so that the scope of the book will get smaller and smaller as time goes by.

As it is, the whole shape of the book has been forced into changes by new Dylan records coming out, so that these have had to be dealt with chronologically instead of thematically—making the latter end of this study much closer to a reviewing process than I would have wished.

In addition, my writing has all along been interspersed with long sessions with friends simply playing Dylan records in the normal course of things; and though this has helped immeasurably, it has also reinforced my feeling that in the last resort I have pinned down in these pages much much less than I set out to.

All the same, this is a good time to be writing a concluding chapter, because since the rest of the book was written, Dylan has indeed produced some new recordings—two singles and eleven album tracks (though not a proper new album)—and it is work of real quality and excitement and promise. More than enough, at any rate, to let me end on a convinced note of optimism without being too facile about it—and I'm thankful for that.

Taking these latest releases in order, the first to emerge has been the single of *Watching The River Flow* and *Spanish Is The Loving Tongue*.

Curiously, the combined effect of these two pieces of work is to belie the ideas of Dylan's decline as a performer but confirm the ideas of his decline as a composer.

The single offers one new song and one traditional: and

although it seems to have gone largely unnoticed, the latter is the truly interesting track. *Watching The River Flow* is, in its lyrics, an interesting extension of the "New Morning" promise, saying, bluntly enough:

> Wish I was back in the city
> Instead of on this old bank of sand ...

but this is of limited credibility, basically, and certainly the use of sand to suggest impermanence—Dylan shifting position once again—is casually done and hints at no special consequentiality. Other than this, the song has little flashes of a unique Dylan song-writing technique—where you find a great rush of words crowded into half a line and then the other half spun out with one or two words and large pauses. It's a classic Dylan gesture of wit:

> WhyonlyyesterdayIsawsomebodyonthestreetthatwas
> uh really shook!

And that's about it, except that Leon Russell's piano-work is just unbeatable.

In contrast, *Spanish Is The Loving Tongue,* the first totally solo track Dylan has cut for at least six years, is, it seems to me, one of his most impressive ever recordings. He gives it everything. It breathes hard, it labours, it tells of struggle. It is a real experience, the idealism and spiritualism of transient love, put down with the sort of commitment on Dylan's part that hasn't been heard perhaps since "John Wesley Harding". The words, music and voice cohese perfectly to give us a genuinely enriching experience and not just a bland panacea. For the first time in ages, Dylan has sung a song with tremendous potential and used it, under-stood it, felt it (perhaps that last most of all).

Then in November 1971, released more or less together, came Dylan's astonishing single *George Jackson* and the double-album "More Bob Dylan Greatest Hits".

The single is astonishing because it's a protest song and we all thought he'd given them up in 1963; because it's a didactic, ultra-simple song and obviously totally sincere as a straightforward personal statement (which, from Dylan, is fairly unique); because the acoustic version is another completely solo recording, like *Spanish Is The Loving Tongue,* and yet also marks a return to *exactly* the pre-'64 Dylan protest-song formula—guitar backing till the end of the penultimate verse, then a harmonica solo laid on top, then guitar alone again through the last verse, then back with the harmonica for the fade-out.

It isn't a great song but it says something encouraging about the state of Dylan's soul: and particularly, I think, since Dylan plainly wrote it in response not to some empty rhetorical call but in response to Jackson's incredible, tremendous, salutary letters and the consequent special sense of despair and anger and loss felt on hearing that he was dead.

Dylan starts the song very simply by declaring these responses, beginning by using a classic blues opening-line:

> I woke up this morning

and then tightening up at once into the particular and the special —personalizing it with the rest of the verse:

> There were tears in my bed
> They killed the man I really loved
> Shot him through the head.

The song interests me at two other points—although it *reaches* me, as Jackson's letters do, throughout. The first thing is because I remember that as a part of his argument about Dylan-as-mystic, Steven Goldberg suggested that Dylan's politics would be, these days, reactionary rather than radical: and so it's interesting to find traces of the mystical in the middle of this committedly radical song, as Dylan sings

> They were frightened of his power
> They were scared of his love.

That's the one bit that would never have appeared in a pre-'64 political song from Dylan.

The other point of interest, to me, is the way the end of the song deliberately takes up one of Jackson's most attractive and spirited remarks. Jackson says in one letter that from now on he's going to divide people into just two categories—the Innocent and the Guilty. And in the light of that, the pointed ambiguity in Dylan's final verse is particularly striking:

> Sometimes I think this whole world
> Is one big prison yard

299

    Some of us are prisoners
    The rest of us are guards.

Us and Us, not Us and Them.

The new material on the "More Bob Dylan Greatest Hits" double-album consists of releasing for the first time a live take from 1964 of *Tomorrow Is A Long Time*—a lyrical song from the same period as *Lay Down Your Weary Tune*; three tracks with Happy Traum (an old folk-days friend of Dylan) on bass, second guitar and back-up vocals—*I Shall Be Released* (or rather, two thirds of it), *You Aint Goin' Nowhere* (with almost totally new and really delightful words) and *Down In The Flood*, which all come from the 1967 collection of songs which were previously available only on a bootleg acetate; and, lastly, *When I Paint My Masterpiece,* which was produced by Leon Russell and recorded at the same session as *Watching The River Flow*.

Tomorrow Is A Long Time simply shows how beautiful that old, gruff Dylan voice could be; the three 1967 songs offer yet another new Dylan voice—one which has possibilities but isn't that impressive or exciting at base. It is *When I Paint My Masterpiece* which I find of real interest.

Like *George Jackson,* it gets some of its value from its allusion to a book, although the allusion in *Masterpiece* is less substantial, because the song is one of those which give us fragmentary pictures, and the book only figures in the first of these. The book in question is F. Scott Fitzgerald's *Tender Is The Night,* and the allusion Dylan gives us is to the episode where Dick Diver is in Rome, at the end of his affair with Rosemary. He walks around, lost in reflection, seeing Rome appearing to disintegrate; he goes back to the garden after leaving Rosemary and finds her footprints; he passes the Spanish Stairs; a boy brings him a message that Rosemary is waiting for him in her hotel room. It's dank November.

Dylan begins his song with this:

    Oh the streets of Rome are filled with rubble,
    Ancient footprints are everywhere;
    You could almost think that you're seeing double
    On a cold dark night on the Spanish Stairs

Got to hurry on back to my hotel room
Where I got me a date with Botticelli's niece ...

And the rhyming eighth line (as with each verse) runs

When I paint my masterpiece.

Which brings out the final point of comparison to Dick Diver's situation: because it is at this point in the Fitzgerald novel, while Dick is in Rome, that he comes to realize and to admit to himself that he is never actually *going* to write the masterpiece he'd been aiming at.

So Dylan's title line has this fascinating double-edge: "when" may mean "never", as far as Dylan is concerned. And certainly the repetition of this line through the song adds to this suggestion that he's actually realizing that "his masterpiece" just isn't in him (as, in fact, by a strange quirk of literary fate, it is also in Rome that Casaubon, in George Eliot's *Middlemarch*, begins to see that his own work isn't going to be the great book he intended).

And, as a detail, the parallel with *Tender Is The Night* also lends that nice ambiguity to the line

Ancient footprints are everywhere

—allowing it to embody not just a sense of Rome's antiquity but also a sense of the personal love affair acted out there in the past.

The final collection of Dylan tracks released since the rest of this book was written is the set of five songs performed and recorded at the Bangla Desh Benefit Concert organized by George Harrison in August 1971.[1]

The songs Dylan does are *A Hard Rain's A-Gonna Fall, It Takes A Lot To Laugh, It Takes A Train to Cry, Blowin' In The Wind, Mr. Tambourine Man* and *Just Like A Woman*—and these are really something.

Again, no one could have envisaged beforehand that Dylan would ever sing protest material again—much less actually return to *Blowin' In The Wind,* which in the old days he'd felt so chained to. And it's an immaculate, alive and sensitive version, in fact, which makes the song sound, to me at least, about a hundred times better than I ever thought it could be. And if he can do *that* kind of revitalizing, I feel almost any level of optimism for the future of Dylan's art is justified.

What makes it more solid, and more sure as an indication of future possibilities, is that the *Blowin' In The Wind* rendition is not a once-only achievement. He follows it through—accompanied by George Harrison, Ringo Starr and Leon Russell—on *Just Like A Woman*. The August '71 version of that song is by far and away the most exciting thing Dylan has done for years. It's a dazzling extension beyond what he's done before and onto a new plane of directness and pertinence. *Just Like A Woman* was never done properly before—that's the feeling you get from this new version. And all the parts which go to making this stunning total—timing, phrasing, mood, atmosphere—are just definitive and unbeatable.

So there you have it. A good place to finish.

I'm only tempted to add that, conscious as I am that I've said less than I meant to, there is an undeniable magical element in what Dylan's art does for the listener—an element this book leaves untouched and unexplained.

I don't want to produce this now, as it were, out of a hat, to wave at the reader who feels, as I do, that the book explains less than it should. It's just that if other readers feel roused to pursuing Dylan's art from here onto the records, they should know that they will find there more than this writer has promised.

NOTE

[1]Since this was printed, yet more has emerged: three tracks by Dylan & The Band recorded in 1968 at the Woody Guthrie Memorial Concert at Carnegie Hall—*Mrs. Roosevelt, I Aint Got No Home In This World Any More, Grand Coolie Dam* (all Guthrie songs)—and now released as part of a Memorial Album on Columbia; and one track, also from Columbia, on the album "Earl Scruggs, His Family & Friends", which has Dylan saying "OK" and then playing an instrumental duet with Scruggs of *Nashville Skyline Rag*.

Further: since the hardback edition of this book, Dylan has played on "Election Year Rag" and "Somebody Else's Troubles" by Steve Goodman, both of which were released as a Buddah single—the latter also released on the album of the same name; and on several tracks on the excellent Atlantic album "Doug Sahm & His Band", which includes a new Dylan song, *Wallflower*. At the time of writing, however, (April 1973) there is still no Dylan album—making a gap since "New Morning" of two-and-a-half years: by far the longest gap in his recording life.

Appendices

Appendix A: List of Released Dylan Albums, with Notes

1962: BOB DYLAN

Side 1: *She's No Good* (J. Fuller); *Talkin' New York* (B. Dylan); *In My Time Of Dyin'* (?); *Man Of Constant Sorrow* (arr. B. Dylan); *Fixin' To Die Blues* (B. White); *Pretty Peggy-O* (arr. B. Dylan); *Highway 51 Blues* (C. Jones).

Side 2: *Gospel Plow* (arr. B. Dylan); *Baby Let Me Follow You Down* (R. Von Schmidt); *House Of The Rising Sun* (trad.); *Freight Train Blues* (trad.); *Song To Woody* (B. Dylan); *See That My Grave Is Kept Clean* (L. Jefferson).

SOURCES:

Jesse Fuller was a one-man band (because, he said, he couldn't trust other people), playing guitar, harmonica, drums, fotdella and kazoo, and singing too. He came from Jonesboro, Georgia, was part of the medicine-show tradition, and began playing in Oakland in 1929. Unlike Chuck Berry, who uses about three tunes over and over again for his songs, Fuller had basically just one. It was launched with his famous *San Francisco Bay Blues* and then applied to hundreds of others, including *You're No Good*.

Bukka White, a Mississippi Negro, was on parole from Parchman Farm (where, like Leadbelly, Son House and Pat Hare—Muddy Waters' guitarist—he served a sentence for homicide) when Dylan did *Fixin' To Die*. He has been recorded by the Lomaxes for the Music Division of the Library of Congress. He did vocals, guitar and piano.

Ric Von Schmidt, from Boston, was a personal friend of, and direct influence on, Dylan. (See also Appendix B.)

Dave Van Ronk, a contemporary folksinger, brought *House Of The Rising Sun* to Dylan's attention. (Similarly, Dylan's recording of it, and of *Baby Let Me Follow You Down*, resulted in these two songs being chosen for the first singles by The [original] Animals in the early sixties.

Roy Acuff's version of *Freight Train Blues* provided a basis for Dylan's. Acuff was a much-revered Nashville artist and composer.

Blind Lemon Jefferson was born in Texas in the 1890s, was a country blues guitarist and fine singer—one of the very greatest blues men, and the main blues influence on Leadbelly. (See also note 1, page 64).

John Hammond produced the album. He is a key figure in getting blues men and others onto record and, among other things, was organizing "Spirituals To Swing" concerts at Carnegie Hall in the late 1930s.

Don Law was to have been the producer. He had produced Robert Johnson, and many early recordings on Columbia & labels like Okeh. Dylan met him in New York in 1962. He attended the studio sessions at which Dylan's "John Wesley Harding" album was recorded in 1968. He has never, in the event, produced Dylan.

Walter Jacobs, Sonny Terry, Merle Travis, Ramblin' Jack Elliott, Hank Williams, Jimmie Rodgers, Jelly Roll Morton, Woody Guthrie, Mance Lipscomb, Rabbit Brown, Big Joe Williams, the Everly Brothers, Carl Perkins and Elvis Presley are also mentioned as being of relevance on the informative back-cover of the album (by Stacey Williams). Some of these are dealt with elsewhere in this book in relation to Dylan. With the exception of Rabbit Brown about whom I haven't been able to discover anything, the others are dealt with below:

Walter Jacobs came to Chicago from the South, encouraged by Big Bill Broonzy, at the beginning of the 1950s, playing harmonica that was very Down Home. He played on Maxwell Street, and cut his first record for its tiny label, Ora-Nelle; then got a contract with the mighty Chess label. His style relied on cupping his hands over microphone and harmonica.

Sonny Terry, blinded as a child, was born in Georgia, later moved to New York. Has had a long, famous partnership with Brownie McGhee. Like Walter Jacobs, Stacey Williams mentions him as an influence on Dylan's harmonica-work. However, Terry has in fact influenced just about everybody—and is so much more technically proficient than Dylan that it's hard to trace any connection. Merle Travis was a stylish Nashville guitar-picker.

308

Jimmie Rodgers worked with black singers in a medicine show that travelled round Texas and New Mexico. He influenced a number of blues men and invented the name "Howlin' Wolf" for Chester Burnett.

Jelly Roll Morton was born in 1885, was playing in New Orleans by 1902, and, directly influenced by as well as an influence on jazz, added a ragtime flavour to the blues with his piano. Big Joe Williams, born in Mississippi in 1903, was a harshly distinctive singer. He claimed to have worked in every state in the union, but was based in St. Louis, where he began recording in the mid-1930s, often with Sonny Boy Williamson on harmonica. He also sang with the Count Basie Orchestra. He also played a nine-string guitar.

Carl Perkins is a countryish rock singer from the 1950s era, who recorded for the pioneering Memphis label, Sun. He wrote *Blue Suede Shoes* and claimed that but for an accident which stopped him promoting it, his version, and not Elvis Presley's, would have been the smash-hit single. He also wrote *Matchbox*. Finally, Susie Rotolo, Dylan's girl, attended the album recording. The guitar on *In My Time Of Dyin'* was fretted with her lipstick holder. Later, she is supposed to have been the girl around which Dylan's *Boots Of Spanish Leather* was built.

1963: THE FREEWHEELIN' BOB DYLAN

Side 1: *Blowin' In The Wind*; *Girl From the North Country*; *Masters Of War*; *Down The Highway*; *Bob Dylan's Blues*; *A Hard Rain's A-Gonna Fall.*
Side 2: *Don't Think Twice, It's All Right*; *Bob Dylan's Dream*; *Oxford Town*; *Talkin' World War III Blues*; *Corrine, Corrina*; *Honey Just Allow Me One More Chance*; *I Shall Be Free.*

All the songs were written by Dylan, but *Girl From The North Country* is based on *Scarborough Fair*, *A Hard Rain's A-Gonna Fall* on *Lord Randall* and *Masters Of War* on *Notamun Town*; the tune of *Don't Think Twice, It's All Right* is that of an earlier Johnny Cash song, *Understand Your Man*; *Oxford Town* is based on an older song, as, of course, is *Corrine, Corrina*. The back cover included some Dylan "poems". Tom Wilson produced the album. The musicians on *Corrine, Corrina* are Bruce Langhorne, George

Barnes, Dick Wellstood, Gene Ramey and Herb Lovelle. They do *not* appear, despite some liner notes, on *Don't Think Twice, It's All Right*.

1964: THE TIMES THEY ARE A-CHANGIN'

Side 1: *The Lonesome Death Of Hattie Carroll*; *Boots Of Spanish Leather*; *With God On Our Side*; *The Times They Are A-Changin'*; *One Too Many Mornings*.

Side 2: *Only A Pawn In Their Game*; *When The Ship Comes In*; *Ballad Of Hollis Brown*; *North Country Blues*; *Restless Farewell*.

All songs by Dylan. Produced by Tom Wilson.

1964: ANOTHER SIDE OF BOB DYLAN

Side 1: *All I Really Want To Do*; *Black Crow Blues*; *Spanish Harlem Incident*; *I Don't Believe You*; *Motorpsycho Nitemare*.

Side 2: *It Aint Me Babe*; *I Shall Be Free No. 10*; *My Back Pages*; *Ballad In Plain D*; *Chimes Of Freedom*.

All Dylan songs, but several based on older ones. *I Shall Be Free No. 10* takes its inspiration from Leadbelly's *We Shall Be Free* (see Chapter Two); and even the very distinctive *To Ramona* is founded on an older song, a common country version of which, with entirely different lyrics, is called *Anita*. Dylan plays piano for first time on record generally released, on *Black Crow Blues*,* *Motorpsycho Nitemare* is based in one sense on the Alfred Hitchcock film *Psycho*.

Tom Wilson produced the album. Further Dylan "poems" are published on the back cover.

*but see note on *Mixed up Confusion*, Appendix B.

1965: BRINGING IT ALL BACK HOME

Side 1: *Subterranean Homesick Blues*; *She Belongs To Me*; *Maggie's Farm*; *Love Minus Zero/No Limit*; *On the Road Again*; *Outlaw Blues*; *Bob Dylan's 115th Dream*.

Side 2: *Mr. Tambourine Man*; *The Gates Of Eden*; *It's Alright Ma, (I'm Only Bleeding)*; *It's All Over Now, Baby Blue.*

All songs by Dylan. The first album with rock musicians on it; the last produced by Tom Wilson. The back-cover includes a prose piece by Dylan; the front-cover includes, in its photograph, two paintings—one propped on the mantelpiece and one up on the wall above it—which strikingly resemble the cover painting of Dylan by Dylan on the later "Self Portrait" album.

1965: HIGHWAY 61 REVISITED

Side 1: *Like A Rolling Stone; Tombstone Blues; It Takes A Lot To Laugh, It Takes A Train To Cry; From A Buick 6; Ballad Of A Thin Man.*
Side 2: *Queen Jane Approximately; Highway 61 Revisited; Just Like Tom Thumb's Blues; Desolation Row.*

All songs by Dylan. Produced by Bob Johnson. Back-cover includes a very fine prose-poem by Dylan. The British album leaves the musicians uncredited, but the American album lists the following personnel: Dylan—guitar, harmonica, piano & police car. Mike Bloomfield—guitar. Al Kooper—piano & organ. Paul Griffin—piano & organ. Bobby Gregg—drums. Harvey Goldstein (i.e. Harvey Brooks)—bass. Charlie McCoy—guitar. Frank Owens—piano. Russ Savakus—bass. However, NB. according to Al Kooper, Bruce Langhorne (guitar) also appears on the album.

1966: BLONDE ON BLONDE

Side 1: *Rainy Day Women Nos. 12 & 35; Pledging My Time; Visions of Johanna; One Of Us Must Know (Sooner Or Later).*
Side 2: *I Want You; Memphis Blues Again; Leopard-Skin Pill-Box Hat; Just Like A Woman.*
Side 3: *Most Likely You Go Your Way And I'll Go Mine; Temporary Like Achilles; Absolutely Sweet Marie; 4th Time Around; Obviously 5 Believers.*
Side 4: *Sad-Eyed Lady Of The Lowlands.*

The first Dylan double-album—it may have been the first double-album in the rock music field. All songs by Dylan. Produced by

Bob Johnson. Recorded in Nashville. Dylan plays lead guitar on *Leopard-Skin Pill-Box Hat*, and harmonica on all tracks except *Obviously 5 Believers*, on which Charlie McCoy plays. The other musicians are: Wayne Moss; Kenneth Buttrey; Hargus Robbins; Jerry Kennedy; Joe South; Al Kooper; Bill Aikins; Henry Strzelecki; and Jaime Robertson.

McCoy has played on every subsequent Dylan album, as has Kenny Buttrey. Joe South has since cut many records of his own, and was the composer of his own million-seller *The Games People Play*, and of *Walk A Mile In My Shoes*—a song done brilliantly by Presley on his "On Stage" album (1970).

Al Kooper was a founder-member of Blood Sweat & Tears, was featured on the CBS album "Supersession" with Mike Bloomfield (which will perhaps suggest how much status he now enjoys as a rock musician) and plays also on Dylan's "Self Portrait" and "New Morning" albums. He plays organ and piano.

Jaime Robertson is the genius behind The Band, the group Dylan has often been backed by—as he was at his 1969 Isle of Wight Festival performance. On some British copies of "Blonde On Blonde", *Memphis Blues Again* is listed as *Stuck Inside Of Mobile With Thee*; on early British copies of the album also, *One Of Us Must Know (Sooner Or Later)* has been balanced differently, so that the piano which should dominate the "gaps" between verses is very much subdued, especially between the first verse and the second.

1967: BOB DYLAN'S GREATEST HITS

Side 1: *Blowin' In The Wind*; *It Aint Me Babe*; *The Times They Are A-Changin'*; *Mr. Tambourine Man*; *She Belongs To Me*; *It's All Over Now, Baby Blue*.

Side 2: *Subterranean Homesick Blues*; *One Of Us Must Know (Sooner Or Later)*; *Like A Rolling Stone*; *Just Like A Woman*; *Rainy Day Women Nos. 12 & 35*; *I Want You*.

A badly-selected regurgitation of old recordings put out by Dylan's record company during his long silence after "Blonde On Blonde". The balance on *One Of Us Must Know (Sooner Or Later)* is better than on the early issues of the British album of "Blonde On Blonde" but is still not as it should be. The back-cover has photo-

312

graphs of the covers of his other albums but misses out the fourth one, "Another Side Of Bob Dylan".

It would not be a good idea to start listening to Dylan via this LP.

1968: JOHN WESLEY HARDING

Side 1: *John Wesley Harding*; *As I Went Out One Morning*; *I Dreamed I Saw St. Augustine*; *All Along The Watchtower*; *The Ballad Of Frankie Lee & Judas Priest*; *Drifter's Escape*.
Side 2: *Dear Landlord*; *I Am A Lonesome Hobo*; *I Pity The Poor Immigrant*; *The Wicked Messenger*; *Down Along The Cove*; *I'll Be Your Baby Tonight*.

Produced by Bob Johnson in Nashville. All songs by Dylan, but there is a return to the old reliance on older material. Thus, for instance, *I Dreamed I Saw St. Augustine* is based on the old political song now associated with Joan Baez, *I Dreamed I Saw Joe Hill*. Dylan plays guitar, harmonica and piano. The musicians are: Charlie McCoy on bass; Kenny Buttrey on drums; and, on *Down Along The Cove* and *I'll Be Your Baby Tonight*, Pete Drake on steel guitar. If you turn the front cover upside down and stare hard at the top visible bit of the tree in the photograph, you can see, for no particular good reason, the faces of John Lennon, Ringo Starr and others. (Dylan was later to play a session with Starr in Hollywood in 1970.) Apart from this, the "John Wesley Harding" album cover is a classic piece of packaging: its dun colour, its quietness, the photograph in black-and-white, the bare winter trees fit perfectly the image of the album.

1969: NASHVILLE SKYLINE

Side 1: *Girl From The North Country*; *Nashville Skyline Rag*; *To Be Alone With You*; *I Threw It All Away*; *Peggy Day*.
Side 2: *Lay, Lady, Lay*; *One More Night*; *Tell Me That It Isn't True*; *Country Pie*; *Tonight I'll Be Staying Here With You*.

All songs by Dylan; production by Bob Johnson; recorded in Nashville. Dylan drops the harmonica altogether on this LP. The musicians are: Dylan on guitar; Charlie McCoy on bass; Kenny Buttrey on drums; Pete Drake on steel; plus Norman Blake, Charlie Daniels and Bob Wilson, who also play on the "Self Portrait" album.

Johnny Cash sings with Dylan on *Girl From The North Country* and contributes the appalling "poem" that appears above the foggy colour photograph of Nashville's skyline on the back cover of the album. Again, the front cover is a great piece of packaging, with its warm blue sky, the sun behind Dylan's head, his beautiful shiny guitar with flower-design, and his hat-tipping, smiling pose.

An interesting album for comparison is "Nashville Airplane" by Flatt & Scruggs. The strong resemblances are not entirely co-incidental.

1970: SELF PORTRAIT

Side 1: *All The Tired Horses*; *Alberta No. 1*; *I Forgot More Than You'll Ever Know*; *Days of '49*; *Early Mornin' Rain*; *In Search Of Little Sadie*.
Side 2: *Let It Be Me*; *Little Sadie*; *Woogie Boogie*; *Belle Isle*; *Living The Blues*; *Like A Rolling Stone*.
Side 3: *Copper Kettle*; *Gotta Travel On*; *Blue Moon*; *The Boxer*; *The Mighty Quinn*; *Take Me As I Am*.
Side 4: *Take A Message To Mary*; *It Hurts Me Too*; *Minstrel Boy*; *She Belongs To Me*; *Wigwam*; *Alberta No. 2*.

Songs by various people. Produced by Bob Johnson; recorded in Nashville in June 1969, at the Isle of Wight 2nd Festival of Music on August 31st, 1969, and in New York around November 1969.

C. A. Null composed *I Forgot More Than You'll Ever Know*.

Gordon Lightfoot composed *Early Mornin' Rain*.

M. Curtis, G. Becaud and P. Delano wrote the English-language version of *Let It Be Me*.

P. Clayton wrote *Gotta Travel On*.

Paul Simon wrote *The Boxer*.

Richard Rodgers and Lorenz Hart wrote *Blue Moon*.

Boudleaux Bryant wrote *Take Me As I Am* (*Or Let Me Go*), and, with Felice Bryant, also wrote *Take A Message To Mary*.

Days of '49 is, like *Copper Kettle*, a traditional song.

In Search Of Little Sadie and *Little Sadie* are credited to Dylan but are based on an older song. Johnny Cash has cut three different versions of this: *Transfusion Blues,* recorded with The Tennessee Two on the Sun label (and reissued on an album in Britain in 1970) and two later CBS recordings called *Cocaine Blues,* one of which was done "live" in front of a prison audience.

It Hurts Me Too is also accredited to Dylan but is basically an older blues number done by many other people, including Elmore James. The Isle of Wight tracks are *Like A Rolling Stone,* the Dylan song first put out on the 1965 album "Highway 61 Revisited"; *She Belongs To Me,* the song first issued on Dylan's other 1965 album, "Bringing It All Back Home"; *The Mighty Quinn,* a Dylan song never previously released by him, although it is one of the songs on the 1967 basement tape; and *Minstrel Boy,* which, like Dylan's version of the old Scottish song *Will Ye Go Lassie,* had not been heard before the Isle of Wight performance. (*Will Ye Go Lassie* has not, unfortunately, been released officially, although there have been at least two different bootleg issues of the Isle of Wight performance, which include it.) The tracks cut at Nashville in June '69 include *Living The Blues,* with Dylan on piano (the song he featured when he appeared in the Johnny Cash CBS-TV Show at around the same time); *Take A Message To Mary*; and *Blue Moon.*

All The Tired Horses does not feature Dylan's voice, although it may be his guitar in the background: and it is his song.

The musicians on the Isle of Wight tracks are the members of The Band: Rick Danko, Levon Helm, Garth Hudson, Richard Manuel and Jaime Robbie Robertson. Robertson also played on "Blonde On Blonde" and The Band also provide the backing on the 1967 Basement Tape. All of The Band play several instruments, except Robertson, who appears to play only guitar (apart from singing—which he also does on the Dylan Isle of Wight tracks). Danko plays bass but can also play violin and trombone; Helm plays drums, and can play mandolin and guitar; Hudson plays organ and also clavinette, piano, accordion, sax and slide trumpet; Manuel plays piano, plus drums, and mouth harp. These are not, of course, all featured on the "Self Portrait" tracks.

The violin on *Blue Moon* is by the celebrated Nashville player, Doug Kershaw, who has recently cut albums of his own (and at least one Kershaw single, a brilliant version of *Orange Blossom Special,* has been issued in Britain—in November 1970).

The singers on the rest of the album are Dottie Dillard, Delores Edgin, Hilda Harris, Lillian Hunt, Millie Kirkham, Martha McCrory, Carol Montgomery, June Page, Albertine Robinson and Maeretha Stewart (who provides the pastiche jazz-singing on *If Dogs Run Free* on the "New Morning" album).

The other musicians are: Bryon T. Bach; Brenton Banks; George Binkley; Norman Blake; Dave Bromberg; Albert N. Butler; Kenny Buttrey; Fred Carter Jnr.; Marvin D. Chantry; Ron Cornelius; Charlie Daniels; Pete Drake; Solie J. Fott; Bubba Fowler; Dennis A. Good; Emanuel Green; Frederick Hill; Karl T. Himmel; Martin Katahn; Al Kooper; Sheldon Kurland; Barry McDonald; Oliver Mitchell; Bob Moore; Gene A. Mullins; Gary Van Osdale; Rex Peer; Bill Pursell; Alvin Rogers; Frank C. Smith; Anthony Ferron; Bob Wilson and Stu Woods.

The cover portrait is of Dylan and by Dylan, and is the second of his paintings to constitute an album front cover. The first was a painting of The Band for their first album, "Music From Big Pink"—which included several Dylan songs, notably *Tears Of Rage* and *I Shall Be Released,* both from the 1967 Basement Tape era.

The rest of "Self Portrait's" cover features photographs of Dylan at the Isle of Wight, in the studio, and outside, plus photos of other musicians in the studio. (In two of the shots, one of Dylan's children can be seen lying at his feet.) One shot of Dylan keeps up the tradition of showing him in a suede jacket, which seems to have been on each cover from "Blonde On Blonde" onwards.

1970: NEW MORNING

Side 1: *If Not For You*; *Day Of The Locusts*; *Time Passes Slowly*; *Went To See The Gypsy*; *Winterlude*; *If Dogs Run Free*.
Side 2: *New Morning*; *Sign On The Window*; *One More Weekend*; *The Man In Me*; *Three Angels*; *Father Of Night*.

All songs by Dylan; produced by Bob Johnson. Dylan plays acoustic guitar, electric guitar, organ and piano. (His piano tracks are tracks 2, 3, 4, 5, 8, 10 and 12). Dave Bromberg plays electric guitar and dobro; Harvey Brooks and Charlie Daniels play electric bass; Ron Cornelius and Buzzy Feiten play electric guitar; Russ Kunkel and Billy Mundi play drums; Al Cooper plays organ, piano (it's his piano on the *If Dogs Run Free* pastiche), electric guitar and French horn. The back-up vocals are by Maeretha Stewart, Hilda Harris and Albertine Robinson. Maeretha Stewart is the singer in the background of *If Dogs Run Free*. The front cover, which is without words, has a black-and-white photograph of Dylan taken in 1970; the back cover includes a large photograph (again in black-and-white) of a very young Bob Dylan standing with Victoria Spivey. This was probably taken in 1961 when Dylan played a part in an album cut on the Spivey label (see Appendix C).

1971: MORE BOB DYLAN GREATEST HITS

Side 1: *Watching the River Flow*; *Don't Think Twice It's All Right*; *Lay, Lady, Lay*; *Memphis Blues Again*.

Side 2: *I'll Be Your Baby Tonight*; *All I Really Want To Do*; *My Back Pages*; *Maggie's Farm*; *Tonight I'll Be Staying Here With You*.

Side 3: *Positively 4th Street*; *All Along The Watchtower*; *The Mighty Quinn*; *Just Like Tom Thumb's Blues*; *A Hard Rain's A-Gonna Fall*.

Side 4: *If Not For You*; *New Morning*; *Tomorrow Is A Long Time*; *When I Paint My Masterpiece*; *I Shall Be Released*; *You Aint Goin' Nowhere*; *Down In The Flood*.

An incomparably better collection than the first "Greatest Hits" album, with, overall, a reasonably sane selection of his work, with tracks from every album except the first (although the only track from "Self Portrait" is an Isle of Wight concert track). *Tomorrow Is A Long Time* was cut in concert in 1964; *When I Paint My Masterpiece* was cut at the same short session as *Watching The River Flow* and produced by Leon Russell, who plays piano. The last three tracks on side four were cut in October 1971 with Happy Traum on bass, banjo, second guitar and vocal harmonies. The words to *You Aint Goin' Nowhere* are radically altered from the 1967 version; a third of *I Shall Be Released* is not included in this version.

Appendix B: Other Officially Released Dylan Recordings, with Notes

1. COLUMBIA RECORDINGS

(a) SINGLES:

This list does not include, of course, the Extended Play releases put out by Columbia in Britain in 1964 and soon deleted. Tracks which are not available on Columbia albums are asterisked. The dates given in brackets refer to the issuing-dates of the singles, not the recording dates.

... *Mixed Up Confusion** c/w *Corrine Corrina** was issued as a U.S. single before the release of the "Freewheelin' Bob Dylan" album but withdrawn almost immediately afterwards (1962). It was issued again in Holland in 1966 (CBS 2476) and is still available in Germany and the Benelux countries. *Mixed Up Confusion* has Dylan on piano and harmonica. *Corrine Corrina* is not the same cut as issued on the "Freewheelin' " LP. It has different words, a slightly different pace, and accompanying musicians more prominent that the "Freewheelin' " version.

... *Let Me Die In My Footsteps** c/w ? was scheduled for release in 1963 in the Schwann Catalogue (U.S. only). If it actually was released, however, it was immediately withdrawn.

... *On The Road Again* c/w *Bob Dylan's 115th Dream* (1965).
... *Gates Of Eden* c/w *She Belongs To Me* (1965).
... *Like A Rolling Stone* c/w *Gates Of Eden* (1965).
... *Positively 4th Street* c/w *From A Buick Six* (1965).
... *Can You Please Crawl Out Your Window** c/w *Highway 61 Revisited* (1965): NB. In the U.S.A., there were two issues of this, the first incorrectly labelled as being *Positively 4th Street*.
... *One Of Us Must Know (Sooner Or Later)* c/w *Queen Jane Approximately* (1966).
... *Rainy Day Women Nos. 12 & 35* c/w *Pledging My Time* (1966).

318

... *I Want You* c/w *Just Like Tom Thumb's Blues** (1966):
NB. This B-side was recorded in concert in Liverpool, England,
May 1966.

... *Just Like A Woman* c/w *Obviously Five Believers* (1966).

... *Leopard-Skin Pill-Box Hat* c/w *Most Likely You Go Your
Way & I'll Go Mine* (1966).

... *Rainy Day Women Nos. 12 & 35* c/w *Like A Rolling Stone*
(1966).

... *Positively 4th Street* c/w *Can You Please Crawl Out Your
Window** (1966): NB. This was issued in stereo by Spanish CBS
only, as a free bonus to the first 2,000 purchasers of the "Blonde
On Blonde" album.

... *Just Like A Woman* c/w *I Want You* (1967).

... *If You Gotta Go, Go Now** c/w *To Ramona* (1967) was
scheduled for U.S. release but in fact only got issued in Europe
(and not including Britain). It is still available in the Benelux
countries (CBS 2921). *To Ramona* is the same take as issued on
the "Another Side Of Bob Dylan" album in 1964. *If You Gotta
Go, Go Now* was recorded at the same time as the "Bringing It
All Back Home" album in 1965, and includes Bruce Langhorne on
guitar.

... *I Threw It All Away* c/w *The Drifter's Escape* (1969).

... *Lay, Lady, Lay* c/w *Peggy Day* (1969).

... *Tonight I'll Be Staying Here With You* c/w *Country Pie*
(1969).

... *Copper Kettle* c/w *Wigwam* (1970).

... *Watching The River Flow/Spanish Is The Loving Tongue**
single (1971).

... *George Jackson**/*George Jackson**: one side a solo acoustic
version, the other a rather incongruous sing-along version with
back-up musicians & chorus (Stereo) (1972).

(b) ALBUMS:

CAROLYN HESTER—Carolyn Hester—Columbia CL-1796. Producer: John Hammond. Dylan plays harmonica on three tracks:
Come Back Baby; *Swing & Turn Jubilee*; *I'll Fly Away*. The first
of these was suggested and taught to Miss Hester by Dylan. The
album was recorded September 1961, and issued in 1962.

A TRIBUTE TO WOODY GUTHRIE, PART ONE—Various Artists—Columbia KC-31171, CBS-64861. Producers: Harold Leventhal & Millard Lampell. Dylan & The Band perform on three tracks: *Aint Got No Home In This World Anymore*; *Mrs. Roosevelt*; *Grand Coolee Dam*. (This was Dylan's first appearance in concert since 1966 and so is of special interest. His voice is more or less as it was to be on the John Wesley Harding album.) The recording was January 20th, 1968; the album was issued in 1972.

EARL SCRUGGS, HIS FAMILY & FRIENDS—Earl Scruggs & others—Columbia CBS-64777. Producer: Neil Wilburn. Dylan plays guitar with Earl Scruggs (banjo), Gary and Randy Scruggs (guitars) on 1 track: *Nashville Skyline Rag*. This track was recorded 1969; the album was issued 1972.

2. OTHER RECORDINGS:

(a) SINGLES:
    ...*Election Year Rag/Somebody Else's Troubles*—Steve Goodman—Buddah. 1972. Dylan plays piano on both tracks.

(b) EXTENDED-PLAYS:
    ...*With God On Our Side*. Dylan, Seeger and Baez. Vanguard. Issued UK on Fontana TFE 18009. 1964. Dylan duets with Joan Baez on "With God On Our Side". Recorded live at the 1963 Newport Folk Festival.
    ...*Blowin' In The Wind*. Dylan, Seeger and Baez. UK: Fontana TFE 18010. 1964. Dylan sings "Blowin' In The Wind". Recorded live at the 1963 Newport Folk Festival.
    ...*Ye Playboys & Playgirls*. Dylan, Seeger and Baez. UK: Fontana TFE 18011. 1964. Dylan and Seeger duet on "Ye Playboys & Playgirls". Recorded live at the 1963 Newport Folk Festival.
NB. The three EPs listed above were deleted soon after issue.

(c) ALBUMS:
    ... "Midnight Special". Harry Belafonte. RCA LSP 2449. Recorded: 1961. Released: May 1962. Dylan plays harmonica on the title-track.
    ... "Three Kings and The Queen". Big Joe Williams, Lonnie Johnson, Roosevelt Sykes and Victoria Spivey. Spivey Records. Spivey 1004. Recorded: 1961. Released: 1964. Dylan's first recording. He plays harmonica on *Wichita* (Big Joe Williams) and har-

monica and back-up vocal on *Sittin' On Top Of The World* (Big Joe Williams).

... "Three Kings and The Queen Vol. 2". Big Joe Williams, Lonnie Johnson, Roosevelt Sykes and Victoria Spivey. Spivey Records. Spivey LP 1014. Recorded: 1961. Released: 1973? This has been scheduled for release but may not have actually been released. The tracks with Dylan were cut at the same session as for LP 1004. Dylan plays harmonica on *It's Dangerous* and *Big Joe Dylan And Victoria* (Big Joe Williams).

... "Evening Concerts At Newport Vol. 1, 1963". Various artists. Vanguard. VSD 79143. 1964. Dylan performs *Blowin' In The Wind* live at Newport Folk Festival 1963.

... "Evening Concerts At Newport Vol. 2, 1963: Newport Broadside". Various artists. Vanguard. VSD 79144. 1964. Dylan duets with Seeger on *Ye Playboys & Playgirls;* duets with Joan Baez on *With God On Our Side*, and joins in chorus with Seeger, Baez, The Freedom Singers, Theo Bikel and Peter, Paul and Mary on *We Shall Overcome*. All recorded live at the Newport Folk Festival, July 1963.

... "Broadside Ballads No. 1". Various artists. Broadside. BR-301. November 1963. Dylan appears as Blind Boy Grunt on *John Brown, Only A Hobo* and *Talkin' Devil* and does back-ups for Happy Traum on *Let Me Die In My Footsteps*. Cut 1963.

... "We Shall Overcome". Various artists. Broadside. BR-592. 1964. Includes two verses of *Only A Pawn In Their Game* by Dylan recorded live at the Civil Rights March on Washington, 1963.

... "Dick Farina & Eric Von Schmidt". Dick Farina and Eric Von Schmidt. Folklore Records. F-LEUT-7. 1965. Dylan provides back-up harmonica and vocals on *Glory Glory, You Can't Always Tell, Christmas Island, Cocaine* and *London Waltz*. Recorded in London on January 14th, 1965. Dylan again appears under the name Blind Boy Grunt.

... "Blues Project". Various artists. Elektra. EKS 7264. 1965. Under the name Bob Landy, Dylan appears on several tracks as follows: *South Bound Train* (vocal: John Koerner, harmonica: Dylan); *Downtown Blues* (vocal: Geoff Muldaur, piano: Dylan and Eric Von Schmidt); *Blow Whistle Blow* (vocal: Eric Von Schmidt, harmonica: Dylan); *She's Gone* (vocal: Mark Spoelstra, harmonica: Dylan). Recorded in 1965 — the album from which the group "Blues Project" built up.

321

... "Concert For Bangla Desh". Various artists. Apple STCX 3385. 1971. Dylan live at Madison Square Gardens, August 1st, 1971, backed by Leon Russell (bass), George Harrison (electric guitar) and Ringo Starr (tambourine). Sings *A Hard Rain's A-Gonna Fall, It Takes A Lot To Laugh, It Takes A Train To Cry, Blowin' In The Wind, Mr. Tambourine Man* and (with back-up vocals by Russell and Harrison) *Just Like A Woman.*

... "Somebody Else's Troubles". Steve Goodman. Buddah BDS 5121. 1972. Dylan appears (under the name Robert Milkwood Thomas) on the title track (which was also issued as B-side of the single *Election Year Rag* listed already) on piano and harmony vocals. Recorded late 1972.

... "Doug Sahm And Band". Doug Sahm. Atlantic SD 7254. Dylan appears on the following tracks: (*Is Anybody Going To*) *San Antone*—back-up vocals. *Wallflower*—lead guitar and vocals (song composed by Dylan). *Blues Stay Away From Me*—guitar solo and shared vocals. *Me And Paul*—harmonica. Recorded Late 1972; released 1973.

N.B. Dylan also reportedly appears on a Tom Rush album on Elektra, *Take A Little Walk With Me;* date and details unknown.

NOTE: This is unlikely to be a complete list, because Dylan enjoys slipping into studios "incognito" and because material recorded but not released at the time of writing may well be released subsequently and because in the early days of his career a lot of things happened with Dylan, not then a big name, unnoted on the periphery of other people's studio sessions. However, the list above, incomplete though it almost certainly is, would not have been possible without Greil Marcus' researches, published in *Rolling Stone* in December 1969.

Index

N.B. Where songs are quoted but not named in the text, their titles are nevertheless given in the index with the appropriate page number listed

325

326

327

329

332

GETTING BACK TOGETHER
ROBERT HOURIET

'A charged and comprehensive report on American communes that is also an odyssey, one man's confession. . . . It's difficult not to be moved'
Cosmopolitan

75p Illustrated

THE SACRED MUSHROOM AND THE CROSS
JOHN M. ALLEGRO

'Allegro boldly sketches in the origins of the primitive fertility cult. . . . It is a dazzling foray into the obscure hinterlands of comparative philology'
Dennis Potter, The Times

60p

PSI: PSYCHIC DISCOVERIES BEHIND THE IRON CURTAIN
SHEILA OSTRANDER & LYNN SCHROEDER

'The most important book about ESP research and the validity of the occult tradition yet to appear'
Los Angeles Times

95p Illustrated

THE BOOK OF THE DAMNED
CHARLES FORT

'Charles Fort has made a terrible onslaught upon the accumulated lunacy of fifty centuries. . . . He has delighted me beyond all men who have written books in this world. . . . He has shot the scientific basis of modern wisdom full of large, ugly holes'
Ben Hecht

60p

THE SECRET LORE OF MAGIC
IDRIES SHAH

'The author of this fascinating guide book to the occult has included
the texts of all the major spell books and grimoires in one volume for
the first time'
Oxford Mail

60p Illustrated

BOB DYLAN
ANTHONY SCADUTO

The first full dimensional biography of America's most popular and
most elusive superstar.

75p Illustrated

THE CONQUEST OF THE INCAS
JOHN HEMMING

'Much the best book on the Incas since Prescott's, which it is entitled
to supersede. . . .'
Sunday Times

£1.75 Illustrated

THE VIEW OVER ATLANTIS
JOHN MICHELL

A revolutionary theory of prehistoric civilisation, already established
as an 'underground' classic.

75p

THE PARADE'S GONE BY . . .
KEVIN BROWNLOW

The classic and acclaimed work on Hollywood during the 'golden
age' between 1912 and the advent of sound sixteen years later.

£1.75 Illustrated

SEXUAL POLITICS
KATE MILLETT

'The seminal book in the struggle for Women's Rights. Supremely interesting . . . brilliantly conceived'
New York Times

60p

EROS AND CIVILISATION
HERBERT MARCUSE

Poses fundamental new questions about Freud's views on sexuality and their relevance to political behaviour in modern society.

45p

ONE DIMENSIONAL MAN
HERBERT MARCUSE

'The most subversive book published in the United States this century'
Le Nouvel Observateur

45p

THE ENCYCLOPAEDIA OF ANCIENT AND FORBIDDEN KNOWLEDGE
ZOLAR

'Zolar . . . presents a fascinating introduction to the forbidden and superstition-shrouded world of the occult'
Newcastle Evening Chronicle

90p

GROWTH GAMES
LEWIS & STREITFELD

Over 200 ways to enable you to live a richer life, to feel more fully, and to relate to others more meaningfully.

65p